MW01257950

Flying the Alaska Wild

*The Adventures and Misadventures
of an Alaska Bush Pilot*

by Mort Mason

Voyageur Press

Edited by Kari Cornell
Designed by JoDee Turner
Printed in China

02   03   04   05   06   5   4   3   2   1

Library of Congress Cataloging-in-Publication Data

Mason, Mort D., 1931–
    Flying the Alaska wild : the adventures and misadventures of an Alaska bush pilot / by Mort Mason.
        p. cm.
    ISBN 0-89658-589-1 (hardcover)
    1. Mason, Mort D., 1931– 2. Bush flying—Alaska. 3. Bush pilots—Alaska. 4. Alaska—Description and travel. I. Title.
    TL540.M36737 A3 2002
    629.13'092—dc21
                                                2002002238

Distributed in Canada by Raincoast Books,
9050 Shaughnessy Street, Vancouver, B.C. V6P 6E5

Published by Voyageur Press, Inc.
123 North Second Street, P.O. Box 338, Stillwater, MN 55082 U.S.A.
651-430-2210, fax 651-430-2211
books@voyageurpress.com
www.voyageurpress.com

Educators, fundraisers, premium and gift buyers, publicists, and marketing managers: Looking for creative products and new sales ideas? Voyageur Press books are available at special discounts when purchased in quantities, and special editions can be created to your specifications. For details contact the marketing department at 80 0-888-9653.

Front cover and Page 2 photograph: copyright 2001 Alaska Stock

Acknowledgements

I must, in all good conscience, offer my personal thanks and deepest respect to Dave Klosterman, the best airplane driver I know, who more than once saved my bacon. Though neither of us would go so far as to suggest he might have saved my life, all Alaskans know that sometimes bacon is infinitely the more valuable.

Without reservation, my heartfelt and most sincere thanks go to Kari Cornell, my editor. Kari is at once pleasant, easy to work with, laudably informative, and supremely helpful. She has patiently, and with consummate skill, guided this neophyte through the dark and mysterious halls of the publishing labyrinth, keeping always a remarkable tolerance and gracious humor. I cannot thank her enough.

Last, but surely not least, I want to express my unfeigned gratitude to Michael Dregni, Editorial Director, whose persistence and drive made this on again, off again, back again Finnegan project a possibility in the first place.

Dedication

This book is dedicated, with all possible respect, to the memory of my father, Donald F. Mason, the best man I ever met; to my wife, Peggy, who suffered through more of my late arrivals than I can count, and without whose encouragement this book would not have been possible; and to Donald E. Ziegler, fisherman and philosopher, who alone knows why.

TABLE OF CONTENTS

HOW IT ALL BEGAN

*M*y first flight ever was in an Air Force C-54, one of those four-engine jobbies that civilian airlines called the DC-4. Although I wore an Air Force uniform, I was a passenger on this flight, transferring from Great Falls, Montana, to Silver Lake, Washington. The seating arrangements on board were spartan to say the least. Instead of seats, passengers sat on canvas webbing that had been strung up on either side of the fuselage.

I had made myself comfortable on the dirty plywood floor when an Air Force captain, stocky, blond, blue-eyed, and all smiles, burst through the open doors, holding a crash helmet and a parachute. Once inside, he brandished the 'chute above his head and shouted, "I can see the headlines now: '*C-54 CRASHES—ONE SURVIVOR*'." The panache of a true single-engine fighter pilot, I thought. That flight over the Rocky Mountains didn't last long enough for me. I was thrilled to pass the time listening to the tales of a genuine, in-the-skin fighter pilot. I had always been fascinated by flight and had dreamed of becoming a pilot myself one day.

I shot this young bull caribou while on a hunting break back in 1961. Of course I had to fly to the hunting grounds, which were located on the Upper Susitna River just east of Mount McKinley.

But it turned out that earning my wings while in the Air Force wasn't meant to be. At one point I was enrolled in the OCS (Officer Candidate School) class that would have later led to flight school. But after I found out that I would first have to re-enlist for six more years, I withdrew from the course. It was a tough decision, but I didn't want to give Uncle Sam any more time than the four years I had already signed up for.

Joining the Air Force did eventually lead to flight lessons, however. While stationed at a small RADAR site in Montana, a run-in with a nosy lieutenant landed me in Alaska for two years. Although the assignment was meant as a punishment, it turned out that lieutenant couldn't have done me a bigger favor. I absolutely loved Alaska and all its empty grandeur. At the end of those two years, I took my discharge at Wright Patterson Air Force Base in Cleveland, Ohio, and scooted right back to the Big Empty.

Having been a hunter and fisherman all my young life, I continued to hunt and fish the great Alaska outback. Trouble was, the only way to get from here to there in that wild country was by air. This was it, then. I simply had to earn my pilot wings.

On October 23, 1955, I marched resolutely across the airport grounds to the operations office—a rather grand term, in those days—of Safeway Airways, our local Piper aircraft distributor and flight school. Inside a small lean-to attached to the Quonset hangar, I found the flight office and got my first look at my flight-instructor-to-be, Mr. George Kitchen. Robert Redford he wasn't, but hanging on the wall of his small office was a certificate of commendation from the Civil Aeronautics Administration, that Department of Commerce arm now known as the Federal Aviation Administration. The commendation was for having soloed more than 1,000 pilots! That was the equivalent of 10,000 hours as an instructor, and I know George did a lot more than just instructing would-be pilots.

George gave me my first hour of dual instruction that day. Flying over a world covered in snow, I was lost from the moment the wheels left the ground until we shut the engine down an hour later. When up in the air, everything on the ground looked the same to me, except for the nearby Chugach Mountains. I knew that I could never learn to fly. How in the hell did anyone up there know where he was? I was truly discouraged.

Flying didn't come naturally to me, and I wasn't all that good at it at first. In fact, I was sometimes so disappointed in poor landings, half-accurate spins, or skidding turns that I had decided I would give it up—right after earning my private pilot certificate. Even though I didn't like flying all that much, I wasn't one to quit before achieving my goal. My father never started a job he didn't finish, and that never-give-up attitude rubbed off on me. And I'll be eternally grateful that it did.

By the end of my fourth hour of dual flight instruction, I could perform a two-turn spin—in either direction—and pull back out into level flight within ten degrees of a predetermined heading.

I would solo out on Friday the Thirteenth in April 1956, after seven hours of dual instruction. It wasn't the best day for my first solo flight. At Lake Hood, from where we were flying ski-equipped, 65-hp Aeronca Champions, a hard snow was falling and the crosswind measured 25 knots. My instructor at the time, F. A. White, told me that the weather wasn't suitable for a green student pilot with less than eight hours total flying time. I told him that we were going to fly that day, or I was going to change flight schools. Period. We flew.

Deep ruts marked the takeoff and landing path through the canal that joined Lake Hood with Spenard Lake, Anchorage's seaplane base during summer months. After one flight around the lake, the instructor, who was sitting in the back seat, demanded I land on the right ski, holding the right wingtip only inches above the snow. The landing wasn't particularly difficult, and the instructor directed me to stop and let him out for my first solo flight.

I had heard many hangar tales about wind gusts flipping an airplane onto its back, and I just had to find out for myself whether or not this was true. After the solo takeoff, I climbed directly into the high practice area hard against the Chugach Mountains and began practicing stalls and spins in the moderate to severe turbulence. My instructor told me to circle the practice area, land and return to the tie-down area, and I didn't know enough about all this flying stuff to understand that this was the usual drill.

When I returned an hour later, *without* flipping the plane, he was as mad as a scalded cat about my lengthy disappearance. As far as he was concerned, I had simply disappeared into the snow after takeoff. Despite his well-deserved verbal abuse, I learned a lot that day.

Lack of funds delayed actually getting my private pilot's license until the following March. After I passed both the written and practical exams, and received the license I had worked so hard for, my friends seemed to crawl out of the woodwork, always needing a ride to some distant place. I was so busy I forgot that I was going to quit this foolishness.

After I had "earned my ticket," I realized that personal airplanes, like boats, are pretty much just big holes in the sky into which owners throw large sums of money. I had to somehow earn the money to afford the flying machines. I earned my license as a Territory of Alaska Registered Guide and, over the years, have made just about enough money to keep my airplanes in the air and to pocket the little dab that was sometimes left over. Any thought of quitting never entered my mind.

By the time I had reached my sixtieth flying hour, flying changed dramatically for me. I went to the airport one morning, carefully preflighted the little Aeronca, and, instead of getting into it, I simply put it on, just like slipping into my favorite jacket. The little plane seemed to fit me perfectly. From that day forward, I would slide into the airplane and just go wherever I decided to go. The airplane had no choice but to go along with me. I've learned that not every pilot goes through such a metamorphosis, but I've always been glad that I did.

Of course, I never set out to become Alaska's greatest pilot, bush or otherwise. That's just as well, because I didn't and I'm not. I'm not even close. There are some real whiz-bangs flying around the Alaska outback. I'm just one of those Alaska pilots who paid a whole lot of attention to preventative maintenance and learned one stumbling, bumbling, fumbling hour at a time the limits of my equipment and my abilities.

I did have a few advantages over most Alaska fliers. To begin with, I have maintained my five-foot-nine-inch height at a weight of 159 pounds since high school graduation. My light weight meant that I didn't have to strip all the radios from my airplanes to reduce gross weight. My build also allowed me to crawl in and out of some relatively small aircraft such as Piper's Super Cub and Cessna's 180s and 185s. Secondly, I was blessed with excellent vision. I regularly scored twenty/five on our vision tests. That meant I could see at a distance of twenty feet what the average person saw at a distance of five feet. It is likely this bit of good fortune allowed me to fly with very little discomfort in relatively poor weather.

And, last but not least, I am an incorrigible optimist. I always carry within me the absolute conviction that as long as I continue to command my airplane until it comes to a complete stop, everything will work out just fine. This is no doubt some sort of genetic defect. I know many fliers who are much more sensible in their aeronautical pursuits. Defective or not, I am comfortable working right up to the edge of performance. I've been known to take off in weather

Flying through Alaska's mountain ranges takes you right up to some of the state's most beautiful sites, including Mount Redoubt, near Mount Iliamna in the Alaska Range.

that had ducks and geese huddled together on a street corner, waiting for the next bus.

Despite this genetic defect, I'm not known to be reckless. I learned most of my own limitations early on and have tried not to exceed them. On a few occasions, I have talked myself into doing something that stretched the envelope a little in one way or another. Sometimes, stretching the envelope worked in my favor. At other times—well—I guess it didn't.

In this book I tell many of these tales, from the successes to the near disasters that I experienced in my years as an Alaska bush pilot. The majority of the errors were clearly my fault, and I admit that outright. If you decide I've been a little too casual with my flying, try to remember that these boo-boos were made over a period of forty years, while flying in a country where a real airport is still a luxurious rarity. Still, I agree with you. Some days I was a little too casual.

Could I have avoided my mistakes? Most of them, yes. All of them? Most likely not, unless I had simply stayed on the ground or operated only from controlled airports. Can I avoid them in the future? Most of them. Probably . . .

Chapter 1

FLYING THE BIG EMPTY

*T*here is no chapter on Alaska bush flying in any formal flight instruction manual. What skills I learned I picked up one at a time, through my flying experiences, as all Alaska bush pilots do. Every single Alaska flight adds to the pilot's abilities. Because most Alaska flights avoid improved runways and airports, almost every flight serves up a different set of circumstances and conditions. And, even though a pilot may have landed on the same beach two days in a row, the tides will have changed several times in between these landings, potentially cluttering the intended landing spot with logs, dead seals, or new springs.

Flying a plane in Alaska is a bit different from flying the same plane in the Lower 48. Bush flying demands that the pilot has an intimate knowledge of his aircraft, its systems, and—most important of all—its limitations. It demands, too, that the pilot know his own abilities and limitations. He must fly often enough to be comfortable operating right up against the sharp edge of his own capabilities and the capabilities of his airplane. Comfortable enough that he isn't nervous when his landing spot becomes visible only five or six seconds ahead of touchdown.

In my opinion, unless you fly at least five days a week, week in and week out, you will never be the master of your airplane. I don't believe you can keep a sharp flying edge if you fly less than ten hours in any given week. If you disagree, spend one month of ten-hour flying weeks, then lay off for one week. Oh, sure, you can still fly, but you will have lost your sharp edge. And you will notice it, too. If you truly can't tell the difference, you have been flying by the numbers, and have most likely been flying a pretty heavy aircraft, perhaps a six-place plane that you may never have really mastered in the first place.

Hey, I'm not criticizing you for that. You probably operate off paved and maintained airports, too. With lighted runways, and taxiways, paved tie-down areas, line boys, avgas, and service facilities. It's very likely that you've never had the opportunity to work off-airport. It's likely, too, that you haven't had the chance to do much mountain flying.

By mountain flying, I don't mean flying over some steep hills somewhere along the way. I'm talking about flying low and slow over an unfamiliar ridge, gauging its slope and the prevailing winds, and then putting your little airplane down in the weeds or rocks along the mountain's spine. Unless you're flying a taildragger, one of those critters with the nose gear stuck back there on the rear end where it really belongs, you're better off not attempting such a landing in the first place.

I'm talking from almost 20,000 flying hours, with no more than 3,000 of those hours from airports and landing strips that appear on any aeronautical chart. I'm talking about flying in and out of glaciers, snow fields, lakes, rivers, swamps, beaches, sand bars, and gravel bars—places where there are no weather reports, control towers, or Unicom facilities. Places where you have to gauge the ceilings and visibility by your own past experiences—and by reading tea leaves, coffee grounds, or salmon eggs.

Admittedly, Alaska flying promotes some pretty heavy-handed pilots—pilots who are not particularly smooth on the controls. For the most part, we just put the plane where we want it, using some of the same skills used in acrobatic flying. There are times when the little black ball just ain't gonna be in the middle. As a rule, we don't make very good instrument pilots. Bush approaches usually occur in areas where it's not possible to fly real patterns. That tends to make Alaska pilots somewhat impatient, I suppose. When your first glimpse of the landing area is only eight or ten seconds before the touchdown itself, the outback pilot simply doesn't have the time nor the airspace for a fifteen-second pattern entry, a thirty-second turn from downwind to base, and another thirty-second turn from base to final—let alone those seconds or minutes burned up between each of the turns.

* * *

It doesn't take long before pilots who fly Alaska's outback think of their flimsy little aircraft as nothing more than pickup trucks. The insides soon become smelly, then ragged, then worn and torn, then virtually nonexistent. The pilots have probably pulled out the rear seats and built canvas slings for back-there passengers. The exterior becomes dirty, then ragged, then torn or patched or bent. The shiny new paint almost immediately loses both its shine and its new. Some Alaska pilots even wish the paint would peel off entirely, reducing the plane's empty weight and increasing its useful load. A few pilots go so far as to strip off the paint right away. One of these artisans told me that the paint on a Cessna 180 can weigh between fifty and eighty pounds. Stripping away that much weight adds to the payload, you see.

Many bush pilots modify their airplanes to make it easier to get around in the outback. Oversized tail wheels, stronger tail springs, and beefed-up main landing gear components are commonplace, and I highly recommend them for off-airport operations.

Pilots flying the Big Empty often remove the radios, generators, and batteries before they fly their new planes off into the wild blue—or gray or white—yonder. Too much weight, they will tell you, and they don't fly instruments anyway. That's because there are no navigational aids where they're going. Why load a good aircraft down with extraneous avionics and electronics? Many Alaska pilots aren't thrilled to have to talk on the radio, anyway. Quite a few of them won't even fly into an airport that has a control tower.

Any seaplane pilot is familiar with a float kit, which includes a series of tubes and crossbar braces that are installed between the pilot and the windshield—an obstruction that the pilot doesn't even see after the first two hours of flight. These braces then act as a convenient handhold for both the pilot and his passengers. They also hold the power plant firmly in place during water takeoffs and landings, which can be very rough indeed, by the way. There are no shock absorbers in float installations, so pilot technique stands in for springs, oleo struts, or bungees. A float kit is a sensible addition to any wheel-equipped aircraft that is frequently flown in and out of rough strips.

When flying the outback in such aircraft as a Super Cub or a Citabria, most Alaska pilots remove the rear control stick. Many will cover the remaining rear stick stub with a fiberglass housing modification. Any Alaska pilot who flies the bush during the fall hunting seasons knows that there is nothing more disconcerting than to have a 150-pound moose ham slide forward and engage the part of the rear stick left exposed after the upper portion has been removed. That sort of thing can spoil a guy's whole day.

I've always secured a $^3/_{32}$-inch stainless aircraft cable from the forward davit on one side of my airplane's floats to the forward davit on the opposite side. When safety-wired and properly tightened with a turnbuckle, this cable allowed me to get to either side of the plane in water too deep for wading. When using Alaska's rivers for float operations, I couldn't always arrange to get the pilot's side of the aircraft toward the shore. The cable made that problem almost academic. I could get to either side of the plane by walking the cable, using the dead prop as a balancing aid.

During wheel or ski operations, almost every Super Cub has a set of cables attached to various points of the landing gear. Should the gear collapse during a rough landing or takeoff, at least it will still function without wiping a wingtip.

Some cautious pilots even insert a steel cable inside the tubing and between the horizontal stabilizers so the tail feathers won't fall off due to overlooked rust or corrosion. Even with good maintenance, it's a pain to inspect the inside of the leading edge tubing on the horizontal stabilizer. Pouring boiled linseed oil through all the airplane's tubing isn't a permanent fix, either. As with Peral-Ketone for saltwater float protection, constant observations and inspections are required to eliminate the possibility of eventual failure due to rust or corrosion.

* * *

Weight is a big deal in these little planes. The FARs (Federal Air Regulations) Part 91.38 allows Alaska air taxi operators to increase the maximum certificated take-off weight of their little aircraft by 15 percent. I've always thought that 15 percent overload was a quiet compromise, given that the government can't police all the overloaded aircraft in Alaska anyway. In any of Mr. Piper's Super Cubs, you will find a placard in the baggage compartment area that limits the legal load back there to 50 pounds. A 15 percent allowable overload means almost nothing to this tough little airplane. Most Alaska bush pilots, and every single one of Alaska's flying Registered Guides, will put a whole moose back there. Even a cleaned and boned out moose will weigh 500 or 600 pounds. The legal limit for a Super Cub is the pilot and one passenger. More often than not, these planes carry three souls plus their gear and equipment, with external loads tacked on for good measure.

Take, for instance, Ed Smalley, the diminutive demonstration pilot and sales representative for Safeway Airways back in the mid fifties. Incredible airplane driver, Ed. I once watched him lift off and land five times along Merrill Field's Runway 6 with 2,500 pounds of plumbers' lead shot crammed inside his little white and red Super Cub. He completed one takeoff and one landing every 500 feet, including the airborne distance, on this 4,000-foot runway. The tiny plane creaked and groaned and sagged in the middle, but it certainly didn't balk at the load.

I bought a new Cessna TU206G turbocharged six-place in 1984. The ship, N9975Z, was mounted on Mr. Wiplinger's Wipline amphibious floats. The 310-hp Teledyne Continental turbocharged engine gave outstanding performance in and around my hunting and fishing camps, almost all of which are above 3,000 feet MSL (Mean Sea Level). That amphib has carried five or six souls, endless amounts of camping, fishing, or hunting equipment, and full long-range tanks holding 552 pounds of 100 low-lead avgas many times. I've loaded the plane this way for both land and water operations, and never considered it unusual. But the weight-and-balance calculations showed that this aircraft was outside the gravity envelope with only two passengers, full fuel, and no freight at all. On my very first flight in that aircraft, I overloaded it by 600 pounds. Nevertheless the Cessna leaped off the water at Lake Hood as if it wasn't at all overloaded or off balance. Four souls, full fuel, and plenty of freight was the rule rather than the exception with this aircraft. Do I recommend that you fly that way? I certainly do not! And your insurance company will smile if they find out about such an overload. They won't have to pay off in the event of an accident.

Federal Aviation Regulations aside, when you overload an airplane, you fly outside the envelope, and that's very dangerous flying, no matter who is at the controls. If you've ever staggered and teetered along on the ragged edge of an oscillating stall, you know what I mean. There may be nothing quite so unnerving as feeling your airplane slowly oscillate between a climb and a descent on account of a heavy load placed too far aft in the plane. Especially since there is precious little that the pilot can do about it, unless he has sufficient altitude to lower the nose and pick up additional airspeed to continue a controlled flight. The FARs exist for the safety of pilots and their passengers, and matters of weight and balance shouldn't be set aside.

But if you fly the Alaska outback for a living, you simply cannot compete if you don't bend the rules a little bit. As I have said, Alaska's guides fly a whole moose, horns and all, in one trip with their tough little Super Cubs. To fly the same load legally would require five round trips. The legal pilot's clients will simply refuse to pay that sort of money, moving on to another guide/pilot who doesn't flinch at bending the rules. It's wrong, and it's sad, but it's also true. And, I'm red-faced to admit, it's a way of life in the far north.

These loads are certainly one of the reasons that Anchorage historically reports an average of eighty-eight light aircraft mishaps per week during the fall hunting seasons, when every Alaska flier becomes a bush pilot for a time. To give dubious credit where credit is due, however, I will say that most of these accidents happen to those pilots who can't—or won't—take the time to maintain edge-of-performance flying skills.

I have to admit that I have never seen an Alaska bush flier actually calculate the weight and balance of an aircraft. In the first place, they know they'd have to cart a set of scales around with them in the bush. Barring that, they would have to accurately estimate the weight of every passenger, fully clothed, adding in a figure for all the gear that the passenger drags along. Then there's the freight that's attached to the outside of the plane. The awkward stuff, such as moose or caribou horns, rifles, or snowshoes, is usually tied to the floats or struts. The calculations, as you can see, border on the impossible.

Alaska's pilots simply throw the heavy stuff toward the front and toss the sleeping bags, coats, and boots toward the back. During water operations the beer and canned goods may be dropped into the float lockers. Cased firearms and fishing rods are tied outside somewhere. Some pilots have special tubes—often no more than sections of metal chimney stacks—installed behind the headliner and into the fuselage area for the storage of fishing rods and the like. Such tubes make it possible to stow the rods without breaking them down.

Rare in the South 48, external loads have become so routine in Alaska that no one even looks twice at an aircraft burdened with moose or caribou horns, snowshoes, building materials, or whatever else the pilot hangs out there. The FAA will certify a large number of such loads, if they are properly secured. A lot of Alaska pilots wouldn't lift off during the winter months without one or two pairs of snowshoes strapped to the jury struts. I certainly wouldn't. It's a good place for a cased rifle or shotgun, too. Most of us have carried canoes and riverboats tied to the float fittings and struts. Lumber, tools, and camp gear—you name it. I once watched Dave Klosterman fly into Lake Hood driving a float-equipped DeHaviland Beaver with a whole Super Cub strapped atop the right float.

Probably my most exasperating external load was the large television satellite dish that I tied to the spreader bars beneath N9975Z,

THIS FULL SUPER CUB FUSELAGE
STRAPPED TO THE RIGHT FLOAT OF A
DEHAVILAND BEAVER IS AN EXTERNAL
LOAD TO TOP ALL OTHERS. THE PILOT
FLEW THIS LOAD THROUGH PORTAGE
PASS FROM PRINCE WILLIAM SOUND.

the turbocharged Cessna 206 on Wipline amphibious floats. With those floats, all control cables are concealed, leaving both the float decks and all the mounting struts, spreader bars, and hardware free of cables and pulleys. The five-foot-diameter satellite dish fit quite well when lashed to the spreader bars between the huge floats. All went very well until I tried to land. With dead-calm air and a salt-water bay one mile across and several miles long, a glassy water landing was the best answer, and that's the landing for which I made the approach. But an air cushion seemed to build up and balloon under the inverted dish each time I got within two feet of the water surface. Took a danged mile to land that thing.

* * *

Good, safe flying in Alaska and in any other outback part of the world involves preventative maintenance, skillful piloting techniques, and the flier's sure and certain knowledge of what both he and his aircraft are, and are not, capable. I've known a lot of pilots who own Piper's little Super Cubs yet will pass up landing sites that don't provide more than 600 feet of smooth earth or a paved runway. Their little planes will take off in about 50 feet and can easily land in 200 or less. But, from the air, such short and narrow pieces of real estate just don't look big enough. At cruising speed, these tight spots are easy to miss altogether if you are not used to seeing them for what they really are.

Before you take off, do all you can do to reduce the number of things that can go wrong in the air. If and when things go south for you, at least you'll know what it isn't. And, once in the air, never give up an option if you can help it. When your options are down to only one or two, you're already so far behind the power curve that your chances of catching up are somewhere between slim and none.

Take canned aviation fuel, for example. It's easy enough to play it safe and use a chamois to strain any canned aviation fuel you put into the tank while you're on the ground. A pilot who uses canned aviation fuel without *consistently* using a chamois-covered tractor funnel to filter the avgas while fueling up is looking for trouble. A chamois will trap any water or sediment in the fuel, allowing only clean avgas to enter the tank. And before you use those little wing-mounted gas drains to check for water or other impurities, rock the wings a few times, to move any hidden water to drains at the bottom of the tanks, will ya? It's so very easy to take care of the little things while the keys are still in your pocket and you can still reach everything.

It was just another cool, sunny Alaska day late in the fall and in the middle of hunting season when a young Alaska guide and pilot decided he was running a little short of time. He poured some canned 80-octane avgas directly from the five-gallon cans into the wing tanks of his sturdy little Super Cub. His new bride was watching as he took off from the small gravel strip for what was to be a very short flight. The Cub's engine quit at a very critical time, and his wife watched in horror as the Cub met the earth in an almost vertical dive. He didn't survive the crash, which was later attributed to contaminated fuel. If he had only taken an extra few moments to chamois that canned avgas . . .

Most importantly, take some time to really get to know your airplane. Can you imagine starting out across the country in your car without knowing what will happen if you have to slam on the brakes at a moment's notice? You also should know what will happen if you suddenly find your airplane in a spin. Or if you have to jam one or more of the controls hard against the stops. Emergency situations are never a good time to lock up on the controls, either mentally or physically.

Whether you are a budding low-time pilot or a longtime commercial airplane driver looking to sharpen your skills, travel to a small airport near your home. Find some grumpy ol' mossback instructor and beg him to take you up in his little taildragger. Whether it's a Cub, an Aeronca Champ, a Citabria, a Cessna, or any other tandem gear aircraft, spend a few hours in an honest, responsive, and hard-working airplane. Maybe find the pilot for a local glider or banner tow operation. He probably knows his airplane pretty well.

Finally, if you can find the time and a few spare bucks, take six or eight hours of aerobatic training. These will be the best learning hours you will ever spend in an airplane. Not only will you realize the limits of your airplane, you will learn to recognize when you are approaching them. You'll be a much more comfortable driver after those few hours. Full stalls will no longer make you uncomfortable, and spins won't ever again frighten you.

Did you ever stop to consider that a half-loop and half-roll may be the best way to get out of a blind canyon? Scary? Maybe so, if you haven't done them before. Are they a violation of the Federal Aviation Regulations? You bet, unless you're flying an acrobatic airplane and wearing a parachute. But, look at the alternatives. Besides, I don't recall ever having seen a FAA inspector standing around in bad weather at the head of a blind canyon just waiting for a violator, do you?

Or, if you are certain that you have the altitude, close the throttle and pull the nose up to bleed off a little airspeed, roll inverted and pull it through into the bottom half of a country loop. You can perform this maneuver in about 300 vertical feet, and you will have changed direction by 180 degrees. You will also arrive there at cruise speed. Aerobatic instruction can show what you and your aircraft can safely do. I highly recommend it.

* * *

Most of Alaska's Registered Guides, many of its sport fishing guides, and almost all of Alaska's air taxi operators are very active outback pilots. For that matter, you'd be hard pressed to meet anyone in the state who is *not* a pilot. When the fall hunting seasons arrive, even the weekend pilot becomes a "bush pilot." But, there are pilots—and then there are *pilots*.

A few of Alaska's air taxi operators have become pretty good at what they do, but a lot of them really haven't. It's most noticeable during the summer months, when many of them have to hire "outside" pilots to meet the heavy tourist demand. There is no shortage of stories about outside pilots asking directions from passing pilots, only to find that the outsider has dragged his charges through the wrong pass and is now sitting on a lake that seems to have lost the lodge that should have been there. Unfortunately, many of the unsuspecting passengers find they have to pay the bill anyway.

Although there are quite a few big game guides in Alaska with whom I wouldn't fly around the patch, many are great outback pilots. A few of Alaska's pilots are among the best in the world, and I'd fly anywhere with them. They have become both comfortable and proficient in flying the most difficult weather systems on earth. One such pilot is a dentist from Anchorage who gave up his practice and went south to Mexico to learn to fly the hard way. He became a very accomplished pilot, and a top-notch guide, too.

Another seemingly unlikely fellow from Anchorage wasn't satisfied with owning and operating a successful fine arts and native crafts shop, so he crawled into a Super Cub one day and climbed back out as one of Alaska's most talented and fearless airplane drivers. He and I never hit it off well, but I have to give him credit for his incredible flying skills.

He bolted a 200-hp engine to his little Cub, screwed a constant speed prop to the front end, jammed big thirty-five-inch tundra tires under the thing, then began to land and take off at places a sensible house fly would pass up as too small or too steep. Or both. The guy was incredible.

I was once flying some supplies through Merrill Pass on the way to Aniak when I spotted his Cub on a steep mountainside. From my perspective, the scene looked like a crash site. I was too heavy to fool around gawking at the mishap, but promised myself to swing by and see what I could do to help on my return flight in an hour and a half. When I got back, though, the little Cub was gone! The guy had simply landed on what looked like a piece of 45-degree mountain slope with less than 150 feet on a side—and a while later had just flown away again. Nothin' to it. I don't think most of us could have hit that spot with parachutes!

Some of the pilots flying out of Talkeetna, the guys who consistently fly Mt. McKinley—or Mt. Denali, if you're not a crotchety old sourdough—are more than good at what they do. Any talk of these intrepid Mt. McKinley pilots is shamefully incomplete without mentioning Don Sheldon, the premier McKinley pilot, who had an aeronautical engineering degree. Don knew that mountain almost as if he had created it himself.

As good as Don was, he nonetheless went through fifty-two different aircraft during his quarter-century of backcountry Alaska flying. Of course, he routinely flew into places where a sensible fellow wouldn't fling a dead rat. He was almost always flying off-airport. That sort of flying simply carries its own inherent risks. Almost every landing is a new experience, because almost every landing is made at an unfamiliar place. The pilot may never have been there before—although he will tell you he's been almost everywhere at least twice—and he may well never go back there again.

* * *

Alaska is more than huge—it is truly humungous. The country is sometimes hostile, and an unscheduled landing, whether precautionary or emergency, may turn out to be disastrous. Many times, the site of a downed aircraft is either unreachable or never even found. Like the Cessna 310 that disappeared with noted political figures Hale Boggs, Congressman from Louisiana, and Alaska's own Nick Begich. Along with another passenger and the pilot, the twin Cessna departed Yakutat one fine morning, headed northwest along the coast of Prince William Sound toward Anchorage. The weather deteriorated quickly, and the aircraft just seemed to vanish into thin air. Splashed down into the sea somewhere, most of us figured, or banged into a mountain along the route. In spite of a search that included every new electronic aid known to the military and civilian flying world, not a sign of the aircraft or any of its occupants has been seen in the several decades since. Even the XB-71 Blackbird was involved. There was talk of an overconfident pilot, icing conditions, fuel management problems—even possible political sabotage. Still—all these years later—absolutely nothing.

A young service station owner by the name of Yeager did much the same thing, a number of years ago. Flying a Cessna 172, back in the days before Cessna had swept the vertical stabilizer back to streamline it, young Yeager had apparently decided to climb above an overcast in order to reach better visibility and some smoother air. It was later presumed that he didn't calculate the crosswind component and ran out of fuel. He hasn't been seen since.

One fine day, a startling discovery was made by Ward Gay, a longtime Alaska pilot and big game guide who owned Alaska Aeronautical with his brother, Al. Ward took off from Lake Hood and flew northwest, beneath the restricted corridor serving Elmendorf Air Force Base jet fighter operations, and across Knik Arm—the silty body of water that enjoys the second-highest tides in North America, sometimes as high as thirty-nine feet. He was less than two minutes beyond liftoff when he saw something red sticking above water. Low tide on that day must have been very, very low to allow Ward to see anything at all in the water. As he circled around his discovery, Ward was able to get the tail numbers from a huge vertical stabilizer poking above the cold, gray water. Air Force investigations later revealed that the number had been assigned to a B-29 Superfortress that had disappeared in 1949 while on a one-mile final to Elmendorf Air Force Base near Anchorage. No one knew for almost forty years what had become of that huge airplane and its crew. On a one-mile final to a large air force base at Alaska's biggest city? Incredible, isn't it? Everything in Alaska is bigger than it's supposed to be. The mountains, the tides, the massive interior—it's not hard at all to lose an airplane in such a vast place.

One night in 1953, a flight of two F-94 Starfighters departed Elmendorf Air Force Base on a routine CAP (Combat Air Patrol) flight. "Gaydog Yellow Leader" reported a complete failure of his attitude instruments immediately after liftoff. The Civil Aeronautics Administration, which at that time monitored all Air Force radio traffic, broke in on the Air Force Controller's frequency, then working under the call sign "Savoy Nine," saying, "Gaydog Leader, switch to Charlie channel."

The lead pilot replied, "Charlie channel."

He never came up on Charlie channel, though. He simply disappeared forever during the climbing turn he had already initiated. That was almost fifty years ago, and the pilot wasn't more than 500 feet above the runway when he made his last transmission. His wingman, "Gaydog Yellow Two," almost instantly punched up into the same low overcast. He never saw his lead ship again, and the mystery remains to this day.

* * *

Alaska's famed pioneer pilots would be the first to tell you that they were really no different from the best pilots in Alaska today. Contemporary Alaska pilots still fly in the same terrible weather and unforgiving geographical environment as did their predecessors. Modern equipment is far better, of course, and unquestionably more reliable. Flying is certainly more comfortable than it used to be. Maintenance is much better these days, too, and good maintenance is available at many small airports throughout Alaska and the rest of the country. Avionics have put today's airplane drivers in touch with almost anybody they really care to talk to, though this is not true in some of Alaska's more remote areas.

Navigational aids have improved so dramatically that there is virtually no way to compare them to the low frequency Adcock radio ranges used in the 1930s and 1940s, which had unreliable, wandering signals, static-filled reception, aural nulls, dit-dahs and dahdits. Loran-C was great during the late 1970s and early 1980s, even in Alaska's remote and mountainous terrain. ADF (Automatic Direction Finding) may still be the most used tool today's Alaskan pilots have at their fingertips, unless flying exclusively in the instrument environment. Low Altitude Flight Planning Charts, VORs, ILS (Instrument Landing System) Glide Slopes, SIDs (Standard Instrument Departures) and STARs (Standard Terminal Approach Routes), and Instrument Approach Plates are all available to the instrument pilot. Most recently, an amazingly accurate array of satellite-supported GPS systems allows pilots to pinpoint destinations in a state where you can still fly in a straight line for more than 1,000 unbroken miles without crossing a single beer can, cigarette butt, or candy wrapper.

* * *

Virtually everyone in Alaska flies a light aircraft. The per capita number of pilots in this staggeringly empty land boggles the mind. Among these, though, also reside the very few who dedicate themselves to flying the Alaska outback, no matter the season and no matter the weather.

Those who fly the grub and supplies to the trapper who lives "'bout a quarter-mile upstream from that big rock just down from the big bend in the Stony above Lime Village. You know the one I mean. Yeah, I know it's a long flight, but I'll have some canned avgas for ya on the bank there." Boy, he'd better have! Three and one-half hours out on four hours' fuel? The pilot couldn't get back without it!

The bush pilot flies alone—but never lonely—against a backdrop of mountains and glaciers so dazzlingly bright in the sunshine, and yet so absolutely ominous in bad weather, they defy description. Treeless plains of tundra so vast and limitless as to appear larger than the state of Montana. Mountain ridges so new and sharp that a careless climber might cut his fingers on them. If they were within reach and climbable, that is.

And the weather? Without argument the weather is the worst you'll find this side of the South Pole. In 1991, a winter snowstorm with 110-knot winds and seas above eighty feet hit Prince William Sound. The U.S. Coast Guard performed a helicopter rescue in these conditions, saving the lives of three fishermen who had survived ten hours in the sub-Arctic water—at night! What kind of pilot purposely flies out under these conditions? I can tell you. The kind that lives by the creed, "You have to go out; you don't have to come back."

Mason Lavelle, a pilot I knew some years ago, was caught in a snowstorm while en route to Merrill Field from the village of McGrath. He turned up the wrong canyon and, when things suddenly didn't feel right, turned to get back out. He felt a bump, then another bump, then a series of bumps. Several days later, he returned to look at the canyon he had earlier—and mistakenly—flown into. As best he could figure, he had decided to make that turn a split-second before impacting a glacier at the head of that canyon. In the blinding snowstorm, he had taxied across the face of the glacier—*at cruise speed!* I guess you just don't slice it any thinner than that.

It's a really big country. It's really an empty country. Above all, it's a truly unforgiving country. It is here that the Alaska bush pilot plies his edge-of-the-world trade.

It has often been said that there are old pilots and there are bold pilots, but there are no old, bold pilots. In Alaska, it is only the bold pilots who survive to become old pilots. Come fly with me and see what it's really like.

Chapter 2

DRIFT RIVER

We had first tried to make the flight to Drift River on the cold and unfriendly Saturday morning of November 10, 1974. Stratus clouds hung low at 200 feet, blanketing everything from Anchorage to beyond St. Augustine Island. Conditions didn't look all that ripe for success.

Drift River itself is a nothing little stream that flows eastward from a crack in the Alaska Range that separates the Neacola Mountains from the Chigmit Mountains. The small stream meanders for more than fifteen miles across flatland, encouraging a few scattered patches of scrub willow while discouraging salmon runs or native trout populations.

By the same token, it lies within a small area that was of interest to petroleum exploration efforts and, according to the aeronautical charts, sports a 3,000-foot runway 43 feet above sea level just south of its lethargic outflow into Cook Inlet. The headwaters of Drift River, to give more than warranted class to this small stream, lie between the two mountain ranges. Peaks above 6,000 feet rise within ten miles on either side of this river birthing area. It's not a place for the beginning pilot to be nosing around during scabby weather, though the land is virtually flat between the stream's upper end and its confluence with Cook Inlet. Most of this is flat wet grassland and thin willow scrub. The colors nonetheless are picture postcard pretty in sunny weather. In poor visibility, the landscape is virtually without feature. The area's claim to fame, beyond its small-scale petroleum activities, is a healthy moose population. The moose, of course, were the reason for the planned excursion.

The next day, word from Anchorage Flight Service was more encouraging. I had requested a Zone Clearance and earned the Special VFR for a Chester Creek Departure. That would at least get us away from Anchorage and started on our way. The little 125-hp Super Cub, Arctic Gray, was about the same color as the world around us when we lifted off.

We dashed low and westward from the mouth of Chester Creek across frigid Knik Arm to Point McKenzie to the northwest. Knik Arm is a body of glacial, silt-laden water with an awesome thirty-nine-foot maximum tide. No amount of flying experience negates its threat to the pilot. I stayed well within the flight restrictions of "below 500 or above 2,000" established to prevent civil aircraft from encountering jet fighter traffic from nearby Elmendorf Air Force Base. I banked to turn slightly south toward Drift River, cruising the west side of Cook Inlet, open now and free of fog all the way past Kodiak Island and to the North Pacific Ocean. My two passengers were anxious to set up a winter moose hunting tent camp near the east end of Lake Clark Pass and at the headwaters of Drift River. They were excited about several good bulls they had seen yarded up there during a previous scouting flight.

The weather still wasn't really much more than marginal, but it began to improve once we had passed Point Kustatan, south of the private West Foreland Petroleum Company strip. Farther ahead, the west side of Trading Bay looked almost sunny all the way to the mouth of Drift River. My passengers' enthusiasm was now definitely on the rise.

Turning right and heading west up Drift River, as we did then, would have taken us in the general direction of Lake Clark Pass, though not directly into the entrance itself. I had planned to land on a small sand road just northeast of the pass itself, where my two moose hunters wanted to set up their wilderness tent camp. As we approached that area, we saw several big bulls wandering around in the willows within 300 yards of their proposed little campsite. We circled wide to land so we wouldn't disturb them.

Unloading and camp setup took only a short time, and I was soon on my lonely way back to Merrill Field. The hunters were to stay until the following Saturday, when I was scheduled to pick them up and haul them back to town.

On the following day, however, a fierce winter storm had reportedly swept across the Bering Sea to breach the sea wall at Nome. Winds had blasted across the International Dateline, scouring both Big Diomede and Little Diomede Islands, battering the famous gold beaches of that far north city. One billiard parlor operator told reporters that the ocean had roared through the front of his modest shop with such force that it had swept his best snooker table right on out through the rear wall! I supposed he had lost the cuspidors, too. And there was no sign of a letup.

When the Kuskokwim Mountains didn't slow down the storm in the least, it appeared that the Alaska Range wasn't going to stop it either. Early Wednesday morning, several days ahead of schedule, I strapped my little 1952 agricultural model Super Cub to my backside and lit out in a sky that was just about the same gray color as my little fabric airplane.

All Alaskans have seen snow, but this was really *SNOW!* I was bobbing along at about sixty feet in moderate to severe turbulence when I passed Tyonek, twenty-five minutes out. I was still too low to see the village strip atop the 110-foot cliff hard off my right wingtip. With twenty years of Alaska flying behind me, and the Bigfoot Cub belted to my bottom end, I wasn't really uncomfortable yet. I did have one advantage over most Alaska pilots—I was blessed with excellent vision, much better than twenty/twenty. My vision was actually twenty/five, which meant that I could see at a distance of twenty feet what most people could see at five feet. This little bit of good fortune allowed me to fly with very little discomfort in relatively poor weather. Still, it's always darkest before it goes completely black, someone had said, and it was definitely getting darker. I found I was actually looking *up* at the small strip at Nikolai Creek—at an elevation of only thirty feet—when I passed that. By the time I had skirted the private strip at Trading Bay, I was holding twenty feet and watching the pucker meter edge its way upward toward eight, on the way to its imaginary redline at ten.

I flew past the strip at West Foreland—fifty-five feet above the little Cub—still at twenty feet and was by then following every little dimple in the shoreline. By the time I found the west end of that cape at Point Kustatan, I knew I shouldn't go any farther. All I could see ahead of me was the black circle of the spinning prop against a white background. Looking straight down, I could barely see through twenty feet of streaking white to the frigid gray waters of Redoubt Bay, where the snow was now falling faster than it could melt into the dirty, white-capped water.

I landed straight ahead on the beach at the tip of the peninsula and climbed out to sit on the 25x11x4 tundra tire under a protective right wing. For a while I just watched the storm as it raged around me, mostly sheltered from the wind by the trembling fuselage. The snow was *really* coming down. Fierce winds shot the snow horizontally across the sky. After a time, during which I measured four inches of fresh snowfall in only fifteen minutes, I thought the storm might finally be letting up a little.

Never one to pass up an opportunity to do something truly stupid, I climbed back aboard, clamped down my aerobatic seat and shoulder harnesses, fired off the little Lycoming engine, and lit out once more to the south. By the time I had scooted across the mouth of Drift River, it was again snowing too hard for me to consider leaving my only link with the earth, the silty waters just below the left wheel. I couldn't see the scrub willows just a few feet off my right wing, and there was nothing else around there to see. If I turned upstream at that point, and if the wind blew my bouncing little plane off the correct compass course by only a few degrees, I would be less than 300 seconds from flying into the face of solid rock. Holding an accurate liquid compass heading in the turbulence roaring down from the Neacola Mountains just ten or twelve miles ahead would be absolutely impossible. It was now snowing so hard that I could only faintly make out the gray, silty waters of Redoubt Bay, just ten feet beneath the Cub's big left wheel.

I felt, more than saw, the shadows of three spruce trees blink past my right wingtip, and I knew I was coming up on Harriet Point, six or eight miles south of the mouth Drift River. I had already passed by my two stranded hunters and was just about to fly off into history. That didn't seem to make much sense. Besides, I was now flying in heavy turbulence with full flaps, holding less than 50 knots at an altitude of only ten feet above an unfriendly cauldron of snow and slushy gray water.

I had to ease out over the bay and nudge the Cub's nose up a little just to keep my right wing out of the water as I made the right teardrop 180-degree turn to line up for a landing to the north on the narrow, snow covered, and steeply pitched beach. The pucker meter had edged up past nine.

With no forward visibility at all now, and only a vague visual reference of the slush below, that was one of the longest single minutes of my thousands of flying hours. The landing roll was very short, given a combination of almost three feet of fresh snow, the Cub's huge tundra tires and the terrible wind coming from the front left quadrant. Landing was a balancing act. I had to try to keep the wind from lifting the onshore wing and tossing the Cub into the roiling waters; prevent the deep snow from trying to flip the little craft over on its nose; and keep the Cub from sliding or rolling off the steep beach and into the water, only six or eight feet away. The combination of left aileron up, the right rudder pressed to provide a little directional control, the left brake used as needed to prevent a skid, and power over the elevators to keep me from flipping over, gave me a busy moment. But only a moment, since the Cub came to a halt in somewhere less than forty feet, immediately adjacent to the three spruce trees. These were the only shelter for miles in any direction along this stretch of beach, and they had been my only real target for a Siwash camp. Among other things, they would help break the thundering wind and slow the driving snow.

Just before the little plane lurched to a stop, the huge left wheel hit some sort of obstruction buried under the deep snow. The Cub's nose swung sharply in that direction. The spinning prop sliced a wealth of snow from the top of a three-foot drift at the top of the beach, hurling a blinding white curtain across the windshield. What I didn't know at the time was that the prop tips had also whacked a huge cottonwood log concealed beneath the three-foot drift.

After shutting down and climbing out to the familiar smell of warm oil and the ticking of cooling cylinders, I lifted and grunted the tail in nearly a 180-degree arc to a point at the top of the narrow beach, setting it gently across the huge, snow-buried cottonwood that must have crashed ashore a great many storms ago. At least my fragile little plane was now above the pounding gray slush and below the raging offshore winds that had threatened the landing. After tying down the tail section to the big log and roping the right wing-mounted tie-down ring to another portion of the same log, the little Cub was pointed about 45 degrees southeast down the beach and protected by the trees from most of the shrieking wind. The trees would make a good wind break for my nylon mountain tent, too, and I set about to make a snug little camp against the howling storm. I first tied the control stick back with the seat belt, and then began to take stock of my situation.

While I was unable for the moment to extricate my two hunters from the upper reaches of Drift River, I knew they had comfortable and weatherproof tents, heat, and plenty of food. Moreover, they were both skilled and experienced Alaska outdoorsmen. While I suspected they might be less than back-home comfortable, I felt good about their safety at the moment. Since there was little I could do for them while the storm raged on, I bent to the task of setting up house.

I had always kept a lightweight North Face geodesic dome tent in the back of the plane. It was more than suitable for winds in excess of 80 miles per hour. And long ago I had gotten in the habit of packing food and first-aid gear into a carton that was strapped to the longerons aft of the baggage compartment headliner. When I unsnapped the headliner, however, there was nothing behind it but an empty fuselage. Though I was certain that my gear had been stolen, I later learned that a friend of mine had removed it so that it wouldn't be stolen! After all, what are good friends for, right? All I had with me was my custom Holubar goose down sleeping bag, which I had carried to the plane earlier that morning, and a growing unease about the world around me. This didn't promise to be my very best camp-out, by any means. The insulation in the down bag, once it was wet, would be about as useless as the same amount of damp Kleenex, except that it would at least be contained, all in one lump, of course, and jammed to the bottom of the bag. It certainly wouldn't protect me from the elements.

The temperature was holding at a balmy 30 degrees, and every flake of falling snow that hit those spruce trees teamed with others to melt on the way down, eventually becoming part of a large drop of really cold water. The arctic down bag was small protection against this soaking, and my makeshift emergency camp soon became a slushy little lake beneath the low branches of the three dripping spruce trees. For the next two and a half days I would either lay shivering in the wet bag and huddled under the raining spruce trees to stay out of the wind, or sit cramped in the small Cub's front office. In either event, all I could see was snow, and most of that was still blowing across the beach and out to sea in horizontal streaks. I wondered how long the storm could last without some sort of relief. Maybe for a lot longer than I could.

I had no food at all, was reduced to drinking water from the slushy little puddle around my useless sleeping bag, and was without a heat source of any appreciable kind. An open flame under the winter spruce would have stolen my meager shelter, too, if any of the low branches had caught fire. Even if I could have somehow built a fire in the ankle-deep water.

At about nine o'clock on the night of the fifteenth, fifty-two hours after I had landed, I looked north into the darkness and thought I saw an orange glow through the blowing snow. It had to be the off-shore oil rigs, burning off vent gas waste. I figured if I could see that far through the snow and darkness, I could see well enough to fly. I prepared to leave as quickly as possible, hoping that the snowfall would hold off for a while.

I counted off 100 paces as I trudged north through the deep

snow along the beach, finding no big holes, logs or dead seals. Even in the deep snow, that 250 feet would be enough to allow the empty Super Cub to bounce off the steep and narrow beach without much concern. A Cub may have relatively poor ailerons, but it has an effective rudder, and I knew I could handle a little slipping and sliding during the takeoff roll.

I found an old spruce limb under the trees and used it as a makeshift broom, sweeping as much snow as possible from the Cub's upper wing, tail and fuselage surfaces. I didn't realize that I was also shredding the fabric on the upper wing surfaces where I could barely reach. If I had, I might just have stayed on that miserable little stretch of beach forever.

I untied the Cub and lifted its tail off the log, swinging it around and down to align the plane with the beach, the nose now pointed north toward home. The cold engine started within seconds, as it always did. It was an old Cub, but well maintained, and I knew that the small 125-horsepower Lycoming engine had more than enough power to lift us off that narrow little beach. As soon as the oil temperature gauge indicated some life, I performed the magneto check, did a quick full-power runup, pulled down two notches of flaps, and roared off in a cloud of blown snow. Performance wasn't exactly what I had expected, but I gave that to the snow left on the wings and tail surfaces. It wasn't until later that I discovered the altered propeller pitch.

I found I could only make it up to 200 feet before slamming into the heavy overcast, but that was still about 190 feet better than I had on the trip down, wasn't it? I wasn't the least discouraged.

I gave Kenai Radio a call, but they weren't encouraging. The FSS wallah told me that the Anchorage weather was 200 feet, sky obscured, one-eighth-mile visibility in heavy snow, with winds at 35 knots. By the time I had received that good news, I had already flown north far enough to realize that it was still snowing too hard for me to make it back home along the west side of Cook Inlet. Especially in the black of night and without instruments.

I banked the little Super Cub east toward the off-shore oil platforms and flew like a moth to the flame of burning gases at the southernmost oil rig. There's something in all of us that takes comfort in a nice, warm fire. Hearth and home, I suppose. Whatever it is, it pulled me around that oil rig twice, warming my chilly imagination until I remembered that I was bobbing along over some of the world's most treacherous water. That cold thought stole any warmth the flames had provided, and I took up a bouncing compass heading for Kenai. The city was still ten long minutes ahead and east across Cook Inlet, home of thirty-nine-foot tides. Several times each year, these tides could come in behind a six-foot wall of water moving at 15 knots.

Those ten minutes were among the longest, and darkest, I've ever passed. With one eye on the wildly swinging compass and the other on the elusive bubble of the turn-and-bank indicator, bucking turbulence I can still honestly call severe, I punched along through the tail end of one of the worst blizzards I'd seen in the past twenty-four Alaska winters.

When I finally reached the hazy shoreline, black against dark gray, and thankfully right where it was supposed to be, I turned south along the beach toward the mouth of the Kenai River. When I took the U-turn at the river mouth, a turn that aligned me with Kenai's Runway 1, I felt home free.

After taxiing clear of the runway and tying down Mr. Piper's wonderful little Super Cub, I entered the Flight Service Station. I learned that my two hunters had already walked the road out to the commercial camp at the mouth of the Drift River. They were not only safe and sound, they were warm and well fed, too. I called my future wife, Peggy, in Anchorage to let her know that her erstwhile partner had done it again, then called a taxi for the trip to a local motel where I could get a really huge meal and a warm, dry bed. It was at precisely that moment when every light from Homer to Talkeetna went out!

A dependent swath of Alaska more than 400 miles long had suddenly, and without warning, gone completely black. It was a power failure of *major* proportions. It is very sobering to reflect that, if all those lights had gone dark just a few minutes earlier, I'd probably be circling around over Cook Inlet to this day!

I didn't tell just everybody, but it was this very flight that pushed me to immediately rip the fabric from the already torn and shabby little Cub and begin a complete rebuild. I installed a new and larger power plant, new fabric, a few of Alaska's special bush modifications, and enough instruments to shoot full IFR approaches, right down to the Glide Slope and Marker Beacons. Never again would I fly that little plane around in the dark, like a moth in the night, looking with straining eyes for a warm and friendly flame somewhere out there in the cold and lonely Alaska night.

Chapter 3

FREEZE UP

*E*very now and again I find myself browsing through some of my flight logs, recalling flights past and refreshing my resolve about some of the things I might do differently during similar flight situations. More than half the "Remarks" columns in those books bring to my mind's eye sharp images of particularly memorable trips. Two of those entries read, "BARTUSSEK/LEICHTHAMMER: ABORT/ WX." On these two flights, made in October 1979, I flew two German hunting companions to hunt caribou. Both these experienced hunters would later become my very close friends.

I've always been something of an easy mark. Too quick with an off-the-wall "yes" to one or another request for assistance. This trait has caused some pretty serious problems a few times in my life.

My "yes" on this occasion was to a telephone call from Anchorage's Captain Cook Hotel. A heavy German accent asked for "Heah Mawt Maz'n," which I took to be me, Herr Mort Mason. The caller identified himself as Alois Bartussek. He and his hunting companion, Wulf Leichthammer, wanted an unguided, drop-off caribou hunt.

I explained to Herr Bartussek that it was already way down in the fall, and that winter was even then huffin' and puffin' at us from the other side of the Alaska Range. It was a little late in the year for a floatplane trip into the hills. I explained that once the lakes began to freeze, it would be some weeks before safe ski operations could be conducted. During that period, use of a floatplane, *ein Wasserfleugzueg*, would be out of the question.

The story my caller proceeded to relate was a sad, if not atypical, Alaska tale. He and his companion had hired a pilot from King Salmon to fly them out and drop them off on a gravel bar in the crystal-clear King Salmon River, where they would set up camp and hunt for bull moose. A price for this service was agreed upon, and the pilot dropped them off as he had promised. He collected his fee for services, then flew almost 500 miles back to Anchorage, caught a commercial flight to Seattle—and vanished. It turned out that the *federales* were just one jump behind him for some infraction or another, and he apparently felt that a change of scenery was necessary.

The two innocent and unknowing hunters, meanwhile, had succeeded in taking a fine bull moose while up the river. Since Germany does not permit its returning hunters to bring the meat of wild animals back into their country, they would donate the meat to others, taking home only the trophy horns.

In the lengthening absence of their original pilot, they finally succeeded in flagging down a passing bush pilot—no small feat in and of itself—and made their way back to King Salmon. At least they were no longer up the river without a paddle, right? The rescue pilot agreed to take their gear along, but wouldn't take the moose that they had bagged, field-dressed, and hung on a meat pole. Without charging another exorbitant fee, that is. And to leave meat in the bush would mean breaking state law. They had to dig deeply into their dwindling resources yet again.

They had just arrived back in Anchorage, but still had a few more vacation days before they were scheduled to return home to Germany. My name was familiar to them from several German hunting magazines, and they located me through the Yellow Pages, where we were listed as guides, pilots, and outfitters.

My caller asked if I could drop the two of them down somewhere in productive caribou country for a short, unguided trip. Even for just two or three days, he pleaded. I explained that, beyond just finding and bagging a caribou, packing meat, horns, and hide back to camp would involve lots of pretty hard work. Two days in camp was an extremely tight time frame. In addition, the short trip would mean only one caribou between the two hunters. Moreover, they wouldn't be able to fly and shoot the same day, under Alaska's strict and well-policed game regulations. They understood all this, Alois said.

He was most persuasive, and I agreed to at least meet with them over coffee to try to discourage such a risky trip. It worked out the other way, obviously, and on the morning of the sixteenth we were at Lake Hood, world's largest seaplane base, loading my Cessna 206 floatplane in some pretty ratty weather.

I had selected a spot near Lime Village, along the Stony River, as a likely place to bag a large bull caribou. Recent snows had driven the biggest bulls down from 5,000 or 6,000 feet where they had been holed up to avoid the flies and bugs of late summer.

Snow and low ceilings brought our planned trip through Merrill Pass in the Alaska Range to a halt. One hour and forty-five minutes after takeoff we were back on the water at Lake Hood.

By the following morning, the weather had improved somewhat. One hour and thirty minutes after takeoff, we landed at

FROM LEFT TO RIGHT IS THE
WEST-TO-EAST ROUTE THROUGH
MERRILL PASS, WITH 90-DEGREE RIGHT
TURN AT THE SADDLE AT THE CENTER
BOTTOM OF THE PHOTOGRAPH. MANY
PILOTS REFUSE TO FLY THROUGH THIS
PASS, EVEN ON BRIGHT, SUNNY DAYS.
WHEN LOW ON FUEL ONE DARK AND
RAINY ALASKA NIGHT, I HAD NO CHOICE
BUT TO FLY THROUGH THE PASS.

Underhill Lake, a small lake deep in the rolling foothills, snug up against some 9,000-foot peaks in the Neacola Mountains. The lake itself sits at an elevation of about 1,200 feet.

We had seen no animals during the flight in, but I knew from experience that this spot was ideal at this time of year. Caribou trails along the ridges above the lake were more than knee deep, engraved in the tundra over who knows how many past decades or even centuries.

I helped Alois and Wulf set up two of my North Face geodesic tents, reviewed a map of the surrounding country with them, and then took off headed back through Merrill Pass for Anchorage. I was scheduled to pick them up again at noon on the nineteenth, two days hence.

Mid morning on Friday, October 19, I lifted the water rudders, advanced the throttle to 2,700 rpm, leaned down from 36.5 to 31 gallons on the fuel flow meter, and pushed the empty Cessna Stationair over onto the step in bright sunshine. With 20 degrees of flaps, the Cessna flew itself smoothly off the sparkling water. But forty minutes later, things weren't looking very good at all.

Anchorage Radio had given me two PIREPS (Pilot Reports) and one weather SPECIAL from Sparrevohn (Cairn Mountain, on the sectional chart for that area), a former USAF Dew Line radar site on the other side of the Alaska Range and about twenty-five miles southwest of the camp at Underhill Lake.

Neither of the two reporting pilots had been able to make it through the pass. It is only fair to state here that many of Alaska's pilots do not like Merrill Pass at all, and some won't fly through it under any conditions. As was my custom, I asked for the airplane types reporting. The first was a Citabria, which I mentally discounted for the moment. The other was a DeHaviland Beaver belonging to a local air taxi operator. I couldn't discount that, since he certainly knew what sort of weather he had seen. I'm not knocking Citabria pilots, but to my knowledge there were no 100-hour Beaver pilots flying floats commercially in the Alaska outback.

Anchorage Radio had reported from Sparrevohn, "three hundred, sky obscured, one-eighth mile in snow." Well, there was always a chance . . .

I had given up on trying to find Merrill Pass in all that bad weather and had climbed to 8,500 feet to cross over the top of the Alaska Range, in hopes of finding a hole in the undercast on the west side. I found the hunting camp by triangulating my position relative to nearby peaks that poked up silently through the solid cloud mass below me. The overcast topped out at 8,000, and I was certain it was solid all the way to the ground.

I tuned Cairn Mountain NDB at 281 on the low frequency radio and followed the ADF needle for exactly ten minutes. Next, I brought up Aniak at 359, got the identifier and a strong needle, and descended in the white to 3,000 feet on the Aniak heading. Nothing but heavy snow all the way down. The ten-minute descent hadn't earned me a thing.

On the way back up to 8,500, I again tuned in Cairn Mountain and checked with them on their comm frequency.

"Sparrevohn, good morning. Cessna seven five six victor romeo with you."

"Cessna seven five six vee are, Sparrevohn, go ahead."

"Roger, Sparrevohn, we're bangin' around here at Lime, climbing back for eight point five. Got any updates on Sparrevohn this morning?"

"Last we had was the Special, about two hours old now. Three hundred, sky obscured, one-eighth mile in snow. You get that one?"

"Yeah, we got that one. Appreciate it, Sparrevohn. Six vee are."

I topped out at 8,000 again and took it on up to eight point five, circling the camp area three times. I was pretty sure that my hunters were listening in the white silence below to the sound of the plane fruitlessly circling overhead. I would just have to give it up, and I was certain they would know that.

The return to Anchorage wasn't much better. I had begun to lose fuel flow and couldn't figure out why. I suspected the Slick magnetos, but they both checked out smooth and with matching drops. Still, I was now being robbed of altitude, foot by foot, because of the insidious power loss.

Crossing the range ahead, still obscured in cloud, meant staying above 8,000 feet, if possible. Several 9,000-foot peaks speared up through all that garbage below, and off to the northeast I could see Mt. Spurr standing above 11,000 feet. I was seriously thinking I might be lucky to hold 6,000, and began trying to visualize the lower saddles in the hidden range, now close enough to be really personal.

I had locked on the Anchorage VOR and was flying direct, the shortest possible route home. It soon began to look as though I was good for the ridgeline. A few minutes later proved that I had, indeed, crossed the jagged ridge. The mountains in this area are relatively "new" mountains, and most of the ridges are so sharp that one could only walk them with one boot on either side. They were sharp enough to slice bread.

I was still losing altitude, and turned slightly north of course to descend toward Chakachamna Lake, the long lake that sits a little above 1,100 feet MSL. I could see the valley in which it lay, but not the lake itself, which was hidden beneath the thick undercast. The mountain range seemed to be holding most of the weather on its western slopes. In all likelihood, the eastern slopes were still wide open.

By the time I had made it to Chakachamna, I knew I would also make Lake Hood. I could keep my home base dead ahead from forty miles out. Lake Hood Tower cleared me straight in for the east waterway, and I crossed Anchorage International Airport's Runway

14-32 on a *really low* short final. Later investigation revealed that it had indeed been a magneto problem all along. I immediately got rid of the Slicks and had new Bendix mags, with heavy-duty harness, installed.

The night of the nineteenth turned severe clear and three-dog cold. I knew that my hunters, on the other side of the Alaska Range and far removed from warm open water, were now frozen in. Great! Now what?

Early the following morning I tied on my 150-hp Super Cub, also still on floats, and headed once more through Merrill Pass for Underhill Lake. The weather was excellent. Two hours later, I knew that my earlier concern had been justified. The lake was frozen solid except for a small circle in the center. The hole looked just a bit too small for landing, and definitely too small for three people, caribou meat, horns, hide, and gear, all piled into a plane, to take off from. Still, I couldn't just leave 'em there 'til spring, could I?

I made a very steep approach, hanging just above a stall, and was able to dig the float heels in and rudder to a stop without climbing the ice. Now came the real problem: getting back out with a truly overloaded airplane.

Everything you've ever read about Super Cubs is true. And more. The baggage compartment placard restricting baggage to fifty pounds is at least one decimal place off. Five hundred pounds, loaded aft, makes that sturdy little plane quite stable. I'm not encouraging that sort of loading. I'm just confessing to it.

Alois and Wulf had heard the Cessna the day before, but it was snowing heavily around them, and they knew I couldn't find the lake in such a mess. After some laughs about the weather, and some back-slapping on account of a grand, hard-earned, fall-color caribou bull, the two hunters set about breaking camp and packing up their gear. I fired up the Cub and began the process of either destroying some ice or bending the floats.

I would ease up to the face of fresh ice, raise the water rudders, pull the stick back to my lap, and advance the throttle. When the empty Cub climbed out onto the ice, I waited for the brittle stuff to break under the point load at the float keels. Time after time, the faithful little Cub struggled up onto the ice only to fall through again. This activity wasn't doing the floats any good, but one more night of freeze would close this part of the world for several weeks, and I knew it. As clear as the weather was at that moment, that freeze would come tonight!

After an hour or so of this racket, I had done all the damage I was able to do. The remaining ice was just too thick to break, and it was still freezing. I had reached the point where the Cub would just sit atop the ice until I could power it around and taxi off to plunge back into open water again.

We successfully loaded the meat, both hunters, and most of their gear into the cramped Cub, filling both float lockers with equipment. We tied the large horns to the float struts outside the plane— and cached some of the gear. I promised to return later in the winter on skis, pick it up, and ship it to them in Germany. (I was able to make that trip several weeks later.)

I certainly didn't like the current situation. I would have to attempt a tight step-turn takeoff in an extremely restricted area. Steep hills on three sides, beginning right at the lake's edge, gave us a one-way departure, with absolutely no options. If by then I had not been at this sort of foolishness for more than twenty years, I wouldn't even have tried it. I thought, though, that if I could just get this overload up on the step, I could make it. It would certainly be unorthodox, but I thought successful more likely than not.

Four or five attempts at getting the overloaded Cub up on the step in a circling high-speed taxi didn't do it, so we unloaded about twenty pounds. Later, another fifteen or twenty went into storage with the first twenty. The meat and both hunters simply had to stay with the airplane. So did the large caribou horns.

Alois was about six feet two inches tall and weighed one 185 pounds. Wulf was slightly shorter at six feet one, but tipped the scales at around 220 pounds. Suffice it to say, the little Cub was loaded. The large caribou rack tied outside wouldn't help our aerodynamics a whole lot, either.

We had burned off a few pounds of fuel by our third attempt with the lightened load. I knew by then that I had just committed us to the takeoff. We were finally on the step and in a tight left turn, headed for the ice at slightly more than 40 miles an hour indicated. We were too close to the ice to stop. Both hunters were trapped in the tiny area just behind my seat, as uncomfortable as size twelve feet in size nine boots.

The Cub was drawing more water than I liked, even on the step, but I knew we'd get up onto the ice with this run. The question I couldn't answer yet was will the ice hold under this added weight?

We hit the edge of the ice with a solid thump, losing some speed with the impact. I could hear the ice breaking even over the roar of the anxious little engine. The air was filled with ice and water, and the prop was throwing both in all directions. Several large chunks of ice thundered off the plastic windshield. The tail was taking a tremendous beating, and so were the floats. And then we were up on solid ice!

I had good directional control through the rudder, though this control was neither dramatic nor quickly effective. A little snow on the ice would have helped. The heavy snow of yesterday had obviously stopped before the temperature had plummeted below zero, and our own private little ice rink was figure-skating smooth.

Flaps still raised, we roared across the short ice field toward the towering spruce trees at the far end of the lake. We were approaching that end of the lake much too quickly, and I gritted my teeth against the temptation to pull the flap handle until the very last possible moment. This was a one shot deal, and I wanted every inch of speed that I could muster before I lowered the flaps.

I held out for about two seconds beyond my better judgment, and then pulled the flaps full on. I could feel the heavy load transfer to the wings and lift free of the ice. The rumbling vibration through the rigid float mountings suddenly stopped. Before I had time to think, the sight of spruce trees filled the windshield.

The determined little Super Cub staggered between two spruce trees that looked to be ten feet apart but must have been forty. We cleared them by at least twelve inches at either wingtip. And then we were flying. Academically, that is. Practically speaking, we were riding ground effect for all it could give us. It would be another mile or more before I would begin to ease the flaps up ever so cautiously and slowly.

A little heavy and a little slow, the return trip to Lake Hood took two plus twenty. I had chamoised in five gallons of cached 80-octane avgas while at Underhill, and that was just about the right amount for the return trip.

When we finally arrived back at Lake Hood, I wondered whether or not I could find a shoehorn big enough to pry my two passengers out of the little Cub. I thought that perhaps neither of the hunters would ever again stand upright.

The two had bagged their big bull caribou, enjoyed more than a little excitement, and arrived home all in one piece, however bent and disfigured by the cramped quarters in the tiny airplane.

Foolish? Yeah, since I shouldn't have taken them through the mountains in the first place. The questionable takeoff? I beg off by remembering more than 600,000 miles of Super Cub flight before that attempt, as weak as that excuse might be. And the hunters? Oh, yeah. Returned to hunt with us the following year. Successfully, I might add. And a whole lot more safely.

Chapter 4

ICE AND WATER

During the late moose-hunting season of 1962, a good friend of mine, Chic Lane, had shot a fine bull for his winter meat supply. He took the moose on Swan Lake, one of three small lakes set into the Chugach Mountains of the Kenai Peninsula, not far from Cooper Landing. On the northeast corner of this small lake sat a small log cabin, and Chic had chosen this for his campsite. It was a snug and sturdy little structure, neat, well scribed and quite well made. It was in this cabin, in fact, that its builder, Doc Romig, a physician from Anchorage, had removed his own appendix using only a hunting knife, a Coleman lantern and a small shaving mirror. And without benefit of anesthetic!

Chic had made himself comfortable there, given that winter moose hunts can sometimes be challenging due to the cold and unpredictable weather. In point of fact, a cold knife blade will freeze instantly to warm meat, and the skinning and butchering chores required to clean an animal as large as an Alaskan moose are demanding at the very least.

Chic had taken his moose slightly up the low mountain on the south side of the lake, and he had packed the butchered carcass down the hill and across the lake. He had then hung all the meat on a sturdy spruce meat pole suspended between two live spruce trees near the cabin.

All the meat had been nicely bagged and separated to provide good ventilation and cooling, as is appropriate with game animals. Each bag swung gently beneath the meat pole, suspended on a short piece of stout line.

After the meat had cooled well, Chic cleaned his camp, loaded his pack with personal gear, and hiked back to his car, parked several miles away. He had left his unused food neatly stored in the cabin for the next guy, which most thoughtful Alaska hunters do. And, in fact, what Alaska law required. After he had driven the 120 miles north to Anchorage, he called to ask if I would fly the meat back for him.

The weather turned unseasonably warm during the next two or three days, and ceilings came right on down to the ground. Flying was impossible, and I just had to wait it out, as did most Anchorage pilots. Since the meat had cooled immediately after it was taken, and had been properly protected against the elements, as well as against predators, human and otherwise, there was little chance of its spoiling or going missing. Neither of us worried about that. While I thought the chances were slim that anyone else would be flying over that area, it was entirely possible that someone might. If they spotted the cache hanging exposed on that meat pole next to the cabin, Chic could lose his winter meat supply. With his big game tag already sealed to the horns, he wouldn't be able to hunt for another moose that winter. That 600 pounds or so of meat meant a lot to him and his family. I was in the air at the very first break in the weather, flying my big-engine Cessna 170A on hydraulic wheel/skis south over the Kenai Peninsula toward Swan Lake.

When I slipped through a small mountain pass to reach Swan Lake, I could see that the meat cache was still intact. No wolves, no coyotes, no wolverines, and no poachers. So far things were going our way.

I circled the lake, gave it the once-over, and pronounced it safe for landing. Almost all ski landings are as smooth as silk, and this one was no exception. I taxied around the lake to the left, always the easiest turn on either floats or skis, and came to a stop near the meat cache. I shut down the 165-hp heavy-case Franklin engine, unbuckled my harness, and stepped down from the cockpit, smelling the warm oil from the engine and hearing the familiar ticking of cooling cylinder fins. I walked around the plane and headed for the meat cache some thirty yards away.

There was no sign that either ravens or magpies had been at the cache. The heavy cotton meat bags had done a fine job in protecting the meat. It had been much too cold for flies, and there were no tracks at all around the cache. So far, Chic's luck was holding in spite of the weather delay.

Before leaving Anchorage, I had removed all the extra seats from the Cessna. I had finished loaded 600 to 700 pounds of meat, including the medium-sized horns that Chic had wanted to save, lashing it all down to the floor-mounted seat rails. I started the big engine for the trip back to Anchorage and noted that the oil temperature was still up where it ought to be. I hadn't been on the ice very long, perhaps thirty or forty-five minutes, and the engine was still pretty warm.

After landing, the skis had frozen themselves to the snow. This is not at all unusual. When a ski-equipped plane moves across snow or ice, the surface beneath each ski melts from the friction. When the plane stops, this melted water immediately freezes again, anchoring the aircraft in place. If the pilot is planning to stay for a while, he usually ties the aircraft down anyway. But, if he plans to leave soon, he might decide to pass up the tie-down effort. This is safe enough on relatively calm days, and avoiding any work at all usually fits perfectly into the Alaska pilot's overall scheme of things.

Because the skis were frozen in place, I was able to run the engine up to 1,700 rpms for the magnetos check. Both mags checked out just fine, with almost no drop in revolutions when each magneto was checked individually. There was no discernible difference in drop between the two. The carburetor heat check revealed no carb ice, which wasn't a surprise. The engine compartment was still warm as toast, and the outside weather was a bit too cold and clear for it anyway. As I applied more throttle for the full power engine check, the airplane broke loose and began to move forward. From there on out, it would be a takeoff run and liftoff.

The plane was pretty heavy and began to move west across the ice only slowly at first. Over the roar of the engine I thought I heard a loud "thump" from somewhere, and thought that it was probably a sonic boom from high above. But then I realized it was the sound of breaking ice! Then, another loud thu-u-u-u-mp.

The Cessna was moving faster and faster now, but not fast enough to allow a straight-ahead takeoff. I would have to circle the small lake and build up to takeoff speed while rounding the last turn, which would align the plane toward the west again for liftoff.

I was still moving west at the early portion of the takeoff run when the ice began breaking up in earnest. Even over the roar of the engine, I could hear the loud booms and thumps, each followed by a roaring "wow-ow-ow-ow," a frightening sound that moaned out ahead of the airplane. I looked back and could see huge cracks appearing in the surface behind me. The pilot's mind seems to slip into overdrive at times like that, and I calculated that I would be pretty light on the skis by the time I had rounded the clubhouse turn and started down the stretch for the final takeoff run westward. In the meantime, the ice might be breaking up, but each second was taking me over new, unbroken ice. I didn't think the lake would break up very far ahead of the moving plane, so I kept the throttle to the firewall as long as I could before each of the high-speed turns. The airspeed indicator stayed between 40 and 45 miles per hour, slow enough to keep me on the ice and fast enough to let the wings take some of the gross weight.

I left the original western heading, turning through south to the east, with the lake still roaring and wowing ahead of me, and cracking up behind me. I was now speeding eastward, sort of on a downwind leg, and I looked out under the left wing to survey the damage. It was a little disheartening, to say the least. It was also a little scary.

I could see no big ice ridges, but the cracks were now blacker than they had been just seconds earlier. Water was seeping through the cracks in the ice, shooting and squirting upward, and soaking the snow as it erupted. This was definitely not an encouraging sight. I thought of trying to ski right off the east end of the lake, but shoreline brush and the steep angle of the mountains rising right from the edge of the ice ruled that out. It was going to be either fly or sink for the heavy Cessna and its tight-jawed driver.

I took the final rounded turn from east through north to west a little too fast, but skis are the most forgiving of all landing gear, and there is almost no way that a pilot can force a plane into a ground loop while on skis. Thank goodness for that, at least!

I held the throttle to the firewall as I came out of the last turn and drove westward as fast as the loaded plane would go. Ahead of me lay a slurry of ice, snow, and water. I was no longer confident my takeoff plan would work.

The heavy plane hit the first water and ice plates at almost 50 miles per hour, skimming over the water like a Florida water skier.

The spray froze as soon as it hit the hurtling little airplane. The underside of the wings, the struts, certainly the horizontal stabilizer and elevators, the rudder, and perhaps even the prop, were freezing up at an unbelievable rate. I hadn't touched the flap handle until I had reached the westward takeoff heading. When I raised the handle, the flaps were reluctant to come down the 20 degrees I was looking for. All of this was happening fast, but I wished it were happening even faster. I wanted off that damned ice!

The roaring breakup must have stopped, or had at least become less noisy than the 165-horse Franklin, because I could no longer hear that distracting racket. With cold lake water and large chunks of ice flying everywhere around me, the nose slowly lifted—and the little Cessna wobbled awkwardly into the air and free of the chaos below.

I held six or eight feet of altitude for the length of the lake, refusing to allow the ship to climb above ground effect quite yet. I was too busy flying to think about the load of ice the plane was now carrying.

Stable at this altitude, if you can call that altitude, I glanced out the left and then the right windows and under the wings. The struts were a mess, as was the underside of both wings and the big Cessna windshield. I couldn't see the prop, but at least there was no telltale vibration. I looked down to find the skis and the big flat-spring landing gear legs almost unrecognizable under the load of rippling, bulging ice. And none of it was smooth, either. I was flying a loaded lump. I knew the tail assembly was also a mess, but I was confident that the upper surfaces of the wings were still in good shape. Airspeed was building steadily now, and it looked as though the Cessna would be able to handle the load of meat and ice.

As I passed the end of the lake, I eased above ground effect and began to slowly raise the flaps. I was sure that I now had enough lift, and I wanted to reduce drag as much as possible in order to build up a little more airspeed. The tough little four-place Cessna responded admirably, and I soon slipped through the narrow slot in the mountains and over the flat land of the Kenai Peninsula.Outside the mountains, and with no high ground between here and Merrill Field, I eased into a slow climb to 2,000 feet. I would need that altitude to safely cross Turnagain Arm, that high-tide, unfriendly body of water along the south side of the stubby peninsula that longtime Alaskans refer to as the Anchorage Bowl.

I went dry feet at the Potter Flats, southeast of Anchorage, and called Anchorage Tower for the clearance through their traffic area. In a few more minutes, I had passed their corridor, contacted Merrill Tower, and was letting down after a straight-in approach to Runway 33.

After I landed and taxied clear, a small group of hangar fliers and onlookers surrounded the plane. The sad looking little ship was an incredibly ugly and frozen lump, for sure. As it sat unmoving under a warming sun, water began to run in streams from the wings, struts, empennage, landing gear, and skis. I wasn't sure why the prop looked so clean and dry, but supposed that it had once been iced up, too. I thought that the prop ice had probably just burned off during the return flight across the Kenai Peninsula.

While this wasn't the last uncomfortable meeting I would have with the vagaries of lake ice, it was among the most sobering. It had been an entirely new experience for me. After more than thirty years, the memory of that roaring and cracking and wow-wow-wowing out there ahead of the loaded Cessna is still vivid in my mind. Just another one of those days, maybe, but man, what a day.

Chapter 5

PAINTER CREEK

*For three months during the summer and early fall of 1984, I
flew for the folks at Painter Creek Lodge, located down on the
Alaska Peninsula. Situated on a plateau on the south side of
Painter Creek, and buried in the Aleutian Range, the lodge was
built beside a fine gravel strip constructed some years earlier by
a petroleum exploration outfit. Although not shown on the aeronautical charts, this strip is large enough for the multi-engine
aircraft that delivers avgas and diesel fuel to the lodge. The lodge
and the strip are both very private. The strip serves the lodge
and its guests only. The fact that it serves what are probably
Alaska's finest fishing waters shouldn't encourage you to plan
an unannounced visit there, unless you have made reservations
as a fishing guest, of course.*

$\mathcal{T}$he entire Aleutian Range is dotted with volcanoes. Some are
relatively active, some are more or less inactive, and some are old
news indeed. As a part of this volcanic chain, Mt. Katmai is probably the best known of these volcanoes. Mt. Katmai erupted in 1912,
dropping volcanic ash on every square mile of the Earth, it is said,
and raising temperatures around the world for several years. This
eruption created the Valley of Ten Thousand Smokes, now a part of
Katmai National Park. Here, glaciers melt to form small streams that,

in turn, flow only a few hundred yards before they vanish in clouds of steam. Parts of the park resemble the face of the moon, while other parts are incredibly lush with flora and fauna. It is the home of famous McNeil River, where huge brown bears fish for the salmon that return here each year to spawn. It is here, too, that visitors can fish the Brooks River, one of the very few places where it's still possible to watch salmon actually leaping waterfalls on their difficult journey back to their spawning grounds. On the northeast edge of Lake Brooks sits Brooks Camp, a facility consisting of several cabins, a dining room, and a park office, in Katmai National Park. Painter Creek Lodge is eighty miles over the hill from Mt. Katmai.

Only twenty-eight miles to the south of the lodge is Aniakchak Crater, an extinct volcano with small Crater Lake centered at the bottom. I once saw a gorgeous, cherry-chocolate brown bear moseying around down there. There are some pretty neat hot springs between Katmai and Anaikchak that not too many people know about. A little dip and a picnic here make a pleasant diversion for those fishing in the area.

The country around Painter Creek is rich with moose, caribou, and the huge peninsula brown bear. It is no doubt that the tremendous runs of Pacific salmon are responsible for the really large brown bear population in this area. And the reason that world-class fishermen place this neck of the woods very high on their lists of places to test the waters.

I used my Cessna 206 amphibian at the lodge for freight and passenger flights, but the planes used for local fishing trips from the lodge airstrip were wheel-equipped Cessna 180s. I would frequently fly the amphibian from Painter Creek to Anchorage in order to pick up about a thousand pounds or so of foodstuffs for the lodge, and quite often would fly from the lodge to King Salmon to pick up guests arriving at that airport. King Salmon, 100 miles from the lodge, is the nearest airport regularly served by commercial air carriers. Lodge pilots almost always provided transportation from King Salmon to the lodge. Peninsula Air out of King Salmon picked up the slack for us at times.

There were usually three pilots flying out of the lodge. Joe Maxey, one of the owners, was among these, though he was usually very busy in the field with one or another small group of lodge guests. Joe would be killed flying one of the lodge's Cessna 150s in August 2001. Joe had his own float-equipped Cessna 170B at the lodge, usually docked downstream where Painter Creek meets the King Salmon River. Not the King Salmon River mentioned later in this chapter, but a second one, far south of the other, larger stream. The King Salmon River nearest the lodge is fed by Mother Goose Lake, while the more northern river begins in the mountains to the east.

Archie Hutchison and I were the other two pilots, and we almost always had one or another of the lodge's two wheel-mounted Cessna 180s in the air. Mounted on 8.50x6 tires and tubes, these tough planes routinely flew into and out of places hardly large enough for the Alaska mosquitoes that are so prevalent in that area.

Beginning about the first of August, one of my favorite fishing spots was a place I'll call Main Creek. It lies over the range and east of the lodge, on the Pacific side of the mountains. Actually, that salt water is all a part of the Gulf of Alaska, but we always just called it the Pacific Side. Main Creek feeds into Amber Bay, a part of the Gulf of Alaska.

Huge storms and serious fog often keep that side of the peninsula out of bounds to aircraft, but at other times relatively good weather would allow us to sneak over there one way or another. Sometimes we could simply climb over the ridge and drop down to the other side to land on the coast. At other times, we might have to sneak through one of several small valleys and wend our crooked way along a much more circuitous route to our favorite fishing spots. And Main Creek wasn't the only good spot on that side of the mountains, either.

Main Creek, though, was unique. I would land on the wet sand, just north of where the stream emptied into salt water, and tie the Cessna to a big log high on the beach. From the beach, I would lead our fishing clients west over about 400 yards of sand and brush to the stream, which meandered first west then north as one travels upstream from its mouth. The stream quickly turns west again, this time to disappear farther up in the steep mountains immediately behind the beach. And, while this stream was little more than a large creek, it had the best silver (Coho) salmon fishing I have ever seen!

Whenever I arrived at Main Creek with a group of fishermen, I would usually lead them to a small gravel bar along the river and point out a particular flat rock on the beach. Lifting that small rock, I would place a $100 bill beneath it, telling each of them to do the same.

"The first one," I would say, "who can cast and retrieve without hooking and fighting a fresh silver salmon wins the pot."

Heck, that would make even poor fishing worth the trip, wouldn't it?

We would fish through the morning, take a short lunch break, and then return to the stream for the remainder of the afternoon. More often than not, each would get his own hundred bucks back. It's the only place on earth where I can truly say that I have hooked and fought a superior game fish on every single cast, day in and day out, for as long as I cared to fish there. It is an incredible fishing stream.

Just north of that spot, and along the same coast, lies another oil-exploration strip. Five thousand feet long, smooth as can be under a fine gravel surface, this strip is shown on no aeronautical chart.

It is immediately adjacent to a tremendous salmon-fishing stream and is almost never visited by other fishermen. No one seems to know it's there! Or didn't, I suppose, until now. Lying just south of Nakililok Bay, this stream is another of Alaska's exceptional hidden secrets. It is in this small, swift stream that I encountered giant silver salmon.

About one of every ten silvers we caught in this stream was truly an oversized fish. While the average silver salmon probably runs to about twelve pounds, and a really large one to seventeen pounds, 10 percent of the salmon from this fast-moving stream ran to twenty pounds or above.

I took one of the huge silvers from this stream back to the lodge one day and froze it. On my next flight to Anchorage, I took the frozen salmon with me and delivered it to the local fish and wildlife biologists, asking if this were really a silver salmon. I thought it might even be a small Jack Salmon, the young version of the huge king salmon. Though these fish looked like silvers, they were really too big, and I knew that. I was told that the sample was indeed a silver salmon, and—by the way—where had I caught it? Oh, no you don't, you guys! I ain't tellin' ya!

I may have lost a friend or two by not telling, but I have never until now revealed the source of those huge fish. Surely the world record silver salmon will come from that stream one day. In fact, hundreds of new record-sized fish must run that stream every day during the month of August. Hey, you didn't hear it from me, right?

The finest rainbow trout fishing I have ever found was in a stream we called Gertrude Creek. I can tell you where that is because you won't land there anyway. Only a fool would, unless he is driving a Super Cub or is really an experienced bush pilot. The landing must be made on a terribly rough gravel bar near the headwaters of the King Salmon River. With brush on both sides, the land ing area itself is not as wide as the wingspan of the Cessna 180s I operated in and out of there. The downstream end of the bar slams into the water at the mouth of Gertrude Creek itself, while the upstream end terminates at the face of a high bank fronting a small hill. The overall length of the strip has been measured at 560 feet, though only a little more than 500 is usable. It's not a strip for the novice pilot or faint of heart, even though a Cessna 180 with four souls and gear can safely use it. The big gravel is hard on horizontal stabilizers, though. Hard on tail wheels, too, unless the air pressure in them is kept high.

The lower reaches of Gertrude Creek are a short walk inland from this gravel bar. Fishing for grayling is quite good in Gertrude Creek, but fishing for rainbows is excellent. Rainbows to twenty pounds are not at all unusual in Gertrude, and twelve to sixteen pounders are the rule of the day. The fishing is best after the salmon runs, when the brown bears have left the stream. As long as the brownies are there, fishing can be a somewhat nerve-wracking experience. Lots of salmon, lots of bears, and lots of brush. You never know when you might walk right up on one of the big fellows, something that's usually not encouraged.

During the last week of September, I flew from the lodge to Gertrude with Rusty and Dee Rhodes, an attractive and tough husband-and-wife fishing combination if I ever saw one. Another great fly-fisher from Texas, Reverend John, joined us. We had separated along the stream, John and I fishing upstream while Rusty and Dee fished down.

It was another gorgeous September day, and the fishing had been excellent. Almost all fishing out of the lodge was fly-fishing, and catch-and-release. That day I had been scoring on very large rainbows while using my favorite wet fly, a black Wooly Bugger.

John and I had separated, too, as fly-fishers usually do along a good stream. I was working my way back down toward Rusty and Dee. We would soon leave the stream and return to the lodge, almost ninety miles south of us, for dinner and a few tall fishing tales. Suddenly I heard Rusty shouting. I couldn't make out over the sound of the stream just what he was so all-fired excited about. The first thing that went through my mind was that he was tied onto one of the twenty-pound rainbows.

I rounded a bend in the stream and found Dee sitting on a sandy bank a few feet from the stream, her husband bending over her. She was holding her head in both hands, and he was holding her shoulders and talking to her about something that seemed pretty urgent.

When I was finally able to get to them, I discovered that she had been making some long casts, and during the pickup for a back cast, her large wet fly had embedded itself in her right eye. We all thought she would certainly lose the eye.

When I stood behind her and tipped her head back so that I could inspect the damage, I discovered that the large hook had penetrated her right eyelid, but had not struck her eyeball. Whoa, Nelly—what a relief!

Most serious fly fishermen carry hemostat clamps. These locking devices are much preferred over the spin- and bait-casting fraternity's needle-nosed pliers. We simply lock the hemostat clamps to the front of our fishing vests where they are readily available to remove hook and fly after netting or landing a fish. And almost all our fishing is catch-and-release. Gentle handling of the catch was extremely important. At Painter Creek, catch-and-release is the law of the land, unless the kitchen had requested a fish or two for the menu.

John arrived at just about that time. I moved to stand behind Dee again, tipping her head back to get at the fly that was deeply embedded in her eyelid.

I locked my clamp on the fly and punched it through the lid so that the point was exposed. Since there is not too much feeling in the lid itself, this was not a discomfort for Dee. Holding the locked clamp steadily with my left hand, I used the special Sargent & Co. fisherman's pliers I always carried while on the stream to nip the barbed end off the offending fly. This short-nosed pliers closes in such a fashion that the cutting jaws are always parallel, the reason that I prefer them to the long-nosed variety. They're also much tougher and can bite through almost anything.

With the barbed end of the hook gone, it was a simple matter to extract the fly with the hemostat clamp. I put a small dab of Johnson's First Aid Cream on her eyelid and told Dee to wash her hands well, then rub the cream in. I suggested that she use this same cream two or three times each day until she left the lodge. I promised that she would never have a scar if she would do that. By the time she and Rusty left the lodge, she couldn't remember which eye had been struck, and the mark was completely gone. Good stuff, that Johnson's.

An interesting thing happened while I was at the lodge that late summer. One of Alaska's Registered Guides had a camp nearby, about halfway between the lodge and Port Heiden. Situated along a lava bed, which the guide and pilot used as his airstrip, the camp consisted of a frame building or two and one ancient outhouse. A one-holer, of course, since a hunting camp is usually a low-density development at best. The guide was widely known as something of a grump. A crude sort of fellow in the bargain, he was not at all long on patience.

On this particular day, he had informed his housekeeper and camp helper, a hard working, pleasant, and rather elderly German lady, that he had to go to King Salmon for supplies. He wouldn't return until after dark, but that wasn't unusual. A lot of bush flying occurs in the dark, though some special provisions must be made for the landings.

He had instructed the lady to listen for the sound of his returning Super Cub, a noise with which she was certainly familiar. When she heard the plane flying overhead, she was to light a Coleman lantern, take it outside, and set it on the end of his runway. And then, of course, get the hell out of the way!

Well, at some point or another after dark, the kind lady realized her need to visit the camp's sterling outdoor facilities. So she lit the spare Coleman lantern, walked some yards to the outhouse, and set the lantern on the ground near the door. You can imagine the rest of the story.

Our hero returned to find the lantern already in place. Marvelous camp help, he must have thought, to have so accurately predicted his arrival. Perhaps he should give her a small increase in salary this season.

Our hero lined his Bigfoot Super Cub up on the Coleman approach light, being careful to note that his magnetic heading coincided with the alignment of the crushed lava strip, and proceeded inbound on a short final, hanging on full flaps and with the throttle almost closed. He was just about to touch down when he flew right through the little outhouse, knocking both it and its occupant for a loop. The Cub came to a dusty stop with a bent prop, a bent strut, one bent wingtip, and a very short-tempered pilot. The lady escaped with only a few bruises and one hell of a scolding. And no salary increase. The humor of the situation seemed to have escaped our hero completely.

It was October before we finally closed the lodge that season. We loaded up three planes with the last of what would go back to Anchorage and lit out in a healthy snowstorm. J. W. Smith, who was the lodge manager, and his wife, Carol, flew with me in the amphibian. Dan Steele and Archie Hutchison took off in one of the Cessna 180s, N4958A. One of Alaska's off-duty airline captains flew the other 180, N2204C. I took off six or eight minutes ahead of the other two planes.

By the time we were fifty miles north of Painter Creek, it had begun to snow in earnest, and visibility was down to less than half a mile. Archie, the airline pilot, and I maintained radio contact on a discreet frequency along the way. I was able to accurately tell them what sort of visibility to expect from moment to moment, and to select for them the best deviations to use in skirting the worst of the snow.

Archie was one of those cool heads. I'd fly with him anywhere. The other pilot, though a salaried airline pilot, was as nervous as a long-tailed cat in a roomful of rocking chairs. I can't really find fault with that, because I was flying the only plane certified for IFR flight. He'd flown the big iron, with all its sophisticated avionics, for so long that he was no longer very comfortable with basic needle, ball, and airspeed flying. Nor was he comfortable with serious contact flying. Still, this was a routine flight in Alaska, where bad weather was the rule rather than the exception. The nervous pilot's voice was becoming noticeably lighter and higher pitched.

When we finally reached King Salmon and had tied down, we all huddled over coffee and lunch. We discussed the weather ahead and wondered whether or not Lake Clark Pass would be an option. My own thought was that the ground between King Salmon and Iliamna, at the southern end of the pass, was pretty low. Unless we managed to drift east into the mountains, that is. We all had working ADFs, so we could find Iliamna without any problems, I was sure. And we should be able to stay on course with the ADF, too, presuming we all didn't fall asleep at the wheel.

Archie said that he would just follow my amphibian, since he knew that both my airplane and I were capable of making the trip regardless of the weather. J. W. and Carol would ride anywhere with me, they said, and were ready to go as soon as we had topped the tanks. Our third pilot, however, decided to stay the night in King Salmon, telling us that he would drive his Cessna on up to Anchorage the following day. That arranged, Archie and I topped off and taxied for the departure.

Archie was to fly just behind and off my left side so that he could follow my lights and strobes. Though it was still daylight, the visibility was really terrible, and Archie's ADF could have been just a little more dependable. My stack of King Silver Crown avionics had been flawless since installation, and I knew that I could pick up the Iliamna NDB on 239 even from the traffic pattern at King Salmon. From the air over King Salmon, both the ADF and the DME would be solidly locked on, so wandering around in the snow wasn't going to be much of a problem for either Archie or me.

We lit out as a flight of two and settled in to fly direct to Iliamna, eighty-four DME miles ahead on a 021° heading. It was now snowing even harder, with visibility down to less than one-quarter mile, and Archie was having a bad time trying to keep my lights in sight. Since the blinding white wingtip and tail strobes softened and seemed to brighten in the heavy snow, appearing to Archie to come from everywhere at once, I turned them off, keeping the navigation lights and red rotating beacon on. This turned out to be the best arrangement, and we flew north for about ten minutes this way. Then Archie began to lose those lights, too.

Archie and I had flown together enough that we could closely match airspeeds, and we were in smooth air at the time. I told him to slide in tight on my left rear quarter, promising to let him know in advance if I was going go make even the slightest turn. Visibility was so poor that, if Archie had looked at his own instruments for only one second while I started a shallow turn at the same time, he would lose sight of me altogether. We weren't concerned about collision, but we were concerned about separation and the resulting likelihood that we would end up flying in close proximity with no visibility.

Eighteen minutes out of King Salmon, I advised Archie that I was beginning a turn from 021° to 045°, setting us up to fly east past Big Mountain, standing about 2,200 feet high and directly ahead of us. Our route had been roughly following the Victor 427 airway (yes, Alaska still has Victor airways!), a VOR instrument flight route. As the published minimum altitude for this route was 7,000 feet MSL, we certainly weren't going to interfere with commercial air traffic.

Soon after Archie acknowledged receipt of my intentions, I let him know that I was beginning the shallow seven-second turn. He followed me through it with no trouble, and we slid past the mountain, which was invisible off our left wings.

Once past Big Mountain, we picked up a new course to the ILI NDB, now less than fifteen minutes ahead and on the opposite side of Lake Iliamna, Alaska's largest freshwater lake.

With a surface area of some 2,000 square miles, Iliamna is a gorgeous, crystal-clear body of cold water about 20 miles wide and 100 miles long. It is the center of what is recognized as the world's premier rainbow fishing area. Thankfully, its remote location keeps it from casual drop-in fishermen. The streams that feed into it, and the Kvichak River which drains it, are home to some of the greatest freshwater game fishing in the world. This includes char, grayling, rainbow trout, and several species of Pacific salmon. It is truly a fisherman's paradise, and a designated Trophy Fish Area. Most of the feeder streams here are fly fishing only, but just mention Tularik Creek, either upper or lower, to a knowledgeable fly-fisher. You'll get the infamous thousand-yard stare of a truly stricken fish chaser.

Author refuels his Bigfoot Super
Cub at Merrill Field in Anchorage.

About midway across the lake, the snow began to let up. By the time we had crossed the Iliamna NDB, ceilings were above 3,000 feet, and the visibility was out to more than fifteen miles. It was turning into a pretty nice day, though still cool and overcast. The Flight Service Station at Iliamna gave us a reasonable weather report from Anchorage, still almost two and one-half hours ahead, and forecast Lake Clark Pass to be somewhere between marginal and open.

Marginal would be just fine, since both Archie and I had flown this pass so many times we could almost sleep through it. By the time we had reached the midway point of long Lake Clark itself, ceilings were up to 3,500, and it looked like smooth sailing for the rest of the trip. The pass really gets hairy at the north end (which pilots and the Flight Service Stations all refer to as the "east" end, and maybe it is). This is where the pass necks down rather tightly between rock faces and requires a 90-degree right turn at the toe of a glacier. Then there's a quick left 45 to get through, and you're out of the pass. Beyond that, it's almost all flatland flying. Lake Clark is not one of Alaska's more difficult passes unless the weather is really scabby.

Archie and I chatted our way through the pass and were soon on the ground at Merrill, where his Cessna 180 would spend the winter undergoing some much-needed attention. Regardless of how careful we had tried to be, flying the gravel bars and cinder beds around Painter Creek had been hard on the equipment. Since my amphibian wasn't much of an airplane for either of these surfaces, it hadn't taken the beating that the Cessna 180s had.

As it turned out, the lodge eventually skinned me out of a considerable amount of money for my time and for the use of my new turbocharged amphibian. But the fishing had been incredible.

The lodge manager had allegedly escaped with a handful of money, I was later told, and was believed to be cooling his heels in the southeastern part of the South 48, where his brother is a prominent dentist. The manager's income was reputed to be in six figures that summer, and since he hadn't reported this spare income to the lodge owners, I have to suspect that he might have forgotten to mention it to the IRS, too.

Chapter 6

JOHNSTONE BAY

*T*here is a considerable pile of ice, rock, and snow to the east of Seward, Alaska, between Resurrection Bay and the Gulf of Alaska. This mountain ridge, and that's what it really is for all practical purposes, generally runs north and south, rising more than 6,000 feet above the surrounding sea. Some of the peaks jump to 6,000 feet in only three horizontal miles. It is, in places, some of the most vertical and rugged terrain found anywhere on earth.

The toe end of this mountain ridge, and where it plunges abruptly into the cold waters of Blying Sound, separates Resurrection Bay from Day Harbor. The city of Seward sits at the northernmost end of Resurrection Bay. Nothing sits at the northern end of Day Harbor. Nothing of prominence, that is to say, because one can nearly always find a small, rough log cabin, however remote the setting, almost anywhere in Alaska, especially at the head of saltwater bays.

The point of land at the base of the ridge is called Cape Resurrection, although I don't know who chose the name and why. Perhaps the same cartographer who, while sailing under Captain Cook on his good ship *Endeavor,* wrote the word "name" on his charts as they traveled north past a prominent point of land along the Bering Sea coast. Later, the scribbled "n-a-m-e" would mistakenly be interpreted as "n-o-m-e." This is how Nome, Alaska, the gold town situated on the cold black sand and gravel beach got its name.

When flying east around Cape Resurrection and north along the shoreline into Day Harbor, the second small bay off the left wingtip is Johnstone Bay. At one time, abandoned wreckage of two light aircraft, both of which appeared to have been there for some time, marked a stretch of beach along this bay. One of them had burned to a crisp, either as a result of the accident itself or by some cold visitor seeking warmth. Close observation reveals very soft, deep sand on the beach, an area not suitable for aircraft use unless fitted with noticeably oversized tires.

Generally speaking, an experienced pilot can determine whether or not to attempt a beach landing by the shade of the sand. Darker sand is more densely packed, making a much better landing surface than lighter-colored, dry, loose sand. Only truly experienced pilots flying bigfoot aircraft and employing only the most cautious of approaches and landing techniques should attempt landing on a dry sand beach. A quick rule of thumb is to land close to the waterline, rather than higher on the beach where the sand is drier. In either event, using brakes during a beach landing is a touchy matter.

On the last day of April in 1961, two friends, Bob Farmer and Bob Dunford, had talked me into making a flight from Anchorage to Johnstone Bay and back. One or another of them had heard what a pretty place it is, and both had wanted to have a look for themselves. Maybe even land there and take in the scenery for a while, if that turned out to be possible.

The trip down in N5417C, a Cessna 170A with a big engine and a climb prop, was smooth. The mountains and glaciers were awesome in the bright, cold air of late April, and we all kicked back and enjoyed the scenery.

When we flew over Paradise Creek, south of Moose Pass, I could already see the town of Seward and, beyond that, the whole of Resurrection Bay, home to Alaska's Silver Salmon Derby. Held during August, this annual event predictably gathered more participants each year than did the Talkeetna Moose Nugget Festival, which features earrings, necklaces, tie tacks and other such quality items made of moose droppings. Enough said about that.

Off to the right perhaps fifteen miles beyond the right wingtip, we could see the spectacular Harding Ice Field, a 1,000-square-mile panorama of bright, mountain-locked snow many hundreds—or perhaps many thousands—of feet deep. In places, this mass of ice and snow descended more than 1,000 feet per mile to reach the bays of McCarty Fiord, Aiglik Bay, and Northwestern Fiord. It was a very dramatic snowscape, and we were admittedly awed by it.

The pilot, though, usually has things on his mind other than drooling over the local scenery. I began to plan my letdown from 6,000 to sea level within the next fifteen miles. At 120 miles an hour, that would have to happen in about seven and one-half minutes, requiring a rate of descent of around 800 feet per minute. Not a normal letdown—I still prefer 500 fpm when conditions allow it—but certainly not a problem. A slower descent just guarantees better and more even engine cooling, that's all.

We slipped through a small saddle in the ridge to the east about three miles before the rocks petered out completely to disappear beneath the cold, clear salt water. We were now just a mile from the beach at Johnstone Bay, and were still a little too high to make an approach from there. At any rate, I had to have a good look at the beach. I had never landed there before, but even if I had, taking a look is still a good idea. I didn't want to be surprised by any springs, seepage, logs, dead seals, or other obstructions.

The beach seemed pretty steep, but I didn't spot any troublesome obstacles. That is, if we didn't land at the very top of the beach, where the burned hull of an airplane lay heaped in a sad, deserted little pile of scrap fabric and smoked metal. Farther along was yet another wreck, this time not so high on the beach. There would still be plenty of room for our landing and later takeoff, though the sand looked pretty dry and very soft. It was probably that dry, soft sand that caused the earlier accidents, who knew?

I circled around and had a good, slow, second look-see to confirm the pitch angle of the beach, the look of the sand, and the length of the available landing space. Other than the condition of the sand, everything looked in order.

The winds were slightly onshore, which was good. There's nothing quite so disconcerting as having an offshore wind sneak under the upper wing, lift the aircraft, and push it out over the water—or tip it over completely! A steep beach could be a problem, too. When on an incline, the tail wheel tends to wander down hill toward the water. To straighten and align the tail wheel somewhat, a pilot will apply the rudder on the downhill side, much like a car driver will turn into a skid. To counteract the turning skid response to the rudder pressure, the pilot must apply a little brake pressure on the uphill side. And brakes on a sand beach are often a little tricky. The soft sand tends to force a plane to a stop before you're quite ready. It's all a little balancing act, but one that becomes second nature after a while. It is certainly easier to perform than it is to describe, much like aerobatics I suppose.

I turned the plane out over the clear, cold water of the bay. We flew "right traffic" as we turned from the crosswind leg onto the base leg and, finally, on around to a very short final. The flaps were full down, which isn't saying much in the A-model Cessna. I pulled the carb heat control to full hot, and attended to the subtle trim changes necessary to slow the aircraft. The approach was a smooth one. At better-known landing areas, we frequently just bang the aircraft around and jam it on. Too casual, but too true. In this soft sand, banging it on would be a fatal error.

I landed with power on and touched down with only the uphill main wheel at first, allowing the wings to lose some of their lift so the right main would touch down a few seconds later. The sand was pulling at the wheels, but it didn't feel as if the craft would overturn. I reduced the power and let the tail wheel settle gently to the sand. We stopped quickly after that—and there we were.

The plane was well above the apparent tide line, so I left it where it was and turned off the master switch. After allowing the engine to cool just a bit more, I pulled the mixture control full out and starved the heavy-case Franklin into silence, then switched off both magnetos. We could all hear the soft hiss of water meeting the sand at the shoreline as we climbed out of the plane to have a look at the truly awesome surroundings.

We were content to just wander around for a time, first inspecting the two aircraft cadavers and then strolling up the little creek for a short distance. I wondered if I might one day build a small cabin farther inland and up against the mountain backdrop there. During a storm, it would be hell around here, but on a day like this, I thought, there couldn't be a more comfortable and relaxing place on earth. Protected on three sides by awesome, almost vertical, rock rising to 6,000-foot peaks, the tops perpetually covered in snow, the tiny valley was truly picturesque.

When we had gobbled up our fill of the scenery, we prepared to leave the quiet little bay and head north again to Anchorage. The sand had proved to be at least as soft and dry as it had appeared from the air, and I decided I had better let a little air from the 8.50x6 tires to give the Cessna a bigger footprint.

With all three souls aboard, I cranked the engine over and settled back to wait for the plane to warm up enough to give me full horsepower for the short takeoff. When the oil temperature needle came well off the peg, I trimmed for takeoff, dropped two notches of the little flaps, checked to be sure that all seat belts were tight, and came up with the power. The throaty engine roared and the wings wagged a little, but we didn't move an inch. I throttled back to think about this for a moment.

After a time, I killed the engine and climbed out to let more air out of both tires. Not too much, though. . . . The second takeoff attempt didn't get us any farther down the beach than the first try had. I knew I didn't dare let any more air out of the big tires, or we would have a hard time landing in Anchorage. It didn't take long this time to figure our only workable plan of action, and I laid it out to my front-seat passenger, Bob Dunford.

I knew that once the aircraft began to roll in the soft sand, I could probably keep it moving. The problem was getting it rolling in the first place. I explained this, and more, to Bob. He would have to get out and rock the right wing up and down while I added enough power to begin moving the heavy airplane. This, I was certain, would free at least the right wheel from the deep, soft sand. Once that wheel began to move, I could rudder the other one into life, and the plane would begin to slowly move down the beach. Since I would have to keep the power on, the plane would begin to move faster and ever faster, looking for takeoff speed. My passenger would have to leap aboard a moving plane. As long as he stayed behind the wing strut, there would be no danger in this maneuver, and I solemnly promised not to leave the beach without him. I must have an honest face, because he believed everything I said and immediately unbuckled to leave the plane.

When he was beneath the right wing strut at its outboard attachment to the wing, I waved to him and eased in the power. He began rocking the wings with a vengeance. The right wheel crawled ahead just a bit. He rocked some more, and first the right then the left wheel climbed atop the sand and began turning in earnest. When I glanced out to see if my helper was going to board, I could tell by his eyes that he had seen the closed door and thought that his chances of getting aboard the moving plane were slim, and getting slimmer with every passing second. He looked like a tree full of owls.

The air stream from the prop had blown the door closed, but hadn't latched it. I was too busy to lean over and push it open, but he didn't need that anyway. From behind the strut, then behind the rolling wheel, he lunged ahead and pushed the door open a bit as he grabbed at the doorframe with his left hand. Boarding the moving airplane was a struggle, but it paid off. In a few moments he was aboard, the door was closed and latched, and he was locking his seat belt firmly across his hips. In the meantime, the Cessna had begun to pick up speed. In a few more seconds, I applied forward pressure and felt the tail becoming lighter on the sand. I raised the flaps to reduce parasite drag and to allow our speed to build a bit more. When I lowered the 20 degrees of flaps again, the little Cessna lifted off the steep little beach, and we were airborne, climbing for the narrow slot in the rocks through which we had first arrived. And I was pretty sure that I had not bled off so much air from the tires that we would have any trouble landing on the paved runway at Merrill Field—*pretty* sure!

By the time we left the mountains over Turnagain Arm and began our descent into the Anchorage area, the shadows were long and the sun was setting behind the Alaska Range. We passed Portage, where the mountains turn north and Anchorage spreads across the flat land to the west, and contacted Anchorage International for the clearance through their area, then the ATIS (Automatic Terminal Information Service) at Merrill for the weather.

Merrill Tower, at our request, was kind enough to give us a

straight-in approach to Runway 33, at that time still a grass runway, a better option for us in the event that our tires were a little on the low side. The landing, though, was smooth and without incident. We turned right to pass the tower, contacted ground control for a taxi clearance, and were all just about ready for a hot meal and a good night's sleep.

I've never been back to Johnstone Bay, though it has nothing do with the soft sand there. I do want to go back, just to sit on the quiet beach once again and soak up the mountains around me. I just haven't found the spare time yet. But, I will. Someday. You can hang your hat on that one. And when I do go back, it will be in a Bigfoot Super Cub.

Chapter 7

MADMAN LAKE

*A*side from the mountains themselves, one of the most enticing features of the Talkeetna Mountain area is the Big Susitna River, affectionately called the "Big Su" by every Alaskan who has been in the state for more than fifteen minutes. This stream, not large at its beginnings, grows considerably wider in the muskeg country of the Susitna Valley. The river originates at the foot of Susitna Glacier, an ice field that lies in the Alaska Range north of the Amphitheater Mountains. Birthplace of the glacier itself is on the southern slopes of Mt. Hayes, a mountain that stands almost 14,000 feet above sea level. Where the Maclaren River joins the Susitna is home to the Toklat grizzly, the most spectacular grizzly bear on the planet.

This bear, *Ursus Horibilus Toklat*, is the closest relative, they say, of the original silvertip griz, *Ursus Horibilus Horibilus*, the Montana grizzly first chronicled in the field notes of Meriwether Lewis and William Clark. The grizzly assumes the protection of his territory most formidably and with admirable, some would even say awesome, vigor. In plain English, he's not to be messed with.

Not far downstream from where these two rivers meet lies Kelly Lake, headquarters camp for my 7,000-square-mile Guiding District in this part of Alaska. This is prime country for moose, caribou, the mighty grizzly bear, and Alaska's unique, snow-white Dall sheep. The griz in this area are not the big, complacent, fish-eating brown bears of Alaska's coastal regions, but the true mountain grizzly—a mean, cantankerous, loner that is, without argument, the world's most fearsome and dangerous carnivore.

Jack O'Conner, a well-known outdoor writer, editor, and world-class big game hunter, was once asked what he considered the world's most dangerous game. He immediately named the Cape buffalo of Africa. He couldn't think of anything in the world more frightening than to find himself surrounded by a milling herd of fifty African Cape buffalo. But, he was asked, had he ever considered standing in the middle of a milling herd of fifty Alaska grizzly bears? Enough said, for one-on-one, the grizzly is the undisputed bad guy. And the meanest in the bunch would simply run off or eat the rest of the grizzly herd anyway! Besides, a herd of Cape buffalo wouldn't last a week in grizzly country, take my word for it. Like caribou, moose, horses and the occasional cow, they would simply vanish one by one.

As the Susitna River flows west and south from the Maclaren, it passes through more than 100 miles of gently rolling, beautifully flowered hills, no-you-can't-climb-that mountains, and everything in between. Finally, the river spills into the flat Susitna Valley, where it is joined by the Talkeetna and the Chulitna Rivers. The word "Talkeetna" is a native word meaning "where three rivers meet." Talkeetna, the historic little outback town that is the jumping-off place for all Mt. McKinley climbing expeditions, is just south of here.

The Talkeetna Village airstrip, elevation 346 feet MSL, sits only fifty-one air miles from the peak itself, and the ground doesn't really begin rising until you have flown almost half that distance out of Talkeetna and directly toward the mountain. This area is vertical real estate at its most awesome.

About fifty nautical miles upstream from Talkeetna, the Susitna River is squeezed down by almost vertical rock walls to hurtle through the infamous Devil Canyon, a stretch of river world-class kayak organizations long ago designated as Class VI water. For you nonkayakers, that means water that is not survivable. Here, hard against Devil Canyon, directly above and just to its south side, lies Madman Lake.

I've never been certain, but I have always believed that this very small lake got its name from the very few floatplane pilots who deigned to land and take off again from its small surface. Sitting in what can only be described as a bowl, this tiny lake constitutes floatplane possibilities for only the very accomplished, and only to those lightly loaded aircraft with the highest of performance levels. Even at that, a pilot has to be certifiably unhinged to even consider making very many trips in and out of that severely restricted space. Yet Alaska Registered Guide Kenny Oldham built a hunting cabin on its north shore back in the seventies. I later bought the cabin from him to use as a place for skilled European hunters, seeking moose and black bears, who were capable of hunting without a guide. Under a program that we advertised in Germany at that time, Alaska Allein, we provided outfitting services to these nonresident hunters qualified to legally hunt certain Alaska big game animals without the expense of hiring Registered Guides. By state law, this option did not include nonresident hunters looking for the white Dall Sheep or brown and grizzly bears.

In September 1978, I had flown a party of two German hunters into the High Lake and Devil Canyon area for moose and black bear. One of these hunters was Udo Saberschinsky, *ein Jäeger* of no small accomplishment. *Presereferent*, or Press Secretary, to a large German hunting club, Herr Saberschinsky had by then hunted successfully in most parts of the free world—and many parts which were not so free—and his estate in Germany included a separate building constructed solely for the purpose of housing and displaying his many world-class trophies.

Things were going well for the party when I dropped in at Madman late on the afternoon of the sixteenth to check on their food supply and hunting successes. Since it was late in the day, I decided to stay the night with the group.

When I was ready to depart the following afternoon, Udo asked if he could fly with me back to High Lake, just three minutes away and across Devil Canyon, then return with me to Madman later in the week. Since I had no other load to fly out that day, I agreed. We piled in, strapped down, and started the Super Cub, taxiing around the small lake to warm the engine.

I had noticed that the trees farther up the slopes surrounding the lake were bending and blowing around quite a bit, but I couldn't tell exactly how hard or in what direction the wind was blowing. The small lake was absolutely protected from most winds, and at our lower elevation the winds were virtually calm. The landscape around the lake limited takeoff options to one single route. Wind or no wind, all takeoffs from that lake were made from a step turn to the west. Period.

During my observations and calculations prior to takeoff, I failed to note that the wind became both a tailwind and a downdraft at the surface of the lake where we were taxiing in complete ignorance. By the time I had discovered this, we were on the step and almost committed. I chopped the power closed and reefed back on the stick, trying to bury the heels of the floats to brake the airplane to a stop.

By then we were simply too close to the far shore, and the plane was still on the step when I tried to turn right to stay within the lake boundaries. It didn't work, and I drove the Cub up into shallow water where the rocks immediately raked a two-and-one-half-foot-long slash through the bottom of the right float. The sudden stop told me I now had some serious trouble. Trouble? If we hadn't been in such shallow water by that time, we would have been sinking in place!

Udo and I climbed out and stepped off the right float into the cold and rocky water, only about eight inches deep at that spot. There is no real water flow through the lake, and the rocks there are not smooth, by any means. They are equivalent to the same number of broken concrete blocks, sharp on every face, edge, and corner. I knew the float would require maintenance available only in Anchorage, 120 miles south of Madman Lake. But how was I going to get out of there with a sinking airplane?

I told some of my camp help to cut two nearby spruce trees, and to buck and limb them (I think professional loggers call that rossing and spiking) to form relatively smooth poles. I then aligned the two poles about ten feet apart with their upper ends resting on the bank of the north shore, near the cabin, and the lower ends disappearing into the lake water. What I now had was a two-pole ramp of sorts.

I walked back to the aircraft and removed enough rocks from behind the floats to let me drag the injured plane backward into water deep enough to float it again. The damaged right float was nearly sunk, though it still had enough flotation to help support the plane. The right wingtip was still above the water, anyway, so taxiing was possible. If I didn't hurry it, that is. After turning the plane around by hand, I climbed aboard, started the engine and began a very slow taxi back to the lake's north end and the newly constructed ramp just in front of the cabin.

I approached the ramp so that it was on the right side of the Cub, swinging the right wing over the high bank to allow one of my helpers to grab the wingtip and pull the plane snug up against the spruce logs. Then I climbed out, walked one of the logs to the top of the bank, and temporarily secured the plane.

Next, I rigged a block and tackle and secured the lines to the right float fittings. That allowed me to drag the Cub sideways up the ramp until the right float was well clear of the water. This time, I secured the plane firmly, because that is where it would remain until the following morning.

I climbed to the cabin roof where I removed two sections of the metal smokestack that served our wood-burning Yukon stove. While I opened each stack section to flatten it a little, one of my helpers pumped two water-filled float compartments as dry as possible. I cleaned the two flattened stack sections as best I could. Now I had a dry float to work on and the materials with which to construct a big patch that would, hopefully, seal the long gash and give me enough water time for another takeoff.

First, I covered the rearmost length of the long gash with one section of the flattened smokestack, taping it securely in place with bright yellow duct tape. I favored yellow tape because the Cub was painted Piper's bright yellow, and this tape seemed to have a better adhesive than most silver duct tape. I placed the second smokestack section to cover the forward portion of the damage, lapping it generously over the rear section, much the way fish scales overlap. After taping this temporary patch securely in place, I heated the whole thing with a small propane torch from the cabin, setting the mastic of the tape. The little Cub was again ready to fly. I hoped.

The following morning after a good camp breakfast, the small group of guides, hunters, and helpers gathered to listen to my instructions to one of my assistant guides. He was to hold the single anchoring line, now tied with a slipknot, while I started the engine and warmed it until I was sure I could get full horsepower from it. At my signal, he was to yank the knot loose and let go of the line. I would apply power as the plane slid back down the ramp. By the time the Cub was free of the ramp, the engine would be turning up to full takeoff power—and I would be moving. With no load but the pilot, the Super Cub should be up on the step and moving in only three or four seconds.

The whole exercise went even more smoothly than I had hoped, and I was soon in the air, climbing sharply and looking back to see a shower of sprayed water behind the float. A *big* shower of spray. Even with all the precaution, the damaged float had taken on quite a load of Madman Lake's clear, cold water.

The one-hour-and-twenty-minute flight back to Anchorage's Lake Hood seaplane base was smooth and comfortable. I notified Approach Control of my intention to land at Lake Hood. First, however, I would request a fly-by from Anchorage Tower, immediately adjacent to the lake itself. That tower serves both Lake Hood and Anchorage International Airport, though on separate frequencies. I hoped that, with their 10x50 binoculars, they would be able to tell whether or not I still had the smokestack patch on the torn right float. The bright yellow duct tape would make it easy to see if it was still in place. I certainly couldn't see it from my little world inside the plane.

When Approach Control passed me to the tower, I learned that the controllers were already aware of my problem and my request. It was granted immediately, and I began the low approach at slightly below cruise speed, between Runway 14 and the tower itself. I passed the tower in knife-edge flight so the controllers could get a good look at the float hull, and they reported that the yellow tape, as well as the smokestack sections, seemed to still be in place.

I switched to 120.4, Lake Hood Tower, whose controller is in the Anchorage International Airport tower, and requested a landing on the lake from the east. I also requested permission to taxi on the step directly to, and almost onto, the beach at the west end of the lake. I told the tower that I was sure the plane would sink in place if I stopped short of the beach. That request, too, was granted, and the rest of the flight went without a hitch.

I had beached the aircraft almost next door to my maintenance facility, and the mechanic arranged immediately for the hoist that would lift the Cub from the water and place it on the ramp in front of his hangar door. The rest soon became a five-day, $3,500 delay. Seems I had also bent a few interior bits and pieces, along with damaging the keel. Humpf! Taught me to be a little more careful the next time I visited Madman, anyway.

The hunting party, along with my camp help, had to pack their way up nearly 3,000 feet of mountain to reach my camp at Shadow Lake so that Dave Klosterman, owner of Alaska Bush Carrier, could pick them up in his DeHaviland Beaver for their return to Anchorage.

All told, not the best of trips for anyone. At the end of the trip the hunting crew had all been guests in our home. They had slept in our spare bedrooms, and my wife had fixed their dinners and breakfasts while they were there, even driving them to the airport so they could catch their Lufthansa flight back to Germany at the end of their stay. And yet they had neglected to pay my wife the $8,000 balance for the their trip before they waved good-bye to her at the airport. Well, they didn't exactly neglect it. They told her that they had paid me while in the bush. So much for honesty among big game hunters.

Chapter 8

NORTH TO SOUTH

*P*eggy and I suspected that our planned flight from Anchorage, Alaska, to West Palm Beach, Florida, might be a little more than just another long flying routine. After all, it's a trip that nudges right up against 5,000 air miles. It represented roughly forty hours in the air with our turbocharged Cessna 206 amphibian, N9975Z. We were traveling in the dead of winter, too, with our five-inch wheel clearance, which would be cutting it close on snow-covered runways. Because we planned to leave in early Nobember, we could expect the temperature spread to be 130 degrees between Alaska and Florida. The temperature on the ground at Northway, Alaska, stood at -44 . Northway is the only coffee and lunch stop for that trip. It is also the required U.S. Customs stop for those arriving in Alaska from Canada. We expected the leg from Anchorage to Northway to be a two-hour flight.

Because of one delay after another, we hadn't raised the gear handle until about midday on November 14, 1985, in crystal-clear weather and blinding sunshine. When we were about fifty miles north of Anchorage, and as we passed abeam Palmer, we were trimmed out at 5,000 feet and looking upstream along the Matanuska River toward the Matanuska Glacier that spawned it. I decided that it would be a good idea to cycle the gear a few times right about then, although our mechanic had only just remounted the big amphibious floats under the ship for us. The gear had retracted properly after liftoff, but I wanted to check its operation in the extreme cold. Sure enough, nothing. The six wheels were tucked up where they belonged inside the float hulls, but they wouldn't extend again. Looking for open water all along the route wasn't in our plans, and wouldn't have been productive at any rate, since we were traveling the "inside" route through Canada rather than off-shore over salt water. There was no choice but to turn back to Anchorage for some minor maintenance work.

We had departed Merrill Field, but with the frozen gear, Lake Hood would be the better place to land. Lake Hood, now mostly asleep for the winter, is adjacent to Anchorage International Airport and directly across the city from Merrill Field. Lake Hood is actually two lakes, Spenard and Hood, connected by a manmade channel used for both east and west waterway takeoffs and landings, and by all taxiing aircraft. Some days during the active summer months, this canal gets a real workout. Compared to frantic summertime floatplane activities there, however, a day of winter operations on the ice is generally pretty slow.

I contacted our mechanic, Brian Cox of Wilbur's Aviation, on his company frequency, requesting that he meet us at Lake Hood. Then we punched up, in order, the Anchorage ATIS, for the current weather; Anchorage Approach Control, for traffic separation; and Lake Hood Tower, which has its own frequency of 120.4, but is actually located in the Anchorage International Tower, for landing instructions. We were "cleared to land west" and rolled from right traffic onto final at 400 feet. Flaps, by the numbers, went to 40 degrees. I had to work a little for the landing, since floats are hard-mounted to an airplane and there is absolutely no elasticity to smooth things out for poor landings. We were pretty well loaded, too, and I didn't want to wrinkle anything, especially with my wife aboard.

The frozen surface was glass smooth, with only occasional small patches of very thin snow cover. After I had glued the heavy Cessna to the ice, I began steering as best I could with the rudder, aiming for every one of those little snow patches that lay close to our landing path. I was using them to slow the airplane, now sliding along on the heavy aluminum keel of the floats. It was like moving on a huge pair of ice skates, but the small snow patches were helping a little bit. It was still just plain old dumb luck, I suppose, that brought the airplane to a stop exactly at the spot where it belonged. We had stopped precisely against, and parallel to, the wood floatplane dock of the repair station where our mechanic was already waiting.

It didn't take Brian very long to clean the hydraulic lines and screens where moisture had become trapped and froze, clogging the screen filters with an icy hydraulic fluid slush. A short test hop and a few gear cycles convinced me that Peggy and I were ready for an early departure the following morning.

We lifted off on schedule the next morning, rocking good-bye to our back yard. We had one of the flight services pilots aboard with us, one of the Wilbur family in fact. While he was snoozing in the back seat, the amphibian was picking up a load of rime ice. I called and requested 13,000 feet, which was approved, but the loaded aircraft was a little reluctant to make the climb. I called again and cancelled the request for 13,000, staying at 11,000, banging along in the white for a time. The ice buildup seemed to give up after a while, and we cruised along with about one-half inch or so on the wings, struts, floats, and stabilizer.

Two hours into the four-hour trip we put down at Northway

for our pie and coffee. The weather there was severe clear, and even at forty below the sun began to melt the ice we had picked up. By the time we were ready to depart, it had vanished completely.

The next two hours into Canada's Yukon Territory was beautiful, though a little bumpy. By the time we reached Whitehorse, the town where we would spend the night, the cloud cover was back, and it seemed to be riding on quite a breeze.

It felt frightfully cold in the Whitehorse valley, through which the Yukon River winds on its heavy 2,400-mile trip toward the Bering Sea. Peggy and I both were wearing full goose-down underwear, Alaska down parkas, and cold weather boots. We were suited up for extreme cold, mostly in case of an emergency that might put us down somewhere in the interior. The big 300-horsepower Teledyne Continental engine poured plenty of heat into the cabin for us while flying at temperatures that I knew would reach as low as -60° at altitude.

But the outside air at Whitehorse was brittle cold, and it was now being pushed along on a really serious wind, 35 knots or better. I told Peggy to scurry inside while I placed the engine, wing, windshield, and tail covers in place. I also hooked up the extension cord that would allow us to plug in our engine and cockpit heaters through a forward, custom-mounted electrical connection. By the time I had completed those chores, about fifteen minutes or so, I was beginning to fear frostbite. This shouldn't be, with insulated Sorel boots, serious down gloves, and all the other arctic gear I was wearing.

When I met Peggy at the weather office, though, I learned that *the chill factor was standing rock solid at 155 degrees below zero!* In Canada, that was 187 degrees below freezing. By George, that's *serious* cold!

We telephoned for a taxi, which arrived within ten minutes, and rode in warmth to a local hotel owned by Peggy's longtime friend and then-governor of Alaska, Bill Sheffield. We enjoyed a good, hot dinner and then wandered the streets for an hour or so before deciding we might even then be freezing in place. Back to the hotel for a good night's sleep. We were well fed and rested the following morning when our taxi delivered us to the airport.

I filed an IFR Flight Plan with flight operations at the field, then stepped reluctantly outside to preflight the Cessna. After unplugging the extension cord and stowing it, along with all the covers, in the baggage compartment, we loaded up, started the big Cessna, and taxied for the departure.

Our clearance was for the Whitehorse One Departure, which required us to climb on the runway heading to 7,000 feet, then make a right teardrop turn to cross the YXY NDB and shuttle nonstandard to the MEA (minimum en route altitude). Since our rate of climb in the amphib, even in cold, dry air, was only 500 fpm, we had plenty of time to get settled in before nosing over at our on-course altitude, almost eighteen minutes later.

We hit Fort Nelson, Grand Prairie, and Calgary, in that order, for fuel and food. Eight hours and fifty-five flying minutes after departing Whitehorse, we left Calgary and crossed into the United States, headed for Great Falls, Montana.

It was surprising that we had developed clear airframe icing somewhere between Whitehorse and Fort Nelson. It was cold, all right, but it had also been severe clear all the way along. Even more surprising was the fact that we would carry that ice almost all the way to Birmingham, Alabama.

Prior to our departure from Calgary, Great Falls had reported a 300-foot ceiling, with visibility varying between one-eighth and one-quarter mile. More, a Boeing 737 had reported no braking action on clear ice beneath an unspecified snow depth. Our amphibian wasn't really the best of planes for this combination of conditions.

We were cleared at Great Falls for the Runway Three VOR approach. It was snowing lightly, and there was a reported crosswind that might make braking on the ice even goofier than it would be in calm air. Unlike wheeled aircraft, the amphibian tended to swing *away* from the wind, rather than into it. Since the little wheels mounted under the noses of the floats are not steerable and tend to castor under crosswind conditions, I was looking forward to earning our dinner that evening.

When we broke out at about 800 feet, the runway was straight ahead. And it looked clear to me! Now, what had happened to five inches of snow and maybe one inch of clear ice?

We discovered at touchdown that the runway was clear of both ice and snow. All our trepidations had been for nothing. The erroneous runway report is still a mystery to us.

Taxiing clear of the runway and finding rental hangar space was quickly accomplished, though I was astounded to find that there was no *heated* hangar space available. So—on with all the covers again, and plug in the extension cord, too, of course. The thermometer stood at minus thirty-five that night, still pretty cool.

Our first stop the following morning, after an instrument departure from Great Falls, was to be Rapid City, South Dakota. With a wind shear reported at 300 feet and turbulence enough to keep the needles moving, we bounced through the VOR Runway 32 approach after three plus thirty of constant pushing, prodding and shoving at yokes, pedals and trim wheels. While we were topping the tanks at Rapid City, Jerry Dale's most hospitable crew at Westworld Aviation packed surprise lunches for us, without request and without charge! Nice place to visit, Westworld Aviation at Rapid City, South Dakota. The genuine western hospitality reminded us very much of Alaska, where such treatment would not be a surprise at all. Before departure, we had a chance to exchange weather information with some nice folks headed north to Canada in their Cessna 185, another serious and very capable bush airplane.

Rapid City to North Platte went smoothly, the sun setting behind us somewhere along the way. We executed the VOR Approach at North Platte, breaking out at 5,500 feet in the procedure turn. When we rolled out on final, the night ahead of us was crystal clear, and the air was as smooth as glycerin. We were well established inbound, but the runway lights weren't getting any closer. I was working North Platte Radio, since the airport didn't have a control tower. After about two weeks on final, I finally asked North Platte for the surface winds, a number we hadn't been given earlier. "Forty-six knots right on your nose," came the reply. No wonder the airport wasn't getting any closer. We were indicating 90, but doing only 34 over the ground!

The next morning, North Platte to Springfield was a cakewalk, and we filed IFR again from there to Birmingham, Alabama. After exactly seven hours in the air that day, we shut down on the ramp at Jetco in Birmingham. This time we had executed the ILS Runway Five approach in 40 knots. So far, this little trip had been a bit on the windy side.

As nice as folks are around Birmingham, I've never really liked that place. And it's all my own damned fault, as you are about to see.

The next morning, November 21, we were hoping for a flight directly to Atlanta, Georgia. Ceilings there were holding at 300 that morning, so we took our good, sweet time over breakfast and coffee. I was getting a little weary of the long flying days, and an instrument landing down to minimums in high winds at Atlanta didn't pique my interest much just then. When the time finally came to file our flight plan and get moving again, Atlanta was still reporting stay-away weather. We decided to give it a couple more hours, hoping it might get just a wee bit better there. That didn't do much good either, so we finally just filed IFR direct to Jacksonville, Florida, estimating three plus thirty en route.

I knew that Hurricane Kate would be lying somewhere off our right wing, speeding in from the Gulf of Mexico, but I was also confident that we could beat Kate to the east coast, even if she changed direction at the last minute.

I had filed for the Birmingham Two Departure, knowing that I would be receiving vectors to our on-course heading. In large print, the SID (Standard Instrument Departure) for the Birmingham Two Departure notes: "*MAINTAIN 10,000' or assigned lower.*" With high winds, almost no ceiling, rain, fog—and a hurricane lying somewhere close offshore in the Gulf of Mexico—I didn't even pause over the SID. I was simply expecting a wet and rattling stay-on-the-gauges climbout on the runway heading. NEVER AGAIN!

What I got from the controller, just as I raised the gear switch, was a right 90-degree climbing turn. I should have said "no" right then. We were only sixty feet above the runway when that instruction came through the big David Clark headsets. My concern over rain, solid cloud, low ceilings, and an impressive hurricane had caused me to overlook telling Clearance Delivery, or anyone else, for that matter, to expect us to climb at no better than 300 feet per minute. I guess those good ol' boys in Birmin'ham are used to pushing the big iron heavy jets. And thereby hangs my tale. And almost our tails!

Although the IFR departure procedure clearly spelled out the restriction that pilots climb on the runway heading to at least 1,500 feet before turning on course, the controller had turned us almost immediately toward a low range of hills lying to the right of Runway Five. And immediately after rolling into the turn, we slammed into the ragged overcast, flaps still at 20 degrees and the gear slowly looking for a place to get out of the rain inside the big Wipline floats.

The bottoms were very ragged, fortunately for us, and as we passed through about zero nine zero magnetic in our turn, we hit a break in those bottoms. Dead ahead was the series of low hills whose tops were obscured in the overcast. I knew instantly that we couldn't clear a single one of them.

The airport sits at an elevation of 644 feet MSL. I remember having noted that the surrounding hills were in the neighborhood of 850 feet or so, some 200 feet above the runway. Given our disappointing rate of climb, that meant at least one full minute to clear the ridge. More than that, I also recalled that the plates displayed a tower that extended up to 930 feet somewhere much too close for comfort.

I saw the tower just about the time I considered trying a left turn to the north to climb parallel to the ridge. We were staggering along at a turbulent airspeed somewhere around 65 knots IAS, as near as I could interpolate the bouncing airspeed indicator. I thought the tower looked a lot like a fire watchtower that I had once seen years before in Montana. This structure at Birmingham was made of wood timbers, was much higher than our bouncing aircraft, and was now smack in the middle of the windshield. I have no idea how close we really were, but I could clearly make out the bolted connections. The thing definitely looked stronger that it needed to be.

Just to the left of the tower, the hill fell away sharply, forming a tiny pass in the ridgeline. Though I may be wrong, since things were happening in a hurry right then, I swear there was some sort of structure to the left of that small saddle, too.

The pass was clearly wider than our wingspan, and that was good enough for me. With less than twenty feet between the greenery and the ragged overcast, I rolled the wings level and we shot through the gap. I immediately pulled up into the turning instrument climb configuration again. There's not much more a pilot can do in that particular airplane when he's hanging on the prop, gear still en route, flaps hanging out all over the place, and the stall warning horn is sounding, reminding him that he ought to be watching the store a little closer. The controller hadn't noticed our small deviation from his instructions, I'm sure. If he had mentioned it, though, I was prepared to discuss it with him.

As the wooden tower shot past our right wingtip, we slammed into the overcast with a shock, expecting another surprise at any second. The next 300 vertical feet—the next sixty seconds—stand out clearly in my memory as one of the longest single minutes of my entire flying life.

The rest of the climb on course was mildly bumpy and was made in solid, dark, wet cloud up to about 3,500 feet. We broke out between layers into relatively smooth air, settling down at our assigned altitude of 5,000.

Even though the air was smooth enough, the DME was now sticking its tongue out at us. It varied between 60 and 62 knots, while I had filed 120 knots for the trip. Our filed three hours and twenty minutes stretched into four hours and twenty-five minutes. Hurricane Kate slipped behind us somewhere along the way, beating us without mercy with her fierce counter-clockwise winds. I try to think of the Cessna 206 as a comfortable and reliable four-hour airplane, though with good engine management it can be stretched to almost five and one-half. I try to keep individual flights down to a duration of three and one-half hours or less where possible. The four hours and twenty-five minutes were stretching things a bit for my liking, even with the controllable fuel flow. At one point I found myself glaring at the sluggish DME, not at all happy with the idea of putting the loaded amphibian down in a swamp somewhere in northern Florida in the dark. I reckon Peggy wouldn't have enjoyed that, either.

The VOR approach into JAX, with the wind at 30 knots, was

definitely an anticlimax. And a relief, even though I was busy on the controls until taxiing clear of the active.

Almost all my flying had been done in the Alaska bush. I had always been comfortable with high altitude, cold weather, and poor visibility operations. I had failed to consider that the turbocharged Cessna 206 would be noticeably sluggish in warmer climates. And with Birmingham's 10,000-foot Runway 5, I frankly hadn't bothered to consider aircraft climb performance. After all, performance is for takeoff, not climbout, right? *Wrong!* I should have remembered that from all my years of mountain flying.

Never again, should I live to be a thousand, will I take off without thinking ahead about that climbout. I'd rather let starvation wipe me slowly out of sight than see the bolts on that tower right smack in front of the windshield again.

Back up north, the city of Whitehorse, Yukon Territory, lies along the Yukon River. It is ringed with some pretty impressive mountains, and both instrument approaches and departures at Whitehorse are thrills for most transient pilots. But at this airport, the aircraft must climb on a prescribed heading, straight ahead, for almost 5,000 vertical feet before turning on course. Pretty easy, really, and a restful way to start out. A pilot certainly won't get a turn request from the controller very early in the flight at *that* location.

I wasn't bright enough to expect a vector so early in the day at Birmingham, either. And if I had simply used the "Remarks" column of the flight plan form to note our restricted climb capabilities, I surely wouldn't have been vectored into the hills there, either. I'm certain that some controller was just trying to get the little guy out of the way for one of the big boys.

I've been told that, if a frog had wings, he wouldn't hop down the road bumping his little backside. And if I had thought ahead enough to cover the possibilities . . . Yeah, *if!*

Chapter 9

A MATTER OF FUEL

$\mathcal{E}$arly in September 1977, another Alaska Registered Guide telephoned me. He wanted another pilot and me to fly some avgas to a hunting camp he operated just north of Swift River and down the Stony. On the charts, this was not far from the Lime Hills and the small community of Lime Village. His camp was set back against the sloping foothills near the base of the high Neacola Mountains that lay just to the north. Said he was a little short of his projected need for the 80-octane fuel and didn't have the time to fly the additional crates into camp using his own float-equipped Cub. It's not unusual for most of us to cache lots of fuel and oil in the bush against the needs of future hunting and fishing seasons. Like most Alaska pilots, I had done this many times, either for myself or for others. Even then, we sometimes run a little short. So, on the morning of September 7, Roger Christiansen and I loaded our Cubs and lit out for Merrill Pass and the Stony River country beyond.

AUTHOR TOPS THE TANKS FROM ONE
OF HIS MANY SECRET CACHES OF
AVIATION FUEL STASHED HERE OR THERE
AROUND THE STATE. THIS ONE IS
LOCATED ON THE BEACH AT CHINITNA
BAY, AT THE FOOT OF VOLCANIC MT.
ILIAMNA. SUCH STASHES ALLOW PILOTS
TO CONTINUE A FLIGHT WITHOUT
RETURNING TO HOME BASE TO REFUEL.

The pass itself wasn't too bad that morning. We were just a couple of Alaska bush airplanes crammed full of cans and crates, making a routine trip. The Federal Aviation Administration does limit the amount of canned avgas that can be carried inside an aircraft.

FAR Hazmat 175.310 allows only twenty gallons for such flights, though Alaska pilots frequently carry sixty gallons or more in their Super Cubs. The bigger planes could carry much more, of course.

I may as well admit right now that I don't know a single Alaska bush flier who pays much attention to that regulation. No one can afford to, really. It is impossible to fly the Alaska bush without a series of avgas caches stashed throughout the state, and freight hauls of only twenty gallons would be a very expensive waste of flying time.

Roger wasn't familiar with the country on the other side of the Alaska Range, and he certainly didn't know the precise location of the other guide's camp. Without question, he probably could have made the flight alone, but it was just much easier to follow me to the camp. We were a "flight of two," as we had told Merrill Tower when we departed. Roger was slightly in tow as we poured out of the west end of Merrill Pass and cut across the Stony River abeam Two Lakes, heading southwest.

Three hours and forty-five minutes after liftoff from Merrill Field, I lined up my little Cub on the guide's small tundra strip for the landing. Big tundra tires don't leave much of a track in Alaska's vast bush country. The guide's camp was far enough from the strip to make the landing area less than conspicuous to other bush fliers—not at all unusual in Alaska. The camp itself sat on the shore of a lake that the guide used as a base for his own float-equipped Super Cub.

We off-loaded our freight, stacked and covered it for future use, and walked the quarter-mile distance to the guide's camp, wading through one small creek along the way. At the camp we listened to a few bear stories and had a quick bite of late lunch. We all had a good laugh over a freshly skinned bear head with a grass-filled yellow work glove clamped tightly between his impressive teeth. Guides were regaling one of the newly arrived clients with a tale of how the bear had swallowed one of the assistant guides before it was shot. Alaskan September days are short, so it was nearly dark, and it had started to rain as I readied my Super Cub for departure. Roger didn't want to fly the pass at night, generally a wise decision, so he was staying at the camp until morning. I would make the trip home alone.

I had to chamois some of the guide's canned avgas into the Cub's tanks, and had calculated the required quantity pretty closely. My Super Cub had a vernier mixture control and an EGT (Exhaust Gas Temperature) gauge, so I could lean the fuel/air mixture out to best performance with considerable accuracy. Since I knew I wouldn't have to fly full rich, I took from the guide only what I thought I would need to make the safe flight back to Merrill Field that night— no excess for missed approaches or for a forty-five-minute flight at cruise settings to reach an alternate airport. That safety reserve, too, is something that Alaska pilots must often forego.

I took off and climbed out to take up a relatively straight-line course for the mouth of the pass, but darkness and rain had so reduced visibility that I had to abandon that plan almost right away. I began following the Stony River's meandering route upstream, since the river was about all I could make out on the ground. Getting myself as comfortable as possible in the plane's cramped front office, I began to unscrew the mixture control while watching both the river and the EGT. The mixture control was threading its way out, all right, but the EGT was showing no change in its reading. I was sure that I had already turned the red control knob enough to create at least *some* increase in exhaust gas temperature, but—fat, dumb and happy—I continued to unscrew the maddeningly ineffective thing. Suddenly, and without warning, the whole danged thing came off in my hand! The bolted connection at the carburetor must have broken loose, or had somehow come away from its retaining screw, and I was without any mixture control at all. Now I was looking serious trouble right square in the eye!

Before I had changed from a 125-hp to a 150-hp engine, the little Cub burned 7.1 gallons at cruising speed. The bigger engine would burn maybe 10 gallons or so, full rich, but could have been leaned down by several gallons per hour with the EGT and vernier mixture control. The 5-plus gallons I could have saved with the proper fuel/air mixture would have allowed almost another hour of flying time. The flat-back agricultural Cub normally cruised at a relatively high 100 mph. Forty-five minutes of extra fuel would have given me seventy-five additional miles that rainy night. Without that leaner mixture, though, I was soon going to be in some pretty deep doo-doo.

Merrill Pass is so unfriendly that many Alaska pilots won't fly it even on sunny days. I knew one Fish & Wildlife Protection Officer with about 4,000 Alaska flying hours who has tried that pass only once. It's not really as bad as it sounds, but on a dark and rainy Alaska night, it's really not a very cheerful place. Whether I liked it or not, I was committed to this route. In the dark, I could not have returned to the almost invisible little landing strip I had just left. And only engine failure would force me to try to land on a Stony River sand bar under such conditions. I would just have to punch on through the pass and take stock of my options when I flew out the east end over Chakachamna Lake. At least from there the trip was pretty much downhill.

I had found myself reduced to a single option, just about the worst of all possible situations. In the steady rain, the pass would be almost pitch black. I couldn't safely land, but I might not have enough fuel to get home. And the last stretch of the flight would be across the most unfriendly body of water in all of Alaska.

I knew that I had to take a sharp right turn into the second canyon after passing Two Lakes in order to enter the pass. That is if I could see the two lakes. At the second canyon, I could barely see to make the 90-degree right turn and begin the climb from about 1,200 feet MSL to at least 2,400 feet, the minimum altitude that would see me safely through the pass's very narrow rock saddle. I was so busy looking out under each wing that the rain-streaked windshield didn't bother me at all. I had probably made more than fifty or sixty trips through that pass and was quite comfortable there in spite of its treacherous geography. With steep-sloped peaks rising to at least 8,000 feet just off either wing, and with the volcanic cone of Mt. Spurr rearing up more than 11,000 feet at the east end, I wasn't as comfortable as I would have been during a daylight flight, certainly. I knew, though, that I had enough fuel to get me through the mountains and out to the flats near the mouth of the Big Susitna River before things would go south on me. It was the twenty minutes beyond the flats that gave me a scare.

After making the first 90-degree turn to enter the west end of the pass, there is a left 45- and right 90-degree turn in the climb at the narrow slot right at the saddle, then a gradual left 90 to reach the upper end of the lake itself. From there on out, it's pretty much a cakewalk, even though there is an impressive aircraft graveyard lining the east end of the lake. When the ceiling is low here the narrow gorge through which a plane may pass may be less than forty yards across.

The walls of Merrill Pass itself aren't quite vertical, but they are so steep that very little vegetation can cling to their faces. It is much too narrow to consider turning around in the pass, even in a Super

Cub. Once you're in, you either fly on through or land straight ahead. With boulders half the size of a modest home, landing is a bad idea. You're left with flying through the pass.

I crossed the saddle at about twenty feet and rolled into the right 45 over the wreckage of an old military plane. Then I began a slow descent to the left through the curving little valley on the west end of Chakachamna Lake, located only six minutes ahead and 1,300 comfortable feet below me at 1,100 feet MSL.

I flew the length of the twenty-mile-long lake at 900 feet AGL. If I could hold that altitude against the rain and possible lower ceilings ahead, I would have 2,000 feet MSL at the end of the flight, altitude that I would sorely need. I fully expected to finish the flight with a dead-stick glide across Knik Arm, a scary body of cold and silty glacier water.

When I reached the east end of Chakachamna, I called Anchorage Radio for information on the oil exploration strip called Beluga located about 15 degrees to the right and twenty-five minutes ahead. The strip was unpaved, but it was more inviting than running out of fuel over the deadly waters of Cook Inlet or Knik Arm. The strip was 5,000 feet long—plenty of room to land the little two-place Super Cub.

Anchorage Radio firmly discouraged a landing at Beluga, so I asked for vectors and straight-line distances to the nearest runway threshold at both Merrill Field and Anchorage International Airport.

International was closer by several miles, but heading for that airport meant crossing almost thirty miles of Cook Inlet. Out of the question. Merrill Field, on the other hand, was a few miles farther, but a beeline for that field would place me over cold water for only about two and a half miles. At that point, if the engine finally starved out on me, I could at least glide to dry land. This route also gave me several emergency landing options that looked survivable, including Point McKenzie, the Chester Lagoon, Chester Creek, Eastchester Flats, the city cemetery, and a generous park strip, used years ago as the city's first airfield. If I could just coax the little Cub that far.

Inside the cabin at the root of each wing the Super Cub has a glass sight tube, marked as a fuel gauge for the pilot's convenience, that contains a small, red, cork ball. The tube is attached directly to the fuel tank in each wing and the little ball floats atop a column of avgas. This foolproof and very reliable fuel gauge is much more accurate than the electric, panel-mounted gauges of more modern aircraft. When the little red ball disappears at the bottom of either of the sight glasses, the pilot can pretty well expect twenty more minutes of powered flight from that tank at cruise settings before the engine starves and dies. When this happens, the pilot normally just switches to the other wing tank and continues the flight. If the engine has actually stopped, the spinning propeller will start it again with the new flow of fuel.

Both little red floats had vanished from the sight tubes a while back, and I was timing flight from each tank as I crossed the dark flats of the Big Susitna River delta.

I had long before throttled back to best glide speed plus five, trying to stretch my fuel load as far as it would go. The slower airspeed was maddening, since I would only be happy once I was safely back on the ground, but I couldn't argue against good engine maintenance and airspeed. I was properly set up for the longest possible time in the air under power. I certainly didn't want to be in the air *without* power that night.

I pestered Anchorage Radio a few more times, then punched up Approach Control, advising them of a low fuel situation and requesting whatever help they might be able to give me. They arranged a straight-in approach to Merrill Field's Runway 6, which would save me some air time by avoiding pattern entries and turns. It would also carry me directly over the city of Anchorage, which I didn't like. I figured, though, that I could always dump the Cub into Ship Creek, the small stream that separates the downtown business district from a residential area and Elmendorf AFB immediately to the north, or maybe slip into the park strip or the cemetery to the south of my assigned route. Things were looking as good as possible when I passed Point McKenzie at 2,000 feet and throttled back for the long straight-in to Runway 6. The city lights slipped by with agonizing slowness beneath the descending Cub's bright yellow left wing.

The approach was smooth, and the landing was as good as any I have made in that Cub. I landed short, took the first available right off the active, and taxied directly to the gas pumps at Gil's Aircraft. The engine was still miraculously purring along, although I didn't know how.

The Cub's tanks held a meager thirty-eight gallons total, when topped off tight to the filler necks, and only thirty-six gallons of that was usable. The meter at the pump read thirty-nine point six after I had finished topping both tanks. Maybe I had larger tanks by a fat gallon. Maybe the pump was not as accurate as it might have been. Perhaps the nose-low attitude of the long, straight-in approach helped some. I couldn't have cared less right at that moment. I'd have paid twenty bucks a gallon for that much-needed gas at that point, too.

I tied the little Cub down, gave her one last affectionate pat, and headed home for a hot shower, a warm dinner, and a dry bed. I fixed that broken mixture control problem before the next flight. Flying full rich isn't really my preferred method of engine management, even at sea level. Much less through a dark and rainy Merrill Pass.

Chapter 10

THE YEAR THAT WAS

*L*ooking back on it, I'd have to say that 1974 was plagued with more problems than any other year I spent in the air. I had gotten a good deal on a 1952 Super Cub that April. The previous owner had stored the little gray plane in a Kansas hangar for twenty-one years. The plane was an agricultural model, with a flat back and a dust hopper. Steel angles had been welded to the front of the main gear hardware for cutting those fences that hadn't ducked out of the way as the owner dusted his crops. It had a metal belly and a metal panel over the baggage area. I later included this panel in a modification that allowed me to load from the top, instead of passing everything through the fold-down door and over the passenger's seat back. The Cub still had the original 125-horsepower Lycoming engine and the original fabric and factory paint job, down to the old Piper bear cub logo on the vertical stabilizer. I paid $7,500 for that little Super Cub, and sold it a number of years later for $39,000. Of course by then I had rebuilt it and added a few more Alaska bush goodies.

Less than a month after buying the little plane, I had to make a flight into the strip at Curry, north of Anchorage and along the Alaska Railroad. Curry is so small that no one bothers to show it on the aeronautical charts any more. The strip was so seldom used that it sported an orchard of small trees and lesser shrubs within its landing zone.

My landing there had to be pretty short. I was leaning on the brakes and pouring power across the horizontal stabilizer to keep the tail of the lightly loaded Cub from coming over my head. Tromping on the brakes burst an O-ring in the right brake cylinder. That wasn't really a problem during the landing, but I had several more flights to make before heading back to Anchorage where I could replace the O-ring, bleed the system, and put things back in order.

The subsequent takeoff from Curry went smoothly enough, and an hour and ten minutes later I landed in Skwentna, to the southwest past Talkeetna. The trip was routine, but the landing required a little attention after the aircraft had slowed to its taxi speed. Still there was nothing I could do about the defunct O-ring until I got the little plane back to Anchorage.

Once back on the ground again at Merrill Field, a little jockeying around got me to the hangar where I repaired the brake system. That was the end of that little problem.

Three days later, and during a night flight back to Anchorage from Talkeetna, I lost the port wingtip running light. It was a little weathery out that night, and I noticed when the soft red glow around the wingtip disappeared. At the same time the radio decided to fold up, too. Approach Control was a little iffy about that, but there wasn't much either of us could do until I had the thing repaired.

Two weeks after that mishap, it began to seem as if just flying in the little Cub brought on bad weather. First there was a noninstrument landing through a layer of low stratus at Seward, a strip tightly hemmed by mountains. Then high winds hampered a particularly tricky beach landing at Skilak Lake, a place so littered with rocks and gravel that I'm sure this is where God threw the leftovers after building Mt. McKinley. An almost endless series of heavy rains, truly unusual for that part of Alaska, made the next few flights a challenge, to say the least.

It was the middle of June by the time I had to fly to the strip at Moose River, down south on the Kenai Peninsula. Only six more months until the new year would break my little losing streak. The Moose River strip appeared to have been unused for several years. The rocky, brushy, and extremely narrow little strip posed a bit of a challenge.

That same day, lightning had started several fires on the peninsula, and on the return trip to Anchorage, I reported the strikes to the proper authorities. I think it was that very day that I spotted a body floating in a small lake near the mountains and reported that surprise to the Alaska State Troopers. I never did hear whose body it was.

Seven days later, heavy west winds slowed a flight from Anchorage to Aniak, a village to the west and through Merrill Pass. I bounced and shuddered through the three-hour-and-thirty-minute trip. With a brisk tailwind on the return trip, turbulence bordered on severe, jostling me through the pass toward home.

Mountain flying on really windy days can be a completely different bag of tricks.

In the mountains, a 30-knot wind in the valley will be a 90-knot wind in the passes. That same wind jumps to 60 knots across the ridges, if the wind is blowing perpendicular to the mountains. So, turbulence can be pretty tough some days, especially for the many light aircraft that don't have the power to lift them to pass altitudes.

By mid July, I had flown so many turbulent or low-visibility trips through Merrill Pass that I didn't care if I never saw the danged place again.

During the last week of July that year, I dropped off a young couple at the mouth of the Chuit River, a river just north of the village of Tyonek that feeds into Cook Inlet, for a salmon fishing weekend. I left them on the beach at the mouth of the river on a Saturday morning, and was to pick them up the following evening.

It was a sunny Sunday at about six o'clock in the evening when I returned to the river for the pickup. Six or eight small planes were parked at various places along the beach and upstream along the river bar near its mouth. Several pilots had parked right where the wind dictated to be the best place to land, but they hadn't thought to leave much space for other landing aircraft. Even in the boonies your neighbors can be inconsiderate, it seems.

While I certainly had sufficient room to land the little Cub, I supposed that one or two of the pilots on the ground might be a little nervous watching me descend to land among their parked craft. I elected to land along the beach of Cook Inlet, just south of the river's mouth.

To let my passengers know that I had arrived for the pickup, I pulled the Cub up into a country loop. After that show-off maneuver, I lined up for a landing south along the beach, driving slightly into the wind that was blowing offshore.

After landing, I swung the nose of the empty Cub up the slope of the beach and tapped the right brake to turn northward so that I could taxi back to the river mouth. Because I was relying mostly on brakes and power at that point, I had the stick in my lap. I made the mistake of keeping it there as I swung the plane past 90 degrees and around toward the 180 degrees I needed to turn around. Bad move.

A sudden gust of offshore wind, now coming under the high wing and quartering from the left rear, snuck under the tail and lifted the empty Cub up onto its nose faster than I could apply the power necessary to keep it down. The prop hit the sand—and there I sat, staring over the nose and straight down at the Cook Inlet sand and gravel beach.

I admit to swearing at my own stupidity as I climbed out and walked around to the front of the abused little aircraft. Grabbing the prop on either side of the spinner, I lifted, watching the tail settle back down where it belonged.

Both propeller tips were bent back, and like most Alaska pilots, I seldom carry a spare prop in the baggage compartment. I removed the big spinner, cut the safety wire to release the six bolts that secured the propeller, and removed the prop, turning it over and over in my hands. The hotshot pilot with the show-off inside loop was now a little red-faced and in something of a pickle. Served me right, of course, for being so casual in my ground handling technique. On the other hand, I still had to get my passengers back home somehow.

I radioed a passing plane, requesting that the pilot contact my maintenance folks and ask if they could arrange to have a new prop to me later that evening. The answer from maintenance was a disappointing negative. Maybe Monday morning? No, I told the other pilot, that wouldn't do at all. But thanks anyway.

Since waiting hardly fit into my plans, I carried the custom Borer low-pitch prop, now looking much like a set of longhorn steer horns, over to a nearby pile of old cottonwood logs high on the beach. Jamming first one blade and then the other deep into the pile, and reefing back against the aluminum, I was able to take most of the frustrating curves out of the blades.

To finish the job off in fine Alaska style, I lay each blade tip flat across a big log and hammered it pretty much back into shape with a heavy driftwood club. When the repaired prop looked just about serviceable, I screwed the thing back onto the front end of the sad-looking little craft and told my doubtful passengers that I was just gonna take it for a short test hop before we left for home.

I found the engine seemed relatively smooth at both the 1,000- and 2,000-rpm settings, which meant I could take off, climb out, cruise and let down again without much vibration. Looked like a good job to me.

My passengers squeezed aboard, with, I suspected, a great deal of trepidation, and soon we were off to the dubious cheering of the small crowd that had gathered on the beach to watch the custom maintenance work and its ultimate results.

Next morning, the propeller repair station at Lake Hood told me that the damage had occurred too near the tips to be success-fully repaired, and that I would have to buy a new prop. Anchorage is a small town, regardless of its official population. There aren't all that many prop repair stations there. All I could do was grit my teeth as I wrote out a hefty check for another propeller. It didn't make me any happier to think that this had all been my own damned fault in the first place. But, dang, I hated to lose the original Borer climb prop, even though its replacement had been built to exactly the same length and pitch specifications. The first one had carried me through a lot of thick—and through no small amount of thin—and I would miss it.

It was almost one year to the day later that I chopped off the left wingtip at the same little beach. A gust of wind dropped the left wing just as I was touching down north of the river mouth, and the left wingtip smacked another big cottonwood log lying along the beach. High tide had taken most of the beach, and what was left for landing was pretty narrow just then. Duct tape took care of that problem for the short flight back to Anchorage, but two feet of the left wingtip, along with the red navigational light and miscellaneous lengths of electrical wiring, linen fabric, and bits of aluminum, were left scattered along the beach that day.

I have to say one thing about Piper's little Super Cub. While there isn't much one can do to improve the wing, there really isn't much one can do to render it useless, either.

It wasn't until the twelfth of September that I ran into another little snag with that Cub. I had taken a Californian through Merrill Pass for some aerial photographs of large bull caribou and maybe a grizzly or two.

We were at 6,000, nosing around some peaks north of the Stony River so that Jim could snap away at the big bulls as they lay in small patches of snow to escape the flies that were still so thick at lower altitudes.

Crossing one sharp ridge and heading south again for the Stony, I throttled back only to hear a grinding noise that would wake the dead. I ran the power back up to get 2,000 rpms and take stock of the situation. The engine seemed smooth and quiet running at that setting, but when I reduced the power again, the same screaming and screeching returned.

I told Jim to check his seat belt and secure his camera gear. We were going to make a dead-stick landing on the nearest Stony River sand bar so that I could have a look under the cowling. Considering this an emergency, really, rather than simply a precautionary landing, I shut the engine down and picked the bar I wanted for my off-airport airport.

The Bigfoot Cub, on its 25x11x4 tundra tires, took the sand bar without incident. I folded the split door halves up and down, and we clambered out. Jim reached back inside for a spinning rod and some other fishing gear while I opened the engine cowling to have a look-see inside. What I found was a pain in the neck, but nothing really serious. That is to say, it was bush fixable. We wouldn't have to spend much time on a sand bar west of Merrill Pass hoping for a passing rescue flight to stumble upon us.

Both generator mounting bolts had broken clean off, admittedly a most unusual occurrence. Only the belt and centrifugal force held the generator in place. When the engine power was reduced, and the revolutions came down, the generator would fall lower to grind away at the bottom portion of the forward cowling. By the time we had landed, the generator had ground its way clear through in one small place and was threatening to saw its way clear through and fall out.

So—off came the spinner, off came the prop, and off came the nose cowl. Lots of "offs" there. Meantime, Jim wasn't catching anything at all, as I suspected he wouldn't.

I pulled the generator, bracket, and belt from the engine compartment and tossed them into the Cub's baggage compartment. It wasn't long before I had the cowling, prop, and spinner back in place. There would be enough left in the battery for another engine start or two, plus a few minutes of necessary radio time later in the day. I wasn't really concerned about that. In the worst possible case, I would simply hand-prop the little beast.

The faithful Lycoming engine torched off on the first prop rotation, though, and we were soon off in a flurry of dry sand and clear air. A few more photographs and we turned again for the pass and the second leg of this flight.

Earlier we had added some avgas to our tanks from a cache I had hidden away nearby months before, and we had one more stop to make yet that day. This time it would be near the foot of Tokositna Glacier on the southern flanks of Mt. McKinley. Jim had made a moose kill there the day before, and I had neglected to retrieve the tongue for the German grandmother of one of my assistant guides. If I didn't bring that tongue home today, it would be my skin the next time I saw the grand old lady. Besides, I had promised. By the time we shut down the little Cub down at Merrill Field that night, we'd put in more than ten hours of flying.

In spite of several camp equipment and meat hauling trips, I didn't have another little misadventure with the Cub until the first week of October that year. This time, I was at the foot of the Tokositna Glacier, located at the head of Twenty Mile Valley. Some of us called it Moose Valley, because of the high population of both cows and bulls there in the fall.

I had helped set up a moose-hunting camp on a little dab of real estate located at the base of a very small peninsula in the rushing Tokositna River, just below the glacier's toe. The strip was nothing more than a very bumpy piece of glacial moraine, carved out by roaring high waters some time in the recent past. Since the peninsula changed with the seasons, chances were we wouldn't be able to camp there next year. The clearing was less than 200 feet long, and at its lower end, I was always forced into a hard 90-degree right in order to stop before plunging into the rushing, silt-laden waters of the river itself.

The peninsula's upper end began at the top of a four-foot cut bank above the water. All told, it wasn't much of a landing spot, but it was enough for a working Cub with big tires. Even a Cub with a small engine. The real problem was that the ground was so uneven the brakes weren't effective until beyond the halfway point. That meant negotiating the far end quickly, braking heavily on the right side. This was hard on both the tail spring assembly and the braking system.

During the last flight of October 8, it was raining, getting dark, and I had one passenger on board. The strip had always been hard to locate, even in good weather. This time, I had to pick it out by the sweeps and bends in the river, all from an altitude of twenty or thirty feet. When I finally zeroed in on the strip and made my hasty approach, I was too close to slow enough for the landing. I aborted the first pass and turned too quickly to get properly aligned for the second, coming in just a bit high. The third approach would have to be the final approach, because it was now almost pitch dark in light drizzle. I could barely make out the scrub willows along the riverbank as I came in for the final approach, looking hard through the streaked windshield for the brush and cut bank that signaled the near-end of the strip.

I held the Cub high enough to clear the bank, almost invisible now in the rain and dim light. Immediately after passing the near-end, I dumped the flaps and slammed it down. I had been carrying two or three extra miles on the short final in case I had to give it up for the day. When we found the ground, we were still going faster than we should have been, and I braked heavily every time the little Cub decided to meet the earth.

I couldn't see the end of the strip coming up, but I had landed here enough times that my inner clock was timing the landing. I jammed on the right brake and almost ground-looped into the final hard right turn, coming to a stop at the water's edge. The tail wheel spring had snapped under the strain, though, and the Cub was there for the night.

We simply crawled out, tied the plane to nearby willows, and turned in for the evening. Next morning, we inspected the broken springs and searched through our camp gear, finding nothing suitable with which to replace them. I wrapped the springs as tightly as I could with a nylon strap, knowing full well that the nylon was much too stretchy to be of much value as a repair material. Still, it held together through the very bumpy takeoff. I had to make one more landing and that was at Lake Hood, where I figured I could get Jake Bryant to dig up another spring for the Cub.

As it turned out, he didn't have a spare lying around. Instead, he took the springs from another model, laid them across a piece of railroad rail and hammered them into shape with a twelve-pound sledge. When Jake thought they looked just about right, we bolted them on and flew away. The modified springs worked just fine until I located a new set the following week.

It was December when I broke the right landing gear on the tough little ship. I had flown with Artie Breautigam, one of my assistant guides, to Wasilla Lake, north of Anchorage, to arrange a freight flight for a fellow who lived near there. The lake had not frozen well that year, and there were a lot of almost invisible pressure ridges on it.

The landing was fine, but the departure took us across one of the ridges just as we became airborne. We hit the ridge with a loud crack, and I knew something had gone. Looking out the right window, I could see that the impact had snapped the right landing gear. The big red ski had swung down to almost disappear beneath the belly of the little Cub. Our next landing would be a little different from most.

I had installed safety cables on the Cub's gear for insurance against just this sort of thing. I knew the landing wouldn't be dangerous or in any way damaging, but I also knew the right wingtip wouldn't be far above the ice and snow on touchdown. As it turned out, it was very close indeed. But I landed without incident, and had the gear repaired the following day. I've never yet figured out why stateside pilots don't incorporate a few of the Alaska modifications into their own aircraft. These little goodies surely do save a fella a lot of grief, from time to time, and they are certainly worth the few dollars they cost the pilot.

Chapter 11

MILLS CREEK

$\mathcal{B}$etween Nugget Bench and Chelatna Lake, and near to the moraine of the Kahiltna Glacier, lies a small gold-mining claim known by some as Mills Creek. It doesn't appear on any maps or charts that I know of, and that's just as well. After all, the owners surely don't want to advertise their claim, which may one day turn out to be lucrative for them.

Nearby, Chelatna Lake, a body of water about seven miles long by three-quarters of a mile wide, lies northwest to southeast. Mountain ridges rising above 4,000 feet surround three sides. The upper end of the lake slams hard up against the foot of a peak that makes a steep climb to almost 6,000 feet above sea level, and 4,500 feet above the lake itself.

The lower end of the lake spills its clear, cold waters into Lake Creek, a very popular trout and grayling fishing stream. Fishing at the lake mouth, and down river to the point where a steel cable stretched across the stream marks it as too dangerous for casual boat

CHELATNA LAKE LODGE OWNER AND
LONGTIME PILOT GRAHAM MOWER
(LEFT) AND I (RIGHT) CHAT WITH THE
LAKE AND MOUNTAINS IN THE BACK-
GROUND. THIS PHOTO WAS TAKEN
THROUGH THE FRONT DOOR OF THE
LODGE, LOOKING DIRECTLY TOWARD
CHELATNA LAKE. MILLS CREEK GOLD
MINE STRIP IS NEARBY.

travel, is one of Alaska's finest fishing spots. Thirty-five air miles downstream to the southeast, Lake Creek meets the Yetna River.

The lake boasts a lodge, which long ago, without much mystery, was named Chelatna Lake Lodge. The last time I visited, Graham Mower, former chief pilot with Merle "Mudhole" Smith's Cordova Airlines, owned the place. There is a little gravel landing strip at the lodge, crowded right up tight against the water's edge. The navigational charts show the strip to be 1,435 feet long. What the charts don't show is that the end nearest the lodge is doglegged at about 45 degrees. It wouldn't be a suitable strip for most stateside pilots. For some reason, these fellows seem to favor coming in a little too high and a little too fast, then floating past the most important part of any runway—the *near* end. You just can't successfully make that sort of casual approach to a landing at Chelatna Lake.

The mountains that surround the lake are a part of the Alaska Range, home to Mt. McKinley, Mt. Foraker, Mt. Washington, the Moose's Tooth, and other well-known peaks. Mt. McKinley, now called Mt. Denali, stands only thirty-five air miles north-northeast of Chelatna Lake, and is 18,885 feet higher than the lake surface. This should give you an idea of how rugged the country around that lake actually is. It's awesome, it's formidable, and it's gorgeous!

About midway between Chelatna Lake and Nugget Bench, lies the small, relatively unknown, clearing called the Mills Creek Strip. It serves Mills Creek mining camp and isn't shown on any navigational charts. It's a private strip, and I'm sure the owners don't want to advertise the strip to every fall season moose and bear hunter who happens to pass their way.

I had seen a few good moose yarded up there on several flights during one late fall and early winter in the early sixties. A good friend of mine, a bow hunter named Keith Johnson, was looking for a good winter moose, and this seemed a promising place to find one.

An excellent hunter and archer, Keith had only recently arrived in Alaska from Montana, where he had been a schoolteacher. Keith later became a teacher on Alaska's Kenai Peninsula, before making more money as a commercial salmon fisherman. He would later become one of Alaska's premier Master Guides. If you're looking for a really good brown bear, Keith is as good a guide as you can find. And, when it comes to record-class Dall sheep, the pure white sheep of Alaska, you won't find a better guide anywhere in the world.

I mentioned the moose at Mills Creek, and Keith was all ready for a cold-weather try at one of them. We planned to make the trip one cold, clear weekend with Jack Rodriguez, a talented electrical engineer and close friend from Anchorage.

We left Merrill Field for Mills Creek on a really cold morning. I had been a little lazy about changing out the 8.50x6 wheels for the usual wintertime hydraulic wheel/ski combination, since there had not yet been any appreciable snow in or around Anchorage. So I decided I'd better fly the long way to Mills Creek in order to check snow depth along the way.

We headed up the Big Su as far as the Yentna River, then turned slightly left to fly up the Yentna to Lake Creek. Along the way, I made several touch-and-go gravel bar landings, finding only one or two inches of snow along the rivers.

What I didn't know was that there had been a hard freeze in the high country, followed by snow, then rain, then snow, then rain, and finally another snowfall. This sandwiched snow-over-frozen-snow would pose a most treacherous threat later in the flight.

When we arrived over Mills Creek, the moose were still yarded up at the north end of the strip near the tool shed that served the camp. The strip was covered with snow, and judging its depth was a bit tricky.

I dragged the strip low and slow several times, but still wasn't sure of the snow pack's depth. On one of these passes, I saw a clear set of moose tracks laid diagonally across the strip, and from these the snow looked to be about a foot deep. There had been no appreciable wind, it seemed, and the tracks looked almost fresh. With all the moose nearby, I presumed that they were.

On the last pass, I reminded Jack, who sat in the front passenger seat, and Keith, in the back, to tighten their seat belts. Although I trusted my own judgment of the snow depth, we wouldn't really be sure about it until after we had landed.

The strip was plenty long, somewhere between 1,800 and 2,000 feet, and appeared smooth under the snow. I made the approach with full flaps, and I intended to make a three-point touchdown to keep the tail low, staying on the throttle as added insurance.

The three wheels entered the snow at the same moment, and for just a second I thought we had it made. Then the main gear went through the top twelve inches and broke through the frozen layer underneath. When that layer failed, the plane had slowed dramatically. I jammed the throttle forward to send a burst of air across the elevators, trying to keep the tail down. It almost worked.

But the tail came up and seemed to hang in mid air for an eternity. We had come to almost a full stop in only about forty feet, but still it seemed we had made it after all. Then, and with an agonizing slowness, the tail came over the top, and we found ourselves upside down on an isolated strip 100 long miles from home. We had settled down so easily that I was sure nothing had been damaged beyond the scope of a quick bush fix. We'd have to dig out a runway, however. We couldn't take off in that snow cover.

Hanging on my seat belt, I went through the ritual of shutting off the master switch and closing the fuel selector valve. The last thing I needed was an electrical fire. Then I began the methodical flipping of other switches, raising the flaps and shutting down the aircraft completely.

Keith was understandably disoriented, hanging upside down in the low-visibility back seat as he was. Built much like a spider and at times seeming to be all arms and legs he was pummeling my head with his cold, hard boots. I was afraid he would knock me out before I could finish the shutdown and get my two passengers clear of the aircraft.

Keith finally found his seat belt buckle, released it—and promptly fell in a heap on the ceiling. I had by then opened my door so he that he had an exit route, and he took that as soon as he figured out that the wing was supposed to be on the bottom when the airplane was upside down like that.

Jack was having no trouble at all. He was soon out stamping around in the snow and remarking at the severe cold around us. I glanced at the outside thermometer and saw that it was -41°. Well, yeah, that's pretty cold, all right.

As soon as I knew there wasn't going to be a fuel spill or a fire of any sort, I turned the master switch and radio back on and called Anchorage Radio. Even with the airplane upside down and with the antenna now buried deep in the snow, our transmission went right through. In fact, it picked up a CAP (Civil Air Patrol) flight that was still in the air just returning to Anchorage from Kenai. The pilot said he would drop by early the following morning. Would we be all right until then? I told him that we were fine and would just hunker down in the mine's tool shed until then. With that, we began to take stock of our situation.

Survival came first, at this temperature, and we had a look-see inside the tool shed, which wasn't locked. It turned out that the small building was also a makeshift bunkhouse, and although it wasn't insulated, it did provide protection from the wind. We found a Coleman stove that would provide sufficient heat. Besides, we all had arctic down sleeping bags and were in no real danger of freezing.

Coffee and hot soup, made from the plane's onboard emergency rations kit, would set us right for the moment. I took an old coffee-pot and walked about thirty yards toward the musical chuckling of a small stream. I found the little creek and rinsed out the small aluminum coffeepot. I scooped up a pot full of the clear, cold water and dashed for the warmth of the nearby tool shed. I arrived only seconds later to find the water already frozen, despite the terrible jostling it had taken during my dash for shelter. Well, at forty below, what did I expect?

While Keith and Jack started some soup, I went back to see how badly the Cessna had been damaged. I found the lead-filled counterbalance atop the rudder had been bent. Well, at forty below zero, I could just chop that thing off with the hatchet I had seen in the tool shed. Nothing else seemed to be hurt except the prop tips and the lower cowling. So far, it looked as though we'd be out the next day about noon. All we had to do was get the danged plane back up on its feet. Little did I know . . .

We had only been at Mills Creek for about an hour when I heard the sound of a Cessna 180 flying somewhere nearby. Although it was now pitch dark (we enjoyed less than six hours of daylight that time of year at this latitude), I wasn't really surprised. Lots of Alaska pilots fly in the dark. This airplane, however, was without question coming directly our way. I suppose my Cessna stood out rather clearly in the middle of the airstrip.

The other Cessna circled the strip once, then lined up for a landing. I wondered who could have heard about the accident so quickly, and could then have flown to this remote strip so soon. Very few people even knew about this place.

Since my Cessna was now parked upside down and almost smack in the middle of the strip, I was concerned that the arriving pilot might bang into it during his landing. I shouldn't have worried about that. The pilot turned out to be Don Sheldon, on his way back to his wife, Betty, and his home in Talkeetna. Don, Alaska's premier bush pilot at that time and subject of the book, *Wager With the Wind*, was probably just returning from a trip to his little five-sided cabin retreat at the 8,000-foot level of Mt. McKinley's Ruth Glacier.

There wasn't much that Don could do for us that night, although he did offer to bring us a new prop the following day. Keith thought he might as well return home to Anchorage, so he piled aboard Don's Cessna and the two of them lit out into the frozen darkness. No doubt Don gave him an earful over our landing at Mills Creek without skis. He would be right to do so, of course. It wasn't a smart thing to do in the first place.

Jack and I settled in for a long, black night of it at Mills Creek, where the temperature would probably drop to minus fifty that night. The sun wouldn't come up until about nine o'clock the next morning, and there wasn't much we could do until we had more light.

About ten o'clock the following morning, an Anchorage Civil Air Patrol DeHaviland Beaver floated in on wheel/skis to lift us out. The pilot dropped the wheels (actually, he raised the skis) just before coming to a full stop. This would securely anchor the heavy Beaver in place. Civil Air Patrol would take us back to Anchorage to gather the necessary supplies. During the subsequent takeoff run, I stood between the pilot and co-pilot seats and furiously worked the hydraulic pump handle to lower the skis. Hardest danged pumping I've ever done. Later I would host the rescue pilots and their families to a good steak dinner at the Driftwood on Third Avenue in Anchorage. They had certainly wasted no time in getting to us, showing genuine Alaska concern for troubled fliers.

After arriving back in Anchorage, I brought a new prop, rented a ski-equipped Super Cub, and prepared to return to Mills Creek. I had to get the Cessna back on its feet and out of there as quickly as possible. Every moment away from the plane left it vulnerable to

Assistant guide Artie Braeutigam,
pictured here on an unnamed lake
in caribou country, helped put the
Cessna 170 Special back on its feet
after the Mills Creek gold mine
camp incident.

raids by Alaska's flying thieves. And, believe it or not, Alaska is filled with flying thieves!

I called Artie Breautigam, a longtime friend and later one of my best assistant guides, to ask if he had time to help out. As always, Artie was quick to say yes. Artie had been a friend since he was only twelve, and he had grown into quite a man. At about 200 pounds, and a professional meat cutter during hunting seasons, he was about as strong as any man I've ever known.

We flew back to Mills Creek and had another good look at the overturned plane. We would have to dig a hole about six feet across and six feet deep to allow the nose to swing beneath the plane as it rotated on the wings' leading edges and returned to a wheels-down position. The tool shed had sufficient picks and shovels, of course, but we hadn't thought a lot about the frozen ground and sub-zero temperatures we would face.

The earth had been water-soaked before the sharp freeze, and frost had by now traveled down through the earth more than four feet. It was all pick work and not easy at that. By the time darkness set in that first day, we had only chopped through about twelve inches of frozen earth. The next morning we supposed that the severe cold had driven the frost down another fifteen inches. Without an insulating snow cover over the exposed earth in the hole, this routine would go on for days. And that's just what happened. We used the pick to chip away every inch of depth. It took us almost three full weeks of short days to dig that six-foot-deep hole. The temperature held steady at forty below during the daylight hours and plummeted to who knew what during the night. Some nights probably got as cold as sixty below. It was truly miserable work, and Artie did more than his fair share of it.

After the pit was deep enough to allow the nose to pass through, we dug another, smaller hole. In this hole, located about thirty feet

ARTIE BRAEUTIGAM (RIGHT) AND
I (LEFT) POSED FOR THIS PHOTO IN
FRONT OF THE WINTER-READY SUPER
CUB. NOTE THE SNOWSHOES STRAPPED
TO EACH WING FOR EMERGENCY USE.
AFTER SETTING UP CAMP AND
WRAPPING AROUND SOME HOT SOUP,
ARTIE PLANNED TO HUNT CARIBOU
FOR HIS WINTER LARDER.

behind where the tail would finally come to rest when the ship was upright again, we angled a spruce pole away from the plane. To that pole, we attached a block and tackle we had found in the tool shed. We secured the line from that series of pulleys to the tail section and, with some pulling, worked to set the plane back on its wheels again. We had almost passed the balance point in hoisting, with the tail pointed beyond straight up, *when the lines snapped!*

Artie dove head first into the snow and clamped the running lines together with his bare hands. I could see blue smoke curling upward from his closed fists as he snubbed the falling aircraft down with sheer brute strength and determination. He couldn't stop its fall completely, but he slowed it down to the point that the only apparent additional damage was a broken windshield. That was small potatoes compared to what might have happened if he had let the whole mess just fall. To this day Artie has stretch marks along his arms as a result of that effort. I can never repay that sort of dedication.

While we were busy hoisting the plane that first time, we didn't notice that we had so strained the fuselage that the belly skin in front of the tail assembly was now wrinkled. We had bent the fuselage during that first lifting operation! Moreover, I also discovered that the starboard wing strut had been bent and would need to be repaired or replaced. At this point, it looked as though we needed a few more supplies.

Another trip to Anchorage secured a piece of quarter-inch Plexiglas, some three-quarter-inch plywood, bolts, several lengths of one-and-a-half-inch steel angle iron, and some new line, of course. Back at Mills Creek once again, we rigged the new lines and soon had the Cessna back on its feet. Now we could work on the repairs, such as they were going to be. We drilled a few holes through the right wing strut and sandwiched two pieces of angle iron on either side of the bent strut. Ugly, to be sure, but sufficient for the purpose.

Next, we placed a long, narrow piece of three-quarter-inch plywood inside the bent fuselage, securing it along the outside with another piece of the one-and-a-half-inch angle iron. We chopped off the rudder counterbalance to allow complete rotation of the rudder, even though I knew I would have to apply a little more rudder pressure during flight.

We installed a new prop up front and then tackled the windshield. Using a plumber's blowtorch from the tool shed, we heated the Plexiglas, bent it roughly to the shape of the windshield. We then drilled holes through the old windshield and its replacement and bolted them together, with the new piece on the outside. We found the pitot tube had been broken off, so I knew I wouldn't have any airspeed indicator for the flight back to Anchorage. That was all right, since I had flown the Cessna enough to be able to feel the airspeed necessary for safe flight. Besides, I suppose all Alaska pilots are still "seat of the pants" fliers.

Through all of this, the mercury didn't climb above forty below. Almost three continuous weeks of severely cold temperatures and neither of us had yet suffered any frostbite. So far so good.

Last but not least, we installed of a huge set of fiberglass skis, borrowed temporarily from a helicopter. They looked gigantic under the broken little Cessna, and they were. But they were just what we needed to ride the top of the snow on the way out of there.

In the hours just before my scheduled departure from Mills Creek, the warm, wet winds of a Chinook blew in, pelting the Cessna, Artie, and me with ice-cold rain. By the time I was ready to depart, I was soaking wet, but warm for the first time in several weeks.

The engine started right away, but while I waited for the oil temperature gauge to come off the peg, the cockpit warmed enough that my wet clothing began to steam, and a layer of fog spread itself across the windshield between the two layers of Plexiglas. Forward visibility was reduced to zero, though I could still see the shadows of the spruce trees that lined both sides of the strip. Ah, well—in for a penny, in for a pound, it has been said.

I made the takeoff without flaps. I didn't have sophisticated avionics or vacuum instruments aboard, so I controlled the aircraft's direction by carefully judging its distance from the trees through the pilot's side window. Since the airstrip was plenty long, and I had added power only gingerly to avoid the effects of torque, this was no problem. A rapid increase in power would have swung the nose to the left and out of alignment with the narrow strip. After only a short takeoff run, the big Cessna wings lifted the empty craft smoothly into the cold, wet air, and I was off to Anchorage, 100 miles to the south.

I was glad that the air had warmed, bringing rain and lower clouds. This constituted a smooth, stable air mass, without turbulence. I had been a bit uneasy about the possibility of turbulence all along, since I didn't really know what went on inside the right wing. I only knew it had been bounced hard enough to bend its strut, and I could only imagine the concealed damage inside the wing itself.

The flight was smooth and uneventful, even though a reduced power setting naturally resulted in an uncommonly slow airspeed. Although I didn't have a working airspeed indicator, the elapsed time finally told me that I had cruised at about 80 miles an hour, rather than the usual 110 or 115.

I had secured the proper ferry permit from the local GADO (General Aviation District Office) in Anchorage necessary to fly an airplane not certified for safe flight to the nearest maintenance facility. I didn't carry any passengers on that flight, naturally.

The landing at Merrill Field was as smooth as any I have ever made, and in spite of the goofy-looking craft that taxied off the active runway that day, all went according to plan. Until my mechanic snuck a peek inside the right wing, that is.

I had broken the trailing spar on that side, and no ferry permit would have been issued against that sort of damage. The wing could have folded up at any time during the flight. The slightest turbulence would probably have guaranteed it. Thank goodness for smooth air!

The final repair bill was almost exactly the same amount that I had originally paid for the Cessna several years ago. I didn't complain about that, though. The plane served me well for several more years.

The last I saw of that plane almost brought tears to my eyes. A subsequent owner had apparently tried to land on a ridge overlooking Turquoise Lake, along the western slopes of the Alaska Range and south of Merrill Pass. The faithful old plane was upside down once more. This time, though, it was destined to remain in the bush. It's still there, a sad reminder of the proud aircraft it had once been. I still hate to fly past Turquoise Lake, for I always have to look down on N5417C. It always chokes me up a little.

Chapter 12

Nugget Bench

On a snowy day during the second week of November in 1957, I stopped in at the Fifth Avenue offices of the Nugget Bench Placer Mining Corporation. A small but stalwart group of hopefuls had started the company in an attempt to shake a few more dollars from a placer mining claim that had, in years past, produced six million dollars in gold. The yellow metal was still worth only sixteen dollars per fine ounce in those days.

The secretary informed me that she had been holding a batch of mail, including paychecks, for their employees at Nugget Bench. None of their pilots had been able to deliver the package for the past week due to bad weather. I knew that their pilots were pretty much weekend fliers, in spite of the fact that at least one of them flew an old L-13 workhorse. Since I was going up that way anyway, I told the secretary that I'd deliver the mail.

It was my fifth wedding anniversary. Looking back on it, I had no business flying that day in such weather. Still, off I went, and as I lifted off Merrill Field with one of our friends in the right seat, I was still looking forward to a fine dinner that evening with my lovely wife.

My passenger, a very talented lady with a degree in architecture from the University of Washington in Seattle, was a bit on the heavy side. Fact is, she tipped the scales somewhere above 250 pounds. But what the little engine wasn't up to, the long wings were, and the Chief lifted us off Merrill without so much as a second thought. We were pretty cramped in the Chief's limited cabin area, but we were airborne.

We headed for the camp's little gravel strip, about twenty-six air miles west of Talkeetna. The strip, cut from a tundra plateau along the Peters Hills south and west of the Kahiltna Glacier, lies on a bench 2,000 feet above sea level. Navigational charts tell of a strip 1,400 feet long, but that is wishful thinking. Nine hundred, perhaps a thousand, might be a little closer to the truth.

I had been to that strip many times in my little Aeronca Chief, N9459E, a two-place, side-by-side taildragger with great wings, no flaps at all, and a dependable, if seriously underpowered, 65-hp Continental engine. With no radio, no starter, no generator and no battery, it was light and absolutely basic in every sense of the word.

For the next hour and thirty minutes the snowfall became heavier and heavier. By the time we had passed abeam Willow, I had finally realized that I wasn't going to make it into Nugget Bench directly from the south. I banked east to fly northward along the east side of the Peters Hills and past the tiny Petersville strip. This little dirt strip is built atop the high Peters Creek bank, along its east side. Someone had thoughtfully placed a barrier of fifty-five-gallon drums across its north end to keep landing aircraft from running off the end and plunging into the creek far below.

Just beyond the end of the red dirt strip, we rolled left and followed a small dirt road through the narrow pass that would spill us out just northeast of the Nugget Bench strip. One lane wide, this short service road was carved into the side of the steep hill on the north side of a narrow little canyon, lush with grasses and willow growth. It's not a comfortable road to drive, and I wouldn't be caught dead on it during periods of rain or snow.

We were now flying in a snowstorm of serious proportions, and I finally had to locate Nugget Bench by finding the huge pile of large steel pipes that I knew to be stored at the mouth of Nugget Creek, just northeast of the camp itself. After swinging up Nugget Creek beyond the stored pipes, we turned left almost immediately over a huge gravel pit to cross directly over the mining camp. As I flew overhead and past the three small, unfinished wood frame buildings that made up the camp, several of the miners and their cook stood outside waving up at us. We roared overhead less than thirty feet above them. They saw us, but we couldn't see them through the heavy snow. I knew I hadn't missed the camp, and wasn't sure why I couldn't see it.

I flew a complete circle that took me directly over the camp buildings again, but still could see neither the roofs nor the men themselves, still waving their wild encouragement from below. After passing the swale I knew to be just off the southern end of the airstrip, I flew south for another two minutes, turned 180 degrees to fly north again, and used the panel-mounted clock to begin counting off the seconds for a letdown to the short strip.

As long as I could keep the wheels out of the scrub willows south of the strip, I knew we would be safe enough. I expected to see the break in those willows that would signal the near end of the strip in only a few more seconds.

When that break appeared just ahead of the spinner, I chopped the power off and allowed the Chief to settle in and touch the snow-covered strip, coasting uphill almost to its northern end where a thick stand of willows provided a definite end to the narrow clearing. Just a few yards farther along—and beyond this last small patch of scrubby, tough, far-north little willows—the world dropped away steeply into the deep Morgan Pit, an excavation that marked the site of the earlier gold mining operations.

It was here that, many years earlier, a thirty-six-inch steel pipe had been laid from a small lake high above the camp in order to provide the water necessary to sluice out this huge excavation in the high Nugget Creek bank. This tremendous pit had been the site where miners found that the six million dollars in gold some years ago.

After tying down the little Chief, we took the mail and payroll checks into the main camp building, which served as the crew's dining room and kitchen. Part of the crew even used this building as sleeping quarters. The camp also had a separate bunkhouse, tool-storage-cum-workshop buildings, and a screened meat house—a typical bush structure that served as the camp's bear, moose, and caribou meat storage locker during all seasons.

We accepted the generous offer of fresh coffee and warm cookies and passed the next half-hour or so bantering and exchanging bush stories. After a few tales, we reminded the crew that we would have to leave soon before full darkness banged down to lock us in for the night. By the time were finally ready to depart, however, it was already as dark as the inside of your hat. We placed two Coleman lanterns at each end of the strip to mark both its direction and its end.

The little strip, which sloped gently down from north to south, was by now covered with about eight inches of snow over four inches of mud. I had hoped the Chief's narrow wheel wouldn't be a hindrance in this slush. After I had tried both downhill and uphill takeoff runs without success, I noticed that I was never able to coax the airspeed indicator above 50 miles per hour. I needed 52 indicated in order to lift off, and I couldn't cheat about that. The difference between 50 and 52 is only about three feet per second, and the average man walks almost twice that fast. This seemingly miniscule difference, though, is really all the difference in the world at a time like this.

Looking for all the help I could get, I hoisted the tail up on a fifty-five-gallon drum to drain fuel forward from the small auxiliary tank, located behind the baggage compartment, into the two wing tanks. I was trying to move the center of gravity forward just a little, hoping that shift would allow us to get out of there. I was still planning on that anniversary dinner.

After I aborted two more takeoff attempts at the last moment, I tried desperately to come up with some other bright idea that would help us out a little. And finally I hit on it!

The strip had been created by simply smoothing out a stretch of tundra. An eight-inch hump still remained at either end where the strip stopped and the tundra began. I calculated that, if I could hit that bump hard enough when we reached the lower end of the strip, the landing gear would bounce us into the air. I could then follow a natural swale at the downhill end and ride in ground effect until the airspeed needle could crawl up to something reasonable. The swale led down to the east and into the narrow canyon that held Cache Creek, the stream into which Nugget Creek emptied less than a mile away. I knew of other pilots who had used this springboard technique in the past, and I had every confidence in the questionable and somewhat risky maneuver.

On the next takeoff run, both of us now tightly belted in and leaning forward for all we were worth, the little plane roared, complained, rocked, slipped, skidded, and slid its way along the snow-and-mud strip until just past the half-way point. I had the Chief's reluctant little tail in the air and the obstinate airspeed indicator nudging 45, then 48—then 50! I was still holding that precious fifty when we hit the runway end—with almost no perceptible "bump" at all!

When we didn't bounce a single inch into the air, but simply left the strip and plunged at 50 miles an hour into the scrub willows, snow, and hummocks beyond, I remembered that those who had tried this maneuver before had been flying airplanes with bungee cord shock absorbers on the landing gear. Bungee cords, really nothing more than a wrapped bundle of rubber bands, returned to their original shape and length in no time. The little Chief's gear was built around oleo struts, small hydraulic cylinders that had simply absorbed the shock of the bump at the strip's end and left us hanging out there on our own. The pneumatics of hydraulic oleo struts provides a notoriously slow speed of return, and we had been trapped by this lassitude. We bounced and wallowed and tore up the willows, finally coming to rest with the nose dipped into a snow bank and almost completely hidden by the brush around us. Not a very glorious end to the valiant, if truly ill conceived, takeoff attempt.

Shorty, Kozlosky and a couple other men from the camp started up their old Dodge Power Wagon and drove it to the strip's lower end, throwing a hitch around the tail wheel to winch the sad little Chief back up to the runway. But the frail-looking little plane wasn't as frail as it looked. It suffered no damage whatsoever, when at the very least I should have lost the gear, the prop, and the lower cowling.

I cleaned out the air intake screen and filter, and then tied the Chief down for the night. We accepted the camp's offer of spare warm beds that night, followed by a good hot breakfast the next morning. On his way home to nearby Talkeetna, mountain pilot

Don Sheldon had flown over just after the incident. He called in to the TKA FSS and reported that a yellow-and-blue airplane had run off the strip at Nugget Bench. He saw no sign of life. That sort of added insult to injury, since the Chief wasn't yellow-and-blue, but yellow-and-red. I chalked that mistake up to poor visibility in snow and darkness. How he missed any sign of life at the busy camp, though, is beyond me. That message got through to my wife back in Anchorage when she called the local CAA office to ask if they had received any word of my whereabouts. You would be right to presume that this wasn't turning out to be the anniversary celebration either of us had planned.

The next morning, with frozen ground now under the wheels, our takeoff was without a hitch. Well, almost without a hitch. Actually, there were two hitches, to be honest about it. The first was that my passenger, during the successful eighteen-second uphill takeoff run, had apparently envisioned our crashing into the deep Morgan Pit immediately beyond the strip. She had begun to rock back and forth in the passenger seat. When she leaned back, her hands would come up to cover her eyes. But when she leaned forward, both hands would drop to grasp the control wheel on the passenger side of the cramped cockpit. I couldn't risk the obvious, so, just before the liftoff, I met her forehead with my right elbow. She went to sleep immediately, napping through the next two or three minutes. Enough, at least, so that I could lower the nose into to the deep pit in order to pick up a little more airspeed and then climb into the southeast turn toward Anchorage. Not a very nice thing to do, I know, but looking at the options and potential consequences, an apology seemed the least of several possible evils.

The second hitch? Well that didn't happen until I arrived at home later that morning. It was not a pleasant welcome home, I can tell you.

Chapter 13

CHRISTMAS, 1981

*D*uring the month of December, back in 1981, I had to make several flights from Anchorage to Tanacross, Tok Junction, Eagle, and other villages along the Alaska-Canada border. Business with the school district in that area had kept me jumping back and forth in the Cessna 206 Stationair, and the big 300-hp Teledyne Continental engine was hardly able to cool between flights, in spite of temperatures that plunged to -40° and -50°.

That far north, daylight lasts just short of five hours. The weather that month had been particularly rotten, though, and the pass at Sheep Mountain had been closed more often than not, interrupting planned flights into the area.

On the first day of that month, I had flown from Anchorage to Tok Junction, stopping first at Tanacross for the fuel I was going to need for my return trip to Anchorage later on. There were nine inches of fresh snow on the Tanacross runway when I arrived, and while not enough to be a problem for my tricycle-geared, wheel-equipped Cessna 206 Stationair, it was only a portent of what was yet to come.

On my later return trip to Anchorage, the pass at Sheep Mountain was again closed up tight. "Ceiling 400 feet, sky obscured, visibility down to one-quarter mile in snow" was the report from the Palmer Flight Service Station, located at the lower end of the pass and fifty road miles north of Anchorage.

Despite the report, I tried hard to make it through the pass that evening, but finally had to give it up. I turned back to spend that night, admittedly well fed, warm, and snug, at the lodge-cum-customs-office back at Northway. The following morning, the pass at Sheep Mountain was still reported closed in snow, but this time, after poking around in there for a bit, I was able to sneak through. The temperature that morning stood at -21°. The report had been correct, though, for it was still snowing pretty hard when I finally did tiptoe through the pass. It certainly wasn't a place for low-time pilots.

My last trip to Tok that month began on the twenty-third. During that trip I was forced to sneak through the back door, first flying due north to Talkeetna, then east up the Susitna River to Kelly Lake, where I had a hunting camp headquarters. From there, I was able to fly to a point abeam Glennallen, turn left to pass over Duffy's Tavern, scoot through a small pass to cross Mentasta Lodge, meander through the slot past Mineral Point, and finally spill out into the Tanana River valley, a wide valley that would lead me southeast and downstream to Tok Junction.

After the school district business had been completed, Spike, the school board superintendent, and his wife invited me to stay the night as a guest in their home hard alongside the strip at Tok. This well-maintained airstrip was located 3,000 feet above sea level, and measured over 1,600 feet in length. It was quite comfortable for the big six-place Cessna. The temperature dipped down to three-dog cold that night, and I was happy to have their Alaska hospitality. Besides, Spike's wife was an excellent cook.

Late the following day, Christmas Eve, I took off after an all-night preheating. I had hard-mounted one small 800-watt automobile engine heater inside the engine compartment and another under the co-pilot's seat. That heater had a quick-release connector and could be removed with the seat during freight hauls. My mechanic, Brian Cox, had installed and faired-in a special external electrical connection for the 120-volt service required to energize the heaters, when and where that service might be available. Near civilization, I could put on the wing, tail, windshield, and engine covers, plug in an extension cord, and know that the plane would be ready for flight at almost a moment's notice.

I stopped to top off the ninety-two-gallon, long-range wing tanks at Tanacross, and then began the long, cold flight home. The thermometer was holding obstinately at -50° when I left, and I climbed out on another of those sharp, brittle-clear Alaska winter nights that are so beautiful they keep most of us from moving to warmer places.

Tok is tucked away in a grand little valley in the Alaska Range, but about twelve miles after departure I squeezed between peaks of more than 6,000 feet and into the narrow slot that, in only a few more miles, would become Mentasta Pass.

I over-flew Mentasta lodge and scooted out the chute over Duffy's Tavern again, taking up the heading of about 190° magnetic that would lead me to Glennallen. Magnetic variation in this area is almost 29° east, so the heading would really have been closer to 210° true. I had tuned the Gulkana VOR at 115.6 on the primary navigation radio and was cruising along at a smooth, cool, and comfortable 120 knots indicated, definitely feeling sorry for all those earthbound folks who couldn't share this beautiful Alaska Christmas Eve with me. Farther north, at North Pole, Alaska, I figured Santa was about to finish loading the big, red sleigh for his annual round-the-world trip. I reckoned that the first leg of his flight would be as beautiful as mine.

All that began to change as I approached Glennallen. Gulkana Radio was reporting heavy snow at Glennallen (hell, I could already *see* that!) and once again, Sheep Mountain Pass was closed. After thinking things over for a bit, I finally decided to follow the highway southwest to Tazlina, and then hang a right ninety that would take me over Lake Louise.

Louise is only about six miles long, some narrows connect it to Susitna Lake and, a little farther along, with Tyone Lake. This whole body of cold, clear water, end to end, is probably eighteen or twenty miles long. Twelve miles beyond the north end of Tyone lay Kelly Lake, the five-acre site of my main guiding camp for this area. The cabin was fully stocked with everything I would need, if I found it necessary to lay over there for a spell. Heat, food, sleeping accommodations—even reading materials. Not the best place to spend Christmas Eve, but not the worst either. It flashed through my mind that my wife might not be too pleased about it. Peggy tended to worry needlessly sometimes, especially if I were late in returning from a flight. Which happened quite often, unfortunately.

I didn't really want to land at Kelly, anyway. I knew I could make a safe enough landing there, and that I would be warm and snug in my cabin until the storm passed. But the snow would be too deep for a takeoff in the wheel-equipped Cessna, and since I didn't use that camp outside of hunting seasons, I didn't store a snow shovel there. Using a snowshoe to clear a path twelve feet wide by a thousand feet long just didn't strike me as a really fun way to spend Christmas Day that year. I supposed Peggy might have found that somehow fitting, however.

It was snowing pretty hard but, even in the dark of night, visibility was still out beyond a quarter of a mile. Moreover, I was flying over very familiar country. And I wasn't carrying any passengers, which is always a factor for me when making decisions about flying in bad weather.

Most of the high ground was now off my left wing by ten miles or so, around two and a half minutes flying time. That margin was plenty safe. The occasional spruce stood out black against the lighter background, making flight still relatively comfortable. If I could only get over the 3,200-foot mountain just beyond Tyone Lake, I would be right over Kelly Lake. At my current airspeed, it would take only 150 seconds to cross between the two highest points on either side of Kelly, but that's a whale of a long time in the air without being able to see. On the other hand, I would have to descend about 700 feet in turns after crossing the first ridge before I had reached the halfway point between these mountains. Kelly Lake sits at less than 2,600 feet above sea level.

By the time I had reached the upper end of Tyone Lake, visibility was out to about a mile, and it looked as though I might not have to spend Christmas Eve at Kelly Lake after all. I decided to turn slightly left, taking up a heading of 280 degrees magnetic. This course would set me up to intercept the Upper Susitna River where its downstream flow to the south turned generally west toward Devil Canyon and, eventually, to the town of Talkeetna, only ninety comfortable miles north of Anchorage. Since Talkeetna sits at about 370 feet above sea level, the low level flight from there southward across flat country should be easy enough.

Between my present position and Talkeetna, however, lay Devil Canyon itself. That gorge, home to one of the most frightening stretches of river in the world, is really steep and narrow, with sides only a few hundred yards apart. The canyon is also as crooked as a nervous serpent.

I found the Susitna River eight minutes later, right where I had left it the last time I has been through here, and began to follow it downstream toward Devil Canyon. I was hoping that I could soon leave the Big Susitna River and slide south a bit to hit the Talkeetna River. That short river also feeds directly into Talkeetna, but it doesn't have the same sort of narrow, winding, and dangerous canyon as the Big Su. Lowering ceilings finally took that option from me, though, and in another twenty minutes I realized it was going to be Devil Canyon for Christmas Eve.

I knew I was passing Mt. Watana, four miles off my left wing, about ten minutes after hitting the Big Su. I couldn't see it, of course, but I knew when I had passed it because I recognized tiny Watana Creek as I flew over it. This creek flows northward from Watana Lake into the Big Su. It would be decision time soon, and the ceiling had dropped even lower. I was probably now flying at 100 feet, and guessed that I was about to be pressed even lower. If I were forced down another 50 feet, I would be within 20 feet of the black spruce below, and still scooting along at more than 120 miles an hour.

Six minutes after leaving Mt. Watana behind, and about halfway along the flats that surround Fog Lakes, I knew for sure that I couldn't avoid the trip through Devil Canyon. I checked my belt and shoulder harness, settling in for the demanding ten or twelve minutes ahead. I remember thinking to myself that this had now become a truly lousy way to spend Christmas Eve. I hoped Santa still had clear skies up where he was flying, 'cause they were ragged as hell down here where I was bumbling along. At least the air was still relatively smooth.

The winding river had now turned me south where Tsusena Creek dashes in from the north to feed the Big Su. Next would come a serious 90-degree right turn. That turn would force me westward past Devil Creek, which also flows into the Big Su from the north. Devil Creek rushes into the Susitna right at the very mouth of the narrow gorge and the gate to the hideous Devil Canyon chute. That gate was now less than 200 seconds ahead. In a few moments I could see that the upper end of the canyon was still below the overcast. I wouldn't be able to fly *along* the canyon—it looked as though I would have to fly *through* it!

I had noticed that the overcast was flat on the bottom and thought it might also be level. No such luck. It sloped downward, much like the raging torrent below. By that time, my options were down to two: continue the flight or dump it into the chaos below. Nuts to that! No one had ever survived a dunking in that torrent, and my chances were no better than anyone else's. If as good, come to think about it, since all of the victims had been boaters of one sort or another. And none of them had come out the bottom end alive. My chances would be less than none. I was flying neither a kayak nor an inflatable. If, by some miracle, I survived a landing at the bottom of that canyon, the waters would sweep me away to drown while making jelly of my chilly carcass on the rocks.

I was flying now with 20 degrees of the huge, barn door flaps hanging out, and had slowed to about 70 knots indicated, guessing the empty stall speed in steep turns to be down around 60 or maybe 65. That would be the best I could do for the next few minutes. I was looking at about 775 seconds of the most treacherous and questionable moments of my entire flying life. Almost thirteen minutes of absolute terror. The good part was that I would be much too busy to realize it! As long as it lasted, anyway . . .

The overcast was still forcing my defiant little airplane ever lower. Buried deep inside the cloud cover, I was flying below the rim of the canyon and could no longer see the top of either wall. I supposed the big tail fin might even be in it from time to time.

I was still VFR (Visual Flight Rules), if only from a most practical standpoint. The weather certainly wasn't legal VFR, but it was still flyable. Barely. To say that I could see much at all was stretching it quite a bit. Most of the turns inside that steep, dark canyon exceeded 60 degrees of bank and frequently reached 90. I supposed that I was rolling through level so quickly after each steep bank that inertia kept the wings from stalling between those banks. I'd roll from a steep right turn into a sharp left as quickly as the ailerons would respond to violent and full-against-the-stops pressures on the control yoke. It seemed an hour before the dark rock prison suddenly opened up at Portage Creek, toward the lower end of the canyon. Years before, a steel cable had been stretched across the canyon, from wall to wall, at the very upper end of the chute. I guess I must have flown under that thing, though I didn't recall having seen it in the dark. Hell, I hadn't even remembered it was there!

I was sweating like a dock walloper, but hardly breathing at all. I might even have been just a wee bit tense, because I didn't notice the airframe ice building up on the windshield. I had long ago turned the pitot heater on, of course, but I had been too busy to watch the airspeed indicator anyway.

The ceiling had finally forced me down to 550 feet, but there was still another comfortable 50 feet below me and an open shot to the valley floor directly ahead of the nose. The remainder of the flight would be much more pleasant, relatively speaking. As I found the lower stretches of the bifurcated Big Susitna River, I finally noticed the airframe icing at the top of the windshield. That meant it would be forming on the struts, wings, and tail surfaces, too. The prop didn't seem to be icing up quite yet. None of the ice appeared to be heavy, and the next forty-five minutes promised to be much better than the earlier part of the flight, which had by now lasted two hours and forty-five minutes. I guessed that the low ceiling in the gorge had trapped beneath it the moisture that rose from the river just below me. My plane had become a veritable petri dish for the formation of airframe icing which coated the aircraft in a white frost.

I held the 550 feet MSL as I cruised down the Big Susitna River past the town of Talkeetna and south along the Alaska Railroad. Anchorage was just another sixty-five miles dead ahead. The snow had let up a little, and rime ice was no longer building on the windshield.

It wasn't long before I punched in the Anchorage ATIS to get their latest weather report, then called Anchorage Approach. I let them know that I had the numbers, requested a transponder code, and asked for any special instructions they might have for me. I really didn't expect anyone else to be banging around up there on Christmas Eve, but, with Alaska pilots, you never know.

Shortly after passing abeam Big Lake, and while over Twin Island Lake, I received instruction from approach to contact Anchorage Tower on 118.3. The tower gave me the straight-in approach to Runway 14.

The landing was smooth, and I turned left at the first available taxiway, headed for my tie-down at Alaska Bush Carrier. It was only after shutting down the big engine and starting the tie-down procedure that I realized the extent of airframe ice on the struts, wings, and tail assembly. The ice was just shy of one inch thick. Although it hadn't yet formed on the propeller, it probably would have soon. A little more ice and I may have been in trouble. The very stable and hard working Cessna had been able to handle the extra load. The ice hadn't become a negative aerodynamic factor, as far as I could tell.

As I drove away toward hearth and home, I silently thanked the guys at the Cessna plant in Wichita for having made such a stable and dependable little airplane. This would be a nice Christmas after all.

Chapter 14

NEW YEAR'S DAY

*I*t was deep down in the frigid winter lockup of 1957. Things had settled down somewhat after November's blunder at Nugget Bench. My mother had come to Alaska for a short visit by then, and we were all pretty much enjoying the crisp, clear, cold December days that only sub-Arctic Alaska can serve up. My father, still in the South 48, was waffling over the long flight from Seattle and had almost decided to drive the Alcan, the Alaska-Canada Highway, in order to avoid that 1,300-mile over-water trip. In those days, the trip was by way of the Domestic Offshore Route, thence along Green Eight, and finally Amber One to Anchorage. All in all, it was more than four and a half hours in one of the old Constellations.

My father had always maintained that he wouldn't step into an airplane until after he had earned his own pilot's license, so a flight for him looked unlikely. Eventually, though, he did make the flight, shipping his car to Seward. Later in life he came to love flying, especially flying the Alaska outback.

I had decided early on New Year's Day morning, to take a short flight and look over the Russian River Rendezvous lodge property at Lower Russian Lake down on the Kenai Peninsula. The lodge had been unattended during the deep winter months. I knew that Nishka Elwell had already set out her winter trap lines at Upper Russian Lake. Nishka had been born Nishka Zane in Zanesville, Ohio, the city named for Zane Gray, the prolific western author and a member of her family. Luke, her husband of many years, would be busy tying flies for the next fishing season. Just another still and tranquil New Year's Day in the Alaska bush.

I had called Rufus, a friend of mine, asking if he might want to tag along in the two-place Aeronca Chief. He did, and we left Merrill Field at about noon, taking off into a hard and brittle-clear winter sky.

The old two-story log lodge, tucked away in a small valley surrounded by steep mountains, was about a quarter-mile downstream from Lower Russian Lake itself. I say was, because the lodge would, sadly, burn to the ground two winters later.

The original lodge property had been the site of a Russian penal colony long before the United States purchased the territory from Russia in 1867. Alaska's 586,400 square miles was home to only 302,000 inhabitants, allowing an average of 194 square miles per person. Compared to Rhode Island, a state which provided no more than 92 square feet per person, that's huge. Alaska is two and one-half times the size of Texas and almost five hundred times larger than Rhode Island.

Facilities at Lower Russian Lake eventually became home to a silver fox farm, before falling into the hands of a schoolteacher by the name of Smith. Each day, Smith walked three miles by a mountain trail to the road at Schooner's Bend on the Kenai River in order to impart some small semblance of education to his young charges.

Most recently, however, the lodge had been owned by Bill Roberts, a retired U.S. Navy chief and a former all-Navy heavyweight boxing champion who had, for several years, lived alone there. He operated the property as a hunting and fishing lodge during the spring, summer, and fall seasons, then huddled in all by himself throughout the dark, cold, and snowy Alaskan winters. After Big Bill Roberts's sudden disappearance from the Kenai Peninsula in 1959 or 1960, it was rumored that he had fallen from a small boat into the San Francisco Bay and drowned. Few of us who knew Bill very well could believe that story, since he was known to be an excellent swimmer. But there it was.

It isn't a long flight from Anchorage to the lake, usually taking about forty minutes in the Chief. We lollygagged around for one plus thirty, though, before finally crossing the Kenai River just below Kenai Lake. We slipped through the little slot in the mountains at the north entrance to the valley and descended toward the remote snow-covered lake.

On the shore of a large bay on the east side of the lake, we could see thirteen moose yarded up in the deep snow. They were all cows and yearling calves—that is to say, calves born the previous June—but we were still surprised to see so very many of them all herded up together in one small snow-covered meadow along the lake's shoreline.

I estimated that there were only eight to twelve inches of snow on the frozen lake and figured we could easily handle that much depth, even though the little taildragger was still mounted on its small wheels rather than on more sensible and practical skis. We had approached the lake from the north. I circled it in the clear air for an approach from the south, and, with the Harding Ice Field directly behind us, made a smooth landing on the snow-covered ice. At this time of the year, the ice itself was probably more than three feet thick and safe enough for heavy truck travel. The snow presented more resistance than I had expected, and I increased backpressure on the control wheel to keep the tail down. In moments, we had come almost to a complete stop.

I applied some throttle and, with careful control yoke pressures, began to taxi toward the shoreline at the north end. I concentrated on holding the tail above the snow and trying to see through the blinding veil of white, all while I worked to keep the prop clear of it. After several minutes of this tedious chore, I looked out from under the wing to discover that we hadn't moved an inch. I was simply balancing the aircraft on its wheels and blowing snow all over the place. I added more power and held the tail low, plowing a swath through the snow until we finally reached the north shoreline. I shut the 65-hp Continental down, and we sat there in the near silence, listening to the ticking of cooling cylinders.

There wasn't much need to tie the plane down, so we just left it alone and set out on the quarter-mile trek through the spruce woods, knee deep in snow, to the cold and empty lodge buildings. After finding very little food or fuel, I checked the smokehouse for forgotten smoked salmon. There were several leftover pieces, but all were moldy. Well, that wouldn't hurt, since we could brush off the greenish stuff easily enough. It wasn't much of a larder, though, considering that we were stuck here until we could shovel out a runway on the lake.

A check of the tool shed revealed that anything of practical use had already been stolen—stariskis, pulaskis, ice augers, peavies, shovels, picks—the works. We found an old snowshoe, fortunately a trail shoe rather than a bear paw model, as our tool of choice. Some choice. What we needed was a snow *shovel,* not a snow*shoe!*

We cranked up a three-burner Coleman stove and boiled some trail coffee, using creek water and an old porcelain coffeepot, evidence of Bill Roberts's Navy years. Washing a coffeepot in the Navy is a court martial offense, Bill had always claimed, and this pot stood silent and unequivocal witness to that tradition. We sipped hot coffee and nibbled on cold and sour smoked salmon, reviewing our options. It had started to snow again, soon working itself into a veritable blizzard outside the big, two-story log lodge. It was getting too dark and stormy to do any real work, and once the lodge began to warm up a bit, we didn't feel much up to it anyway. We rummaged through many dirty blankets before finding four of the cleanest, then settled in for the night.

The snow had stopped by morning, but more than twelve inches had fallen over night. The snow on the ice was now well over two feet deep, and I began to think seriously about butchering one of those moose still yarded up on the east shore to serve as our winter's meat supply. It might be a while before we saw Anchorage again.

By late morning, we had dug a two-track runway pointing south down the center of the lake. I knew I could keep the little wheels inside the tracks, but I wouldn't be able to take off with two occupants. We decided that I would fly alone to Kenai, some forty miles west of us, turn off the air search that must surely by now be in progress, and bring back some food. We still expected to fly out together later that afternoon.

I lifted off without much trouble, circled the lake to wing-wag at Rufe, and lit out through the slot in the mountains toward Kenai. By the time I got there, it had started to snow again. After tracking down a few quick hamburgers, buying a big thermos to fill with hot coffee, and telling the authorities that we really needed no assistance, the weather had deteriorated so much that I had to request a Special VFR clearance for departure. The clearance read: "Cleared below five hundred to five miles east. Remain east of the Control Zone. No clearance will be issued for landing." In other words, don't come back today. Not very friendly, maybe, but it fit right in with my own plans. I didn't intend to go back there that day, anyway.

Snow continued to fall and, by the time I was within ten miles of the lake, my three-dimensional visibility and my depth perception were gone. Everything was either light gray or dark gray, with no real black or white. There was certainly no color around me, except for the little yellow-and-red Aeronca.

I almost missed the sharp right turn that plunged me into a narrow slot just before I reached the Kenai River. With no depth perception in the blinding snowstorm, I just barely avoided flying smack into a narrow, vertical ravine that, in these conditions, looked almost exactly like the turn in the road that I had been following. I was flying at about fifty feet to maintain visual references on the ground. I had been following a narrow road below me, and that was now my only guide through the mountains.

By the time I found the bridge across the Kenai River, once a magnificent old wooden covered bridge just below Schooner's Bend, I knew I couldn't make it into the lake through that little pass again. I decided to land on the road. In fact, I was going to land on that new concrete bridge, since it was plenty long enough for the Chief, and I was certain the wings would clear the low railing on either side. I flew its length to make sure there were no cars coming from the other direction. I knew there were none behind me, but couldn't see all the way to the end of the 500-foot bridge. Seeing no cars, I set up to commit for the landing.

I pulled the carburetor heat control to the hot position just as I rolled into a left three-sixty to circle around for the landing—and the engine revolutions dropped below 1,000. I couldn't hold any altitude with that dab of engine power, so I shoved the carburetor heat control back to cold. That didn't help much, and I knew something had gone haywire up front somewhere. I rolled back out of the turn, pulled the heat on again, and prepared to land straight ahead on the road along the rushing Kenai River just below Cooper Creek, Cooper Landing, and the outlet of Kenai Lake.

Many curves on this stretch of road kept me busy for a few moments negotiating the sharp turns outlined with snow-heavy spruce. The branches seemed to be leaning over as I passed, attempting to grab one wingtip or another. I had just enough wiggle room for the wings and that was about all. I hardly recognized Pat Gwinn's Roadhouse when I dashed past it, still about ten feet over the snow-covered road.

The landing was fine, although snow packed the left wheel and brake, locking it at the last moment. The nose swung left, leaving the aircraft smack dab in the middle of one of the road's many turns. It was still snowing quite hard. I began to worry that someone driving the road would come around the curve and slam into the little fabric airplane, parked where it absolutely shouldn't be.

I raised the cowl on one side and peered into the warm, dark interior. The exhaust muffler on the carburetor heat side had broken at one of its welds. With the heat control pulled out, the carburetor was no longer getting warmed air; *it was inhaling almost pure exhaust gasses.* I thought it might have been a stroke of luck that the little engine hadn't caught fire up there. The muffler would have to be welded before the airplane could be certified airworthy again. In the meantime, I would have to wire it in place with some stainless steel safety wire that I kept aboard for such repairs.

It was decision time, and I decided that I couldn't leave Rufe stuck at the lake without food and with no way to get out of the valley. After all, I had turned off the air search that would have lifted him out without much trouble. So, when the snow let up just a little, I took off from the road and headed back through the little slot to the lake again. It was a thrilling takeoff, with the falling snow and those big spruce trees bending over the road trying to snag my struggling little airplane.

By now, the hamburgers weren't as warm as they had been, but the thermos of hot coffee had held its temperature. Rufe and I enjoyed a good ol' American fast-food lunch. Rufe had polished our little runway a bit in my absence, in spite of the newly fallen snow, and it looked like we would make it out yet that afternoon. I would just have to be a little judicious with the carburetor heat control. I decided that I could probably perform that little balancing act, so we lined the airplane up in its own tracks and prepared to takeoff to the south.

The takeoff run was a bit long because of poor directional control, but we lifted off without much trouble, the Harding Ice Field fixed dead center in the windshield. After a climbing turn back over the lake, we were once again on our way west through the little saddle, crossing the Kenai River, and cutting through the mountains ahead. Before long we were winging our way northward across the Kenai Peninsula, toward Merrill Field and the promise of hot showers, more food, and a welding job on the stainless steel muffler.

When we reached Anchorage, we learned that our holiday absence had even made the Seattle newspapers, though they had erroneously reported our disappearance to the north, rather than to the south, of Anchorage.

My mother, always a very strong lady, seemed not to have worried about our disappearance in the bitter cold and heavy snow of the New Year. She did bake my favorite cake the next day, though.

Chapter 15

LOWER RUSSIAN LAKE

$\mathcal{P}$at Crowley was so gorgeous it made your eyes hurt just to look at her. Her husband, Captain Joe Crowley, an Air Force pilot, was as handsome as a bull caribou in fall colors. Together, they must have been the most eye-catching couple on Elmendorf AFB. To top it all off, the couple tooled around the base and nearby Anchorage, where they lived off-base, in an immaculate, black Austin Healy 1000.

Early on August 6, 1960, a Saturday, Joe called and asked what I had planned for later that day. Nothing, I admitted. And it was a sunny day, too, though a little gusty. Joe said that he and Pat were planning to drive to Schooner's Bend on the Kenai River, where a trail leading to the Russian Lakes began. They were going to spend the weekend at Lower Russian Lake, but Pat wasn't looking forward to the three-mile walk from the parking area to the lake. Joe wondered if I would meet them at Kenai Lake to fly Pat to Lower Russian Lake, just around the corner. We picked a time to meet at a small lodge and roadhouse along the sixty-mile stretch of Kenai Lake.

Later that morning, I drove to Lake Hood to preflight an Aeronca Champion, N7465B, a 90-horsepower floatplane. Other than needing fuel, all seemed in good order. I slipped the lines from the float davits, started the two-place plane, and began to sail across the lake to the gas dock at Alaska Air Guides, on the north shore.

The tower advised me that the lake was closed due to the high winds, now gusting to thirty-five, but I exercised the pilot's option, advising them of my intention to top off the tanks in preparation for a departure to the south. They acknowledged my transmission, and that was the end of that for the moment.

When winds are so high that a combination of air and water rudders fails to steer a floatplane on the water, the pilot must control the craft with a maneuver called sailing. In floatplane sailing, the vertical stabilizer and rudder are used in the same way as a boat's sails. Under most conditions, pilots also use ailerons and flaps in this sailing maneuver. In the powerful winds of that August day, I sailed the plane across Lake Hood to the gas dock.

The line boy met the Champ at the dock and threw a line on it, snubbing the float to a davit on the deck of the wooden dock. Since he was quick to begin the fueling operation, and I wasn't inclined to climb out into the wind, I simply sat on my lazy backside and waited for him to finish. The Champ doesn't carry much of a fuel load, so he had finished in no time. I signed his gas ticket, and he cast off the line so I could depart.

I started the Champ again and advised the tower that I was going to sail backward into the north cove for a takeoff south, requesting clearance for a low departure across International Airport's Runways 6R and 6L, not an unusual procedure there with winds out of the south. I was again informed of the winds, and then granted the clearance. By then the Champ and I were well into the north cove of Lake Hood. I ran the magnetos checks during the pre-takeoff run.

The mags were fine, and I performed the full-power check on my way up onto the step for departure.

The takeoff was rough because of the choppy water, but in only seconds the little plane leaped off the water. I climbed to cross the two international airport runways and then headed south toward the shoreline at Turnagain Arm.

Crossing Turnagain Arm in that sort of breeze was an experience in and of itself. The winds came from the left, through Portage Pass and directly off cold Prince William Sound. I maintained an airspeed just slightly above approach speed to avoid stressing the lightly loaded airframe. For the next fifteen minutes, I was busy just trying to keep the danged plane headed southeast and in a steady climb to 2,000 feet, the recommended altitude for this water crossing. The USAF had estimated a survival time of only 100 seconds in that cold and silty water. Between the silt loading down your clothes and the extremely cold water thickening your blood until your heart can no longer pump it, the water found on three sides of the city of Anchorage makes arrivals and departures anything but casual.

After reaching the south shore of Turnagain Arm, I flew a very bumpy route along the flatlands of the Kenai Peninsula just west of the Kenai Mountains. I was flying parallel to the mountain range itself, and the wind was crossing the ridgeline on a perpendicular heading. As far as mountain flying is concerned, this is the worst of all possible wind conditions.

Winds reaching 30 miles an hour over low areas can funnel down to hurtle through the passes at a speed of 60 miles per hour. Where these same winds cross the mountain ridges, they can triple, reaching speeds of 90 miles per hour or more. From a practical standpoint, and with a cruise speed of between 90 and 100 miles per hour, many light planes simply can't get over the mountains or through the passes. Period.

Under such circumstances, a small, underpowered aircraft may find it impossible to climb to the altitude necessary to safely fly through the mountain passes. However, I hadn't yet learned how to determine this, since I had only a few hundred hours under my seat belt; I had also taken my flight instruction in the early days, when we flew without radios, and the private pilot written examination consisted of only fifty questions that could be answered during a short lunch break (as mine were). Oh, I could come out on a predetermined heading from a two-turn spin all right, but I didn't have any idea what I was getting myself into on that windy day in the mountains. I only knew it was really bumpy up there.

I tried to climb to several passes that would lead me through the mountains, but the little Champ just couldn't compete with the winds and resulting downdrafts. I was bouncing and bounding along like a cork on rough seas, wondering what would possess me to fly on such a day.

I finally found a pass the little Champ could manage and was able to slip through a very rough route that dumped me out over the west shore of upper Kenai Lake, now far below. I flew to the center of the lake to make my letdown, careful to avoid the power transmission lines that crossed the lake.

These high power transmission lines are clearly marked with large orange warning balls threaded onto the lines themselves. But given the overall scope of the surrounding geography, these large balls aren't very large at all. They are very hard to see, no matter what the weather conditions or the available light. At least one light aircraft had tangled with this line in the past, and as you could have guessed, the airplane came out second best.

Lower down, and nearer the lake's surface, the winds slacked off a bit, and I was able to land in the sheltered area right where Joe and Pat were waiting alongside their snazzy little black Healy.

After beaching the Champ and shutting everything down, I climbed out to turn the plane around, placing the float heels up on the gravel beach for easy departure. We loaded the groceries into the plane so that Joe's pack wouldn't be so very heavy, and then Pat climbed into the back seat, buckling herself in securely. I had warned them both that the flight would be a little bumpy. On the plus side, though, the flight should take less than fifteen minutes, if we flew directly to Lower Russian Lake. Since it would take Joe more than an hour to hike to the lake, we could take some time to flight-see during our trip. I was sure that I could find a calm little valley for this short side trip.

Pat and I took off directly from the beach, climbed only a few hundred feet, and leveled out, still protected by the surrounding mountains. Lower Russian Lake was located almost due east of us at that moment, but it was over a high mountain ridge and past long, narrow Cooper Lake, which lies about midway between the Kenai and Lower Russian Lake.

We headed almost north to pass Quartz Creek, then slipped past Cooper Landing to turn in at Swan Lake for a look around its small valley. After about a half an hour of tooling around, I turned the Champ eastward to cross the Kenai River, which dumps out of the southern end of Kenai Lake, sliding through the small saddle in the mountains to cross over to Kenai Lake. It was right at that moment when the engine decided to quit! The engine was quiet as a grave. Not a good simile right then.

The old Aeronca Champion doesn't have a fuel gauge, per se, but I knew that I had left Lake Hood with a fat four-hour fuel load. And I knew I had only been in the air for about two hours. Surely the little airplane couldn't have run out of fuel!

All that was academic right at the moment, of course, and I had a decision to make. We were on floats, so landing again on the same road where I had put the little Chief down on New Year's Day a couple of years earlier was out of the question. The road was right in front of us at the time, though, and that earlier landing flashed through my mind. I thought that maybe I could land successfully on the river adjacent to that road.

The Kenai River here, and for almost its entire length, is a very fast-moving body of water. During August, when the water is low, it is an impressive and shocking collection of rapids, shallow water, exposed gravel bars, and swirling pools, all seasoned with exposed boulders much too large to be called rocks. As a possible landing strip, the Kenai River was less than encouraging.

But I had no other options. I set up a controllable glide and looked for the wettest spots along the low river. That meant slipping the floatplane down in an unfriendly set of rapids, then trying to rudder the sputtering thing through the deeper spots as I came upon them at 40 miles per hour.

The engine would come to life for a second or two, probably due to the windmilling action of the prop and a few drops of avgas being jostled into the outlet ports, and then it would quit for several seconds. This sporadic performance was enough to carry me very close to the big backwater eddy in front of the tiny village of Cooper Landing. I noticed a few small parties of salmon and trout fishermen along several of the gravel bars off the right side (the roadside) of the plane. Men, waving and shouting gaily at us as we swept past on our wild and reckless dash upstream, made it clear to me that these stalwart outdoorsmen hadn't the foggiest idea that we were in any kind of trouble.

I had noticed that Pat had her head buried deeply in the sleeping bag that she had been holding on her lap. She would later tell me that she had done this so that she could be recognized when she was finally pulled from the wreckage. Riding along back there with absolutely no control over her own fate must have been terrible indeed. I have always remembered that, and I have forever since considered the possible discomfort of my passengers, who put their trust in my hands.

With a lot of luck and at least some small semblance of skill, the aircraft finally gave up and wobbled down off the step, coming to a halt at the only protected stretch of water along the entire length of the Kenai River. I had arrived, if without fanfare then at least without tragedy, at the swirling eddy at Cooper Landing. The little aircraft coasted to a full stop only a few feet from the high bank of the protected eddy. I only had to shut things down, step out on the right float, grab a line from the baggage area, and then get it to the shore so we could tie off.

With what I accepted as no small consideration by a providential guardian angel, there was a large spruce log just off the nose of the right float. I could simply step onto that log, walk along its length to the shore, and tie off to the brush atop the bank there. Up to this point, this whole ordeal had all gone so smoothly that it almost seemed contrived. When I stepped off onto that log, however, all my good fortune vanished in a big splash. The log sank immediately under my weight, and I sank into the cold Kenai River water, right up to my hat.

I must have looked like a Labrador retriever as I swam ashore towing the line behind me. Climbing the cold and muddy bank, I pulled the noses of the plane's floats up tight so that Pat could finally free herself from the failed plane and step gratefully ashore.

The measuring stick told me that we had indeed run out of fuel. The missing right tank gas cap told me how it had happened. Uncle Venturi had struck again, siphoning away our fuel. Fighting heavy turbulence had kept me so busy that I hadn't even noticed the smell of avgas. While I wish I could have given the missing cap to the turbulence, I knew that the line boy back at Lake Hood hadn't secured it properly in the first place. The bumpy air had maybe helped things along a little. After this incident, I would always fuel my own airplane, thank you. Where the fixed base operator's regulations prohibited this, I would nonetheless always check the fuel load and the tank caps. I have never lost another gas cap.

I was successful in begging spare avgas from one of the sterling residents of Cooper Landing, though why they even had any is beyond me. There are no aircraft in Cooper Landing, and there is no airfield or any sort of strip within many miles. To use the river for routine floatplane operations would be sheer madness. The avgas was a lucky find, and I was glad to receive the few gallons that were offered to me. It may have been Pat's extreme beauty that saved the day. Certainly she was a damsel in distress and a gorgeous one at that. For whatever reason, though, I was most grateful.

I cut a small piece from the top of an old rubber hip boot, punched a small breather hole in it, and taped it across the gas tank filler neck.

Pat had decided that the experience really hadn't been so bad after all, and agreed to climb back aboard for the ten-minute flight around the corner to Lower Russian Lake. Joe should just about be there by now. Fortunately, he had missed our antics on the river. We didn't want to arrive late and have him worry that we had gone missing in the mountains.

The cheers of the uninformed fishermen lining the gravel bars accompanied our take off downriver, as we wheeled through the bumpy slit into the lake.

Lower Russian was a sea of whitecaps, of course—not a pleasant sight for the pilot of something as small as a two-place Aeronca floatplane. This wasn't good water even for a Grumman Goose. I couldn't imagine the air being any more turbulent than it was at that moment, either. The landing was something I wasn't looking forward to, given the look of the lake's thrashing surface.

When the distance between the crests of waves exceeds about

20 percent of the length of the floats, the landing is going to be somewhere between marginal and tragic. This one was to be no different.

I approached the water hanging on the prop and hit the wave tops several times with the heels of the floats. When this bumping finally slowed us to stall speed, the airplane neither flipped over nor sank, both of which I halfway expected to happen. Once on the water we were weathervaned and anchored to a single direction: straight ahead. The wind was much too strong to allow water rudder control for steering, so I began sailing sideways, using power and rudder control, along with a bit of ailerons, as best I could in order to reach a quiet bay off to our right side. I could see a small camp near the shoreline of that bay and presumed it was a stream guard station, established for the counting of spawning salmon.

At one time, the Lower Russian River, which drains both Upper and Lower Russian Lakes, was among the world's most famous and productive trout and salmon fishing streams. This was before fishing on the river itself, as well as upstream and downstream from its mouth at the Kenai River, was seriously curtailed out of deference to proper fish and game management. I witnessed the end result of one event that may have ultimately led to the stream closure. During the salmon runs of 1953 and 1954, a large party of young soldiers from Fort Richardson, located adjacent to Anchorage, illegally snagged hundreds of salmon. The inexperienced young fishermen simply didn't understand the huge gross weight of all the fish they had snagged, an unlawful activity at any rate. In the end, they couldn't carry all the fish away, so they left the salmon carcasses on the riverbank, to either feed the bears or rot away.

The Fish and Wildlife Service counted spawning salmon at Lower Russian Lake by rolling a sheet of four-foot-wide white, vinyl flooring across the shallow stream at the lake's outlet and anchoring it in place with large rocks. Once each hour, the stream guard would climb a flimsy log tower to record the number of salmon that swam across the vinyl marker in a fifteen-minute period and multiply that number by four to calculate the approximate number of salmon that passed that spot each clock hour. At the end of the day, the guard would interpolate these numbers into the twenty-four-hour period to come up with the approximate number of salmon passing upstream to spawn each day.

I saw the stream guard come out of the small tent and stand with his hands on his hips, watching our little airplane.

The demarcation line between the calm water of the quiet bay and the horrid mess of the lake itself was quite clear. If I could only sail into that quiet water, we could beach the airplane and take a coffee break as if nothing had happened at all.

I was a little too impatient, though. With the stick in my lap and the engine at idle, I pressed the right rudder pedal full down just before we entered the quiet water of the bay itself. It is likely that I also inadvertently rolled the stick to the right a bit, in effect lowering the left aileron. The water rudder, and the rudder itself, had in that instant found both calm water and calm air, making them both effective once again. The plane began to turn just a little. The wind took this split second to slam the impact lift component against that lowered left aileron and create a tremendous vacuum over the top of the left wing. The vacuum lifted the left wing, causing the right wingtip to dip into the cold water—and disappear right up to the jury strut roots! I was scared to death!

With something like 400 flying hours under my seat belt at the time, I already knew that once a wing went into the water it was pretty much all over. The airplane would simply flip upside down and sink in place.

I jammed the stick to the left, tromped hard on the left rudder, pulled the stick aft as hard as possible, and slammed the throttle forward, shooting full power across the displaced rudder. I was hoping that I could force the little plane's tail to the right, lifting the right wing back out of the water. Lo and behold—*it worked!*

With agonizing slowness, the right wing rose from the cold water. Seconds later, we were upright in calm water, taxiing to the beach with ease.

The stream guard hadn't moved a muscle. He was probably dreading the cold-water swim he would have to make in order to rescue the two goofs in the little yellow floatplane.

When we had tied off and accepted a cup of his camp coffee, he told me he hadn't expected me to overcome the almost certain dunking that had nearly occurred. More than that, he told us that the Fish and Wildlife Super Cub scheduled to bring supplies to his small camp that day had already canceled three flights because of the high winds and rough water. Just too much wind in that little squirrelly valley for him, the pilot had radioed. And, of course, his judgment had been a whole lot better than mine.

It's clear that his pilot had better sense than Pat's, but at least she was down and safe. I knew that I had no right to risk a passenger's safety as I had risked Pat's that day. Doing so was a serious breach of an airman's responsibilities to his charges.

Joe had just arrived on the opposite shore and was now hailing us from there. Since we couldn't cross that cauldron of wild water with the plane, he had to wade the river some yards below us and walk the bank to join our little group. After his three-mile hike, he was ready for some hot coffee, too.

Somehow, both Joe and Pat overlooked my extremely poor judgment that day and flew with me many times after that. Joe even asked me to check him out in light aircraft, which I was happy to do. He was skilled in such machines as F-86 Sabre Jets and the KC-135s. Flying the little ones, he claimed, was much, *much* harder!

Chapter 16

SEARCH AND RESCUE

*M*uch has been written about the many well-publicized Alaska search and rescue missions over the years. The Civil Air Patrol in Alaska historically flies more search and rescue missions each year than do all the other CAPs combined. That's not surprising, since there are more pilots per capita in Alaska than in any other state. The reasons for this are obvious. There is only one set of railroad tracks in Alaska, and many Alaskan cities aren't even served by highways. An airplane is the easiest mode of transportation available.

In an area one-half the size of the continental United States, with more active pilots than you can stir with a big stick, it is no wonder that the occasional light airplane goes missing. Or that, on occasion, one or another of Alaska's many pilots needs some sort of assistance.

In rare instances, a pilot finds himself short of fuel and must put down somewhere, relying upon radio contact to find the help that will eventually get the pilot home. On all too many occasions, inclement weather will overcome a pilot, either forcing a precautionary landing or forcing the aircraft down in such a manner as to constitute a genuine emergency. In the worst cases, these situations can be deadly.

I had scheduled a two-hour time frame for a rental aircraft from Barton Air Service a number of years ago. At the time, Bill Barton had two 90-hp Aeronca Champions available for student instruction. Of the two, N7448B and N7449B, I preferred the former. It was this aircraft, N7448B, that I thought would be waiting for me when I arrived at Merrill Field one sunny April morning in 1957.

N7448B was gone, however. It seems that another pilot had rented it the previous day for a flight to Big Lake, only fifteen minutes north and across the Knik Arm from Anchorage. The plane had not yet returned, but N7449B was on the line. I took that one, preflighted it, and lifted off for the short hop to Big Lake, where I made it a habit to occasionally put away some great homemade pie and good Alaska coffee at the Big Lake Lodge.

Just across the water from Anchorage, and a little north of the Elmendorf runway extension, lies a small strip at Goose Bay. I had to fly over the Goose Bay strip on the way to Big Lake, only two or three minutes farther along. As I passed Goose Bay, I thought I saw something adjacent to the north end of the strip. I circled around and dropped down to make a low pass along the seldom-used gravel runway. As I flew the length of the strip, I saw it. It was N7448B, stabbed vertically into the earth, and with no sign of life.

As it turned out, the pilot and his passenger had reportedly put away a few swallows too many of their favorite beverages during the previous night's festivities at the Big Lake Lodge. When it came time for their departure, the pilot was so inebriated that someone had to show him to his plane. The rest is sad history. He had made it for almost three full minutes in the air before augering in at Goose Bay. One hundred eighty seconds.

A number of years later an American pilot flying from Anchorage International Airport to Tokyo did much the same thing. Except he was commanding a Boeing 747 loaded with cattle. The runway crash site wasn't for the squeamish.

Fortunately most air accidents are not nearly this tragic. But in the remote Alaskan bush, finding airplane crash survivors can be a challenge. When Emergency Locator Transmitters (ELTs) first became a fact of life, I thought they weren't suited for use in Alaska. By virtue of their Very High Frequency (VHF) range of 121.5 kHz (for civil aircraft, and 243 for military operations), these units are only good for line-of-sight transmission and reception. Alaska is, for all practical purposes, one huge jumble of mountains. I couldn't imagine that ELTs would save many lives in that rough country. What I discounted, and shouldn't have, are the several satellites that are always listening on these frequencies. Then there are the many airliners that keep one radio receiver on "guard" frequency, 121.5. All military airplanes and several of Alaska's backcountry pilots, including me, do the same. It didn't take long for me to appreciate the value of those little yellow or international orange boxes required to be secured inside every aircraft that flies the skies of every one of the fifty states. It's the law, and it's a good law. I just wish all pilots would test their ELTs regularly and always keep fresh batteries in them.

When a pilot picks up an ELT signal, he knows that there is very likely a pilot down there somewhere who is in some sort of trouble. First he reports the ELT signal to the nearest Flight Service Station (FSS), if there is one within radio range. In Alaska, there is frequently no one with whom the pilot may speak. Unless he's flying up there in the instrument environment, which is very seldom the case in bush operations, the mountains interfere with the signal. If he is down low, or for some other reason cannot report the ELT, he knows that he may be the troubled pilot's only hope of rescue or other assistance. So he tries to locate the ELT.

Continuing on his flight path, the pilot waits for the signal to get either stronger, meaning he is getting closer to the transmitter, or weaker, indicating that he is flying away from it. Either way, he must set aside considerable time to fly between stronger and weaker, then stronger and stronger, and finally stronger and strongest, until, hopefully, he finally arrives over the site of the downed aircraft. Sometimes it is a genuine crash site. Other times the ELT will emit a signal during a rough landing, and the pilot in question is not even aware that a signal has been sent.

To save runaround time, my own planes were equipped with DF-88 Direction Finders. These units, usually found only on military and CAP aircraft, will home in on an Emergency Locator Transmitter, or any other VHF frequency that its antenna can pick up. Much the same as flying ADF, the pilot has only to follow the needle to the site. Direct. It's a great time and fuel saver, and it is accurate to a fault.

I once lifted off the Big Susitna River just north of Alexander. When I rose above the tall cottonwood trees lining the river there, the DF-88 needle came to life and pointed north-northeast from my position. I immediately swung to pick up the track and, for the next thirty minutes at 120 miles an hour, followed the needle toward the Talkeetna Mountains.

As I crossed Alaska's only railroad track and climbed above the foothills, the needle began to oscillate slightly, then suddenly rotated to a point behind the plane. I looked down just at that moment to see that I was flying over a Super Cub lying inverted on the hillside below. There were two people standing by the machine, and I could tell that neither was badly injured.

I wagged the Cessna's wings and flew west far enough to be able to contact Anchorage Radio, reporting the site and my observations. They advised me only moments later that a CAP plane would be off the ground within the hour. I took an old leather glove from my jacket pocket and wrote a note on it with a ballpoint pen. I advised the two on the ground that the CAP would be along shortly, and that I'd check on them in about one hour when returning from a flight I first had to complete. I stuffed a potato (which I often carried around just for this purpose) in the glove, tied the top with some string, flew low over the site, and dropped the glove out the window. Several weeks later, I received the glove and a thank you note in the mail. The downed men had each eaten half of the potato.

Many times guides or pilots who seem to have gone missing turn up later at some remote lodge or village in the company of a female companion. This is the primary reason that search missions are not routinely commenced based solely upon the frantic call of a wife, girlfriend, or mother. At other times, the missing party is one of those resourceful characters who somehow manages to extract himself from whichever dilemma in which he is at that time embroiled.

When Peggy Brown called me one morning to report that her husband had not returned on schedule, I paid attention to her. George Brown was the owner of a prominent Alaska fast food restaurant, a world-class skeet and trap shooter, and an all-around fine fellow. He was also a former B-29 pilot who wouldn't normally get himself into something that he couldn't get back out of pretty quickly. This time, though, he had not come back from what should have been a very routine flight of less than forty miles round trip.

Peggy told me that he had planned to fly their small Piper across Turnagain Arm, just east of Point Possession, to check out some of the areas there with an eye to the coming year's duck-hunting season. He was due to return later that same day and had taken no provisions for an overnight stay in the bush. It had been two-dogs cold, and the lakes, frozen two-feet thick, were covered with snow. These conditions didn't point to a comfortable evening on the beach for George. When he didn't return, Peggy had become rightfully upset and called me.

I didn't have an available aircraft at the moment, but told Peggy that I would go to Merrill Field and rent one within the next hour. I'd call her when I got back from the search flight. I called two friends and asked them to come along and help me look. We planned to meet at Safeway Aviation on Merrill Field. I then called to arrange the rental of a Piper Tri-Pacer, the only four-place available at the moment, and geared up for the flight. The Tri-Pacer was probably the world's worst choice for that sort of work, but it was the only aircraft available at the moment, so I took it.

The weather wasn't cooperating, as usual, and we only made it six miles across the city to International Airport before being forced down in snow, low ceilings, and low visibility. We loaded up on pie and coffee at the small coffee shop in the old terminal building.

The weather seemed to be lifting a little, so we climbed aboard the cramped little four-place and took off again. Our route would take us south across Turnagain Arm to Point Possession on the Kenai Peninsula, and then across the flats toward the mountains fifteen miles or so to the east. We had barely left the Anchorage shoreline when we climbed into the overcast and I had to go on the gauges. We were still in the tower's control area, and I reported our dilemma, telling them that I would be descending to VFR conditions for the search in a few more miles. I requested a clearance for this unusual procedure, and got the approval without preamble. We do a lot of screwy things in Alaska, I guess.

When the clock indicated that we had reached land on the south side of Turnagain Arm, I pulled the carburetor heat control full on, throttled back, and set up a descent toward better visibility. We broke out at about 300 feet in moderate snow, and turned southeast to begin our search.

It took us only about ten minutes to find George's little plane. We could tell that there had been a bit of a problem. There were two sets of wheel tracks in the snow leading to George's Piper. There was also one set leading away from it, and we knew George had somehow flagged down a ride back out of the remote little lake area. A closer look told more of the story.

George had clearly nosed over in the deep snow on the lake, bending his plane's prop on the ice in the process. Obviously, someone had come by and picked him up. Since we couldn't tell exactly when that had happened, we had to presume that either he had been picked up the day before and flown farther south to Kenai or he had been picked up earlier that morning and flown across the arm to Anchorage. If the latter were true, he would now be warm and safe at home while we were bouncing around in a snowstorm looking for him.

To make sure that our aerial sign reading was relatively accurate, I decided to land and check out the site. Better safe than sorry, now that we were here anyway. I set up for the landing and put the Tri-Pacer down only to find that the snow was about two feet deep. And we were on wheels! Rats!

After examining the evidence we were relatively certain George hadn't been hurt at all in the mishap. We loaded up and tried the takeoff. No soap. I knew that I could get off with one passenger, but certainly not with two! Now what?

As if on schedule, a small aircraft appeared from the south, circled the lake once, and then landed beside our stranded Tri-Pacer. It was Andy Anderson, flying out of Kenai. He had skis, of course, and right away agreed to take both of my passengers back to his home base at Kenai. I would follow and pick them up for the thirty-minute return flight to Anchorage.

Andy and my two friends lifted off, and I followed right behind them, flying through very light snow. By the time we had all landed at Kenai, it was getting dark. The whole day had disappeared, and I hadn't seemed to have done one positive thing the entire time. I loaded my two passengers aboard, and we took off. Once again we ran into more snow as we neared Point Possession. Back to Kenai we went. From Kenai I called Anchorage to make sure that George was safe and sound at home. He was. Then we rented a motel room and turned in for the night. The return trip home would have to wait until morning.

***

It was the last week of May in 1978 when I hauled some parts to a lodge in Iliamna. Flying my Super Cub, N1858A, I was headed south along the west side of Cook Inlet when Homer Radio advised me of a reported ELT signal somewhere in my neck of the woods. I found the ELT without trouble, since the signaling aircraft stood out like a sunflower in a Kansas wind. The signal was coming from a Cessna 180 that had landed on a very small sand island exposed by one of the season's very low tides. Alaskans call them "clam tides," for obvious reasons. The Cessna's pilot and two passengers had decided to pick up some clams at Polly Creek, a known clamming ground, and had landed on the little bar. There were several other aircraft parked on the beach itself, but this pilot wanted to work virgin clam grounds, so he had elected to land on this dangerous spot offshore. The tide was beginning to rise, and the pilot had been unable to start the airplane's engine again for the departure. In another half-hour or so, he and his passengers would have to try to swim to the mainland, leaving the airplane to the salt water that would almost surely cover it.

I dropped the Cub onto the same small sand bar just as the Cessna's prop turned over and the 230-hp engine finally fired up. With a puff of blue smoke, the engine appeared to settle down, and it looked as though everything was going to work out just fine. When I saw the pilot slip his headset on, I chanced a call on 121.5, presuming that was the last frequency that he had used. He replied immediately. I asked him to come up on 123.45, which he did.

It seems that he and his passengers had enjoyed a very productive day with the clams. When it came time to depart, the engine refused to start. I supposed that the pilot, in his haste, had flooded it a little. Fearing that the tide might catch them several hundred yards offshore on this tiny sand island, he had placed a distress call on 121.5, which Homer Radio had passed on to me. The pilot indicated that all was in order now, and that he would take off after me. He would need more of the sand island for take off than I would in my small Super Cub, so off I went. The Cessna 180 and the incoming tide were both right behind me.

On the twenty-sixth of June 1980, I was returning to Lake Hood from High Lake in the Stationair floatplane. I had just dropped Chip and Connie Marinella at the lake and was returning home empty. When I called Approach Control as I passed abeam Big Lake, they asked if I had the time and fuel reserves to look for a Maule floatplane that was in trouble on a small lake between Big Lake and Anchorage. Seems the plane had landed in a puddle a little too small for the subsequent takeoff, and darkness had now caught them without proper survival or camping gear.

I diverted and began looking over the many small lakes in the area. It didn't take long to spot the blue-and-white aircraft, jammed against the bank of a small lake's western shore. I could make out three people and what appeared to be a dog.

The lake had been too small for the Maule to handle. Though the small lake really wasn't much more than a wet spot in the spruce and tundra country of the lower Susitna Valley, it was large enough for floatplane landings—which can be very short indeed—and subsequent takeoffs with less than gross loads. I figured I could fly the downed party out of the smaller lake one at a time, but would need a bigger lake nearby from which to stage the party for the return to Anchorage in a fully loaded plane.

I found a lake nearby that looked large enough for a landing and takeoff in a Stationair with a moderate load, and returned to make a night landing on the smaller lake where the stranded party was located.

When I pulled into shallow water near the party, I discovered that there was a pilot, a father with his five-year-old son, and their family dog. This could have been just another of Alaska's funny stories if the boy hadn't been severely bitten by the hoards of large and hungry mosquitoes that inhabit almost all of Alaska's wet and flat country. I couldn't tell if the lad was having a toxic reaction to the hundreds of bites visible on his face and arms, but I didn't think he would live through the night without medical attention. I had to get them all out of there as quickly as possible.

I flew the boy and his father to the nearby lake, where I built them a small, smoky fire. I told them to sit downwind to avoid as many mosquitoes as possible, and then returned to the smaller lake to retrieve the pilot and the large, wet dog. It wasn't long before I had loaded up the pilot and the dog, landed at the larger lake, and loaded up the father and son for the return trip to Anchorage.

I notified Approach Control of the boy's condition and requested medical aid and transport to meet us at Lake Hood's public ramp area. After having transferred the boy and his father to the care of the attending physician, I taxied away to tie down for the night.

Only a month later, Approach contacted me for help once again.

This time I was returning to Lake Hood from Midway Lake, near the village of Skwentna, where I had dropped off a party of gold miners. Approach told me that a Citabria had gone down in Cook Inlet, not far from the village of Tyonek. Would I fly over that way and take a look-see? Certainly!

When I arrived, I found the Citabria inverted in the cold, gray water about thirty yards offshore. A helicopter, also notified by Approach Control, was circling around the site. I radioed the chopper to see how I could help. He was planning to tow the aircraft ashore before the tides pushed it into deeper water where it would sink forever. But, the pilot told me, he had no ropes or lines aboard, and thought it might take too long to fly to Anchorage and back for the gear he needed.

I had a fifty-foot length of three-quarter-inch nylon line in the Cessna. I told him I would drop the line on the beach if he promised to return the line to me the following day. I made a low pass along the beach, dropped the line, and then watched as the helicopter landed and the pilot's helper got out. He swam one end of the line to the sinking Citabria and secured it there. A really cold and thankless job, by the way.

I suggested that the pilot might want to have his helper slash the fabric along the upper wing surfaces to prevent wing damage as the flooded aircraft was righted in the water. I also suggested that the pilot contact the owner before doing anything else. At that point, the Citabria was wet, but otherwise undamaged. Pulling it upright in the water without slashing the wing fabric was guaranteed to put negative forces on the wings that they weren't designed to accept. I didn't want the rescue pilot to find himself in hot water over the subsequent damage. Who knew what the owner's attitude might be?

While the chopper pilot tried to track down the owner, I received the message that a boat from the nearby village had picked up the pilot and one passenger from the downed aircraft and was already en route from the site to the village. I knew the two would be stranded there. They would have to charter an airplane to get them back to town. Since I was already there, and would be returning to Anchorage at any rate, I could pick them up directly from the boat before it hit the village docks.

I found the boat by following its wake in Cook Inlet. I landed nearby, taxied up to within drifting distance of the boat, and shut down the engine. The two wet, cold, and hungry passengers climbed aboard the Stationair, and we were soon headed home.

It seems that the pilot hadn't really crashed in the inlet. Rather, he had let one of the aircraft's wheels slip into the surf line. The water grabbed the wheel, and the aircraft plunged into the water, turning upside down almost immediately.

I never found out how he squared that with the plane's owner from whom he had rented the aircraft in the first place.

***

Oftentimes, pilots are called upon to come to the aid of others in a predicament. Take the example of the three boaters who, one really dark and particularly stormy night, found themselves between the mouths of the Big and Little Susitna Rivers in something of a fix.

Andrew J. "Bear" Piekarski, owner and operator of King Bear Lodge, and I were returning to Anchorage from his digs on the Yentna River a few miles downstream from Skwentna. As we left the Big Susitna River, Anchorage Approach Control gave us a call asking our fuel situation. I told them that we still had more than three fat hours aboard and asked what we could do for them.

They reported that a party of three boaters had navigated across

Knik Arm and had rounded point McKenzie, entering Cook Inlet on their way to the mouth of the Big Susitna River. Since the tides in this area are dramatic, to say the very least, their trip took them some miles to the south and well offshore before they dared to venture north again toward the river's wide delta on Cook Inlet. Their roundabout route was designed to allow the three to circumnavigate the extensive and dangerous mud flats normally exposed during periods of low tides. These broad mud flats prohibit direct travel between Anchorage and both the Big and Little Susitna Rivers.

Darkness had caught these three boaters first. Then came the rains, followed by rather heavy winds. When the boaters attempted to reach the north shore of Cook Inlet between the two rivers, they faced a heavy onshore wind and a rapidly ebbing tide. The combination of heavy waves and shallow water grounded the small outboard motorboat on the mud flats while still some distance from safe, dry ground.

Keep in mind that foot travel across the mud flats in that area is next to impossible. In some areas, the mud becomes "quick," almost liquid. Over the years, many have lost their lives, becoming bogged down in the mud and then caught by incoming tides. A particularly poor way to go.

To make matters worse, these boaters consisted of two women and one man, all in their eighties. In short, these folks could use a little help. Approach Control asked if we could simply locate them, since a Super Cub had reportedly searched for them earlier without any success.

The weather was really scabby, with very ragged and wispy bottomed ceilings down to about one hundred feet. That gave us plenty of headroom, though, since we wouldn't have to fly above fifty feet. We agreed to find the boating party and see what we might do for them. I didn't really want to land on the mud flats at night with floats, but I'd make that decision later. If it came to that, the winds were right for it, so I didn't completely rule it out.

Bear and I found the boaters quickly by simply flying inshore from the receding water and the shoreline itself. I was able to establish radio contact with them by way of the CB radio unit I had mounted in the Cessna Stationair for contacting many of the Alaska lodges to which I flew and, on occasion, my own hunting or fishing parties in the field.

A very cultured woman's voice advised me that the three of them were in a pretty bad way, and she, aged eighty-four, was about to leave the stranded boat and try to walk to the shore. That would have been a suicide stroll, and I knew it.

I told her that I was at that moment speaking with a helicopter pilot who would be there to rescue them very soon. If she would just wait for a few more minutes, she would soon be warm, dry, and safe. That wasn't entirely true, but I was pretty sure that I could get an Air-Sea Rescue unit in the air through Approach Control.

I notified Approach that we had found the troubled boat and its octogenarian crew, requesting, through ARCC (Alaska Rescue Control Center), that they scramble an Air-Sea Rescue (ASR) chopper and personnel from Elmendorf AFB, into the air as quickly as possible. After a few moments, approach came back to advise me that the ceilings were below minimums, and ASR couldn't get a helicopter off just then. I suggested to them that if a float-equipped, six-place civilian aircraft could bang around in that sort of weather, we expected that a highly trained USAF crew dedicated to air/sea rescue work ought to be able to stagger off the ground, too. Apparently they got the message. Moments later the rescue chopper was in the air.

My elderly correspondent in the boat was obviously becoming impatient with the delay. She again said she would walk ashore, and I could almost picture her, perched with one foot over the gunwale, about to set off into the darkness only to become bogged down and sink forever from view. Aw, Jeez . . .

I punched the CB mike button and asked if she had her purse with her. What, she came back? Your purse—do you have your purse handy? She answered that she did. I suggested that she might want to do a little something with her hair, since I could see the helicopter, with its handsome young Air Force pilots—scarves flying, eagerly looking to wrest the nice folks from the clutches of disaster— thumping its way directly toward them. At least this was true, since the chopper was homing on my transmissions on a VHF frequency separate from the CB band I was using to communicate with my friend in the stranded boat.

It was with a great sense of relief that I saw the chopper arrive to hover above the small boat and discharge one of the air rescue wallahs to the stricken boat below. One by one, the elderly passengers were lifted into the hovering helicopter, and in no time at all, they were chop-chopping their way toward Elmendorf for some hot cocoa and a dry place to sit.

I had been given the names of the three boaters and, the following morning, called one of them to let her know that I would stop by and secure the boat for them. It would be safely waiting for them when they could arrange to have it brought back to Anchorage.

A few days later, I flew one passenger and a dab of freight and grub from Anchorage to Donkey Lake, a flight of about seventy air miles. I was to drop the passenger off at his cabin on Donkey where he would prepare the camp for two friends whom I would fly in the following day. They were setting up for a fall moose hunt.

We were in one of my Cessna 206 Stationairs, and I always kept one of the communication radios tuned to the emergency frequency, 121.5 kHz. In my David Clark headset I heard a call on that frequency, "Anybody with me on guard?"

"Yeah, Roger, N756VR's with you, go ahead."

"Yeah, thanks, 756VR. I'm flapping around down here on the back side of a long lake about ten miles north of Alexander, know where that is?"

"Sure, we gotcha. What'dya need today. We're a 206 on floats, go ahead."

"Yeah six VR, I'm with Fish and Wildlife Protection. I've got one of their Super Cubs over here, and I'm looking for a lost hiker. I could sure use some help."

"Okay—key your transmitter for five seconds so I can get a fix on you, and we'll be right over there, okay?"

"Yeah. Sure do appreciate the help. Here ya go."

My DF-88 Direction Finder hit him right away, and we turned from north to southwest in order to find him. In the meantime, I asked him to come up on 123.45 so we could talk without loading up the emergency frequency.

When he came up discreet, I found that the lost hiker was an eighty-two-year-old man who had wandered away from his family's campsite the previous evening and hadn't been seen since. It gets a little cool in the evenings at that time of the year, and both the Wildlife Protection Officer and I were concerned over the real possibility of a death by hypothermia. An octogenarian low on calories and out in 40-degree weather was a prime candidate for this sort of misfortune.

We teamed up shortly and began a search pattern that centered around long Highline Lake where the family had set up camp. We flew for two hours before we both had to break off and return to Anchorage to refuel. In the meantime, I dropped off my client at Donkey Lake.

In our absence, and most thankfully, the old-timer had simply strolled back into camp on his own. When I returned to Highline, slightly ahead of the officer's Super Cub, all was well with both the family and the elderly wanderer. He even said, no, the mosquitoes hadn't bothered him at all during the night. What a blessing! Once back in the air, I called the officer on 121.5, telling him that all was well at the camp. He would fly in to check it out and make his report anyway, he said. Another disaster avoided, thankfully.

I received a call at about ten o'clock one night from a niece of ours. Her husband had taken two friends from Anchorage via riverboat to Skwentna, giving our niece a definite arrival time back in Anchorage that had long since passed. She was very worried, and would I just slip out there and have a quick look? Sure, I would. Although finding the boat on a stretch of water that was more than 100 miles long in the dark of night was comparable to finding a white duck in a blinding snowstorm. Peggy decided to ride along as a second pair of eyes, which I really appreciated. We saddled up and were airborne within the hour.

The overcast was quite high. The flight would be dark but very smooth. Unless you've flown over completely remote and uninhabited country at night, you don't know what dark really is. There is not a single light to be seen, perhaps for many hours, and there are few, if any, navigational aids for the low-altitude pilot to lean on. It's all compass, dead reckoning, contact flying, and clockwork. It's a way of life for Alaska pilots, but an unusual type of flying for most stateside fliers, I suppose.

We could just make out the lighter splashes of water on the lakes, rivers, creeks, and puddles below. After years of flying this area, I was familiar with almost all of these wet spots, big and little.

We decided to use the low frequency ADF to fly direct to Skwentna, where our nephew, David, had called his wife hours earlier to say that the party was on its way down the Yentna River toward the confluence with the Big Su. We doubted that the party would have gone back upstream from Skwentna.

We circled over Skwentna and made a descending turn to arrive back over the river at about 200 feet. That would keep us above the cottonwood trees, but allow us a good view of the waters ahead and below. We began to follow the crooked river downstream, using 20 degrees of flaps and flying at about 65 knots.

Soon we had passed King Bear Lodge, just off our right wingtip, and banked right, then left, over the big sweep that would take us past Lake Creek and the Lake Creek Lodge. We spotted Dave's riverboat on a large muddy bar just out from shore and almost directly in front of that lodge.

The water was particularly low, and I knew that the river in front of the lodge, just a few yards upstream from where Lake Creek flows into the Yentna River, was both shallow and full of mud bars. We lined up south and downstream from the lodge and landed in the water on the opposite side of the river where the water was deepest.

Dave and his party had heard the big Cessna, of course, and were lining the shore as we taxied up into the shallow water covering the biggest mud bar. We grounded out some distance from the shore, drove the plane up onto the mud to anchor it, shut down, and waded ashore.

It turned out, as it usually does in such cases, that they were having engine trouble. The party had drifted down the river to Lake Creek and put ashore to track down some hand tools. (They should have been carrying such tools in the boat with them out here in the bush, of course!) By the time we found them, they had finished making the necessary repairs and were about to leave. Since there was no telephone at Lake Creek Lodge, they couldn't notify anyone at home about their revised schedule.

I told David that his wife would skin me if we returned without him that night, so he agreed to climb aboard the big Cessna with us. The rest of his party took off for the trip down river and across

Cook Inlet and Knik Arm for Anchorage. That was a trip I wouldn't have made by water, even in the daytime, but I'm an airplane guy, not a boat guy. Every time I get in a boat, I get into trouble.

I boarded Peggy and David, then pushed and prodded until the Cessna pointed into the river. I climbed up to the pilot's seat, started the engine, and then warmed it for a few minutes in place. I advanced the power and drove the plane over the mud and into deeper water. When we were truly afloat, I lowered the flaps to 20 degrees again, added power, and raised the water rudders. In a few seconds we were airborne and on our way back to Lake Hood, heroes, I hoped, to our worried niece. I should have been ashamed of myself for having that thought, since no heroism had been involved.

It was about ten o'clock at night, with rain, winds, and low ceilings hovering over our comfortable home in Anchorage, when the telephone rang. I dreaded picking it up. On the other end of the line was a young lady whom Peggy and I knew well. She was calling because her fiancé, Bear Piekarski, had not returned home from a moose-hunting trip into the Talkeetna Mountains. The pilot who had dropped him off was now saying that the weather was much too bad for flying, as it had been for several days by that time. Since only that pilot and I knew exactly where Bear would be hunting, would I fly into the mountains and bring him back? Tonight?

I told her that at that moment from our living room window I could see a group of ducks and geese huddled together under a streetlight waiting either for a bus or for better weather. She was in tears, by that time, and I don't like to hear women cry. I knew that Bear was warm, safe, and snug in his tight little tent camp on the north shore of Dawn Lake, a site he favored year after year for his annual moose hunt. He always hunted alone there and was always successful. But I couldn't convince his fiancée of his safety. For that matter, I couldn't have sworn to it under oath myself, but I did know

Bear quite well. As Alaska's most penalized hockey player, he was tough enough to go hand to hand with a small griz, and was pretty skookum about life in the bush. Still . . .

I geared up, drove to Lake Hood and preflighted N9975Z, the turbocharged Cessna 206 Stationair amphibian. Forty-five minutes later, I passed Talkeetna and headed up the Big Susitna directly into Devil Canyon, a bad place even on the sunniest of days. I had only my intimate knowledge of the canyon and surrounding area on which to lean, because I could see next to nothing. It was after ten at that point, and it was raining and blowing as it almost always does during the Alaska moose-hunting season. We headed to our lodge on High Lake, just one-half mile north of that canyon.

Dawn Lake isn't very big, but it is big enough for a Cessna 206 Stationair, if the pilot is careful and if the plane isn't packing a big load. I shot a night, slick-water landing on the lake and taxied up to the northwest corner, where Bear always camped. There he was, all warm, safe, and sound—and, sure enough, with the usual big bull moose, all butchered, bagged, and hung on a meat pole.

Bear didn't want to leave his moose cache because of the large number of grizzlies in the area. There was really no good way to cache the meat against the griz, since there were no tall spruce, and the meat was hung rather close to the ground. On the other hand, his fiancée would not be pleased if I returned to Anchorage without him, so he climbed aboard for the flight back home.

Bear has flown with me in some really ragged weather over the years. To the point, in fact, that I had even developed an NDB approach to his lodge on the Yentna River. I could fly the ADF needle and clock downstream from Skwentna to land in the river in front of his King Bear Lodge, seven air miles south of the NDB, in the scabbiest of weather. And had, many times. I had established a decision height (DH) of 120 feet above the ground for these approaches, an altitude designed to keep me out of the tall cottonwoods in the area.

We listened to music through the David Clarks and chatted over the intercom as we passed the next hour of Alaska night flying. I had to return to Dawn Lake with him the next day so that we could get his moose meat back to town. The grizzlies, wolves, and wolverines had not discovered the cache. Bear's fiancée was happy to see him safe and sound, even though he was still a little grouchy about being torn away from his small Siwash hunting camp high in the Talkeetna Mountains.

Back in May 1984, I had bought a Cessna 180 from Kenny Howard, owner of a masonry subcontracting company. It came with wheels, hydraulic wheel/skis, and floats. Although the floats were a bit shorter than I prefer, it had been a good deal, I thought, and the ship served me well. I eventually gave it to a nephew of ours, the same nephew we had picked up on the Yentna River during his interrupted riverboat trip.

It was a month or so after buying the airplane that I landed on the Yentna River and shut down the Cessna 206 Stationair to tie up at the peninsula gravel bar that served King Bear Lodge. Kenny's brother, Charlie, ran from the lodge to meet me, saying that Kenny had broken his back while working at their cabin on nearby Shulin Lake. Would it be possible for me to fly Kenny back to Anchorage in the Stationair and get him to the hospital? There was no way Charlie could load his brother into his own Cessna 185 because of its small doors. Since the Cessna 206 has a four-foot-square loading door on the right side of the plane, this would be no problem for me.

I didn't want to do anything to further injure Kenny, but the air was smooth and the weather very good. If we could load him without killing him in the process, maybe we could get him back to Anchorage for medical attention.

Charlie rode with me in the Stationair so that he could handle his brother during the flight back to Anchorage. It's only a few minutes between King Bear Lodge and Shulin, and we made it in no time at all. We landed and taxied right up to the cabin site. Sure enough, Kenny was there, and he didn't look real good at all.

I aligned the Stationair so that the big loading doors were next to the dock, and then Charlie and I carried Kenny, who lay on a sheet of plywood, to the plane. Lifting Kenny's dead weight and getting him into the airplane was an engineering feat, but we finally managed without doing him in completely. Charlie joined Kenny in the back, trying to keep his brother as quiet and as comfortable as possible. I climbed aboard and started the big engine to taxi to the far end of the lake.

Kenny was moaning and groaning behind me. I knew he wasn't much of a complainer, and the sounds coming from the back made me dread the flight ahead. What if I hit a bump in the air and killed him off right then and there? Could I be charged for that? Would I miss him? Hell, would his wife miss him? Would she miss him enough to take a pot shot at me some time down the road? I was at least sure of the answer to that. Sure she would. After all, he was breathing, talking, moaning, and groaning when we had loaded him into the plane. Would Charlie be a character witness for me, I wondered? Probably not.

The flight back to Anchorage was smooth, and I had arranged by radio with Anchorage Approach Control for an ambulance to meet us at Lake Hood. I let the professionals unload my cargo, since they seemed to know what they were doing. Besides, they had a backboard and all the other stuff required to deal with a back injury.

It turned out that Kenny had only sprained his back and had maybe pinched a nerve in the process. For my own money, though, I had expected the groaning to stop at any moment during that flight.

I had been quite sure that Kenny wouldn't survive the trip to Lake Hood. Good thing I'm not always right.

A number of years ago, an Alaska State Trooper asked me to fly to Little Susitna Station to pick up a gunshot victim. As I made the short fifteen-minute flight from Merrill Field, all sorts of thoughts ran through my mind. Was it a man or woman? Was the gunshot serious? Would this actually turn out to be a matter of flying a dead body back? Who was the victim? Why had he or she been shot? Was some nut still running around out there with a firearm, shooting at anything that moved? Including an airplane and its erstwhile pilot? What the hell was I doing here?

When I landed at the small dirt strip, I could see only one person waiting there. There were several boats on the small river, obviously fishing for the silver salmon that run so heavily past the station at certain times of the year. But there was no crowd and no maniac with a gun—only a young boy.

I shut down the engine and stepped from the plane to ask if the lad knew of anyone around there who might have been shot. Then I noticed the bandage on his right hand. Turned out that he had been fooling around with someone's Colt .45 semi-automatic pistol. The gun had gone off, and he had been burned by the flash. I unwrapped his hand and discovered a little blood and a whole lot of unburned powder buried beneath the skin of his swollen thumb. The injury didn't appear to be life threatening, but I *had* received the call—and now here we both were.

I belted the youngster in, secured my own harness, and we lit out for Anchorage. I told the boy that I was going to have to call the troopers, since a firearm had been involved and the accident had already been reported—and that they would, no doubt, meet the airplane when it landed at Anchorage International Airport. Approach had already told me that Merrill Field was out, since I was carrying a gunshot "victim" aboard.

It took me a while to convince Approach Control, Anchorage Radio, and Anchorage tower that I didn't really need an ambulance for the victim. I did think, though, that a trip to his family doctor might be in order. Approach Control let me know that the trooper would take care of that.

By now the boy was scared to death. Seems he had hitched an airplane ride to the Little Su in spite of his father's specific admonition to do no such thing. And now here he was, shot in the thumb and without a swift way around a truthful explanation. I'm sure he thought he'd get the seat of his pants tanned, and I rather expected he had earned at least that. The trooper met us on landing, and I was quickly relieved of my tearful and repentant little casualty. Just another life-saving rescue in the Alaska bush . . .

Chapter 17

BUSH GUIDE MISHAPS

When almost every facet of Alaska hunting, fishing, and bush flying are dictated by circumstance and constant change, the opportunity for something to go wrong is the only real constant. Change is the only thing that doesn't change, and to expect things to remain as they are at any point in time is not only unreasonable, it is bound to lead to problems.

With virtually no bush weather forecasts available to the Alaska pilot, conditions over the first range of mountains is mostly a matter of judgement based on experience. Even that's only a guess, and the only way to really know about that weather is to fly to one of the passes and see if you can sneak through it. Even then—are you going to be able to fly back through the same pass? Worse, though, is making it through the pass only to discover the weather is so scabby on the other side that you can neither continue on nor return through the same pass. You'd better be carrying a fishing rod and some emergency gear (this is state law, by the way!), because you may be squatting on that little lake over there for several days.

Certainly you can't depend on the wildlife. Oh, you may know what wildlife exists in any particular area, but you don't know what their behavior might be. Are you sure the spawning salmon run you expect will have arrived on schedule so that your client fishermen will have a good day of it? The runs are affected by the weather as well as by the calendar, and they just might be stalled downstream a few miles.

Most tenuous, though are the assistant guides. Is one of them going to do something stupid? If it's a game violation, the state will quickly gather up all your equipment—including your aircraft, boats, motors, firearms, and any other camp gear—in a seizure designed to remind you that you, the licensed guide, are totally responsible for the behavior of your assistants.

Finally it's your clients that can have the biggest affect on your future. Each is a potential poacher, and each is an unknown personality. What you do know is that each of them has paid big money for the trip of a lifetime, and bad weather, poor aircraft maintenance, bad flying, or acts of God are not going to get you off the hook. In their eyes, your job is to provide satisfactory results, period.

A most unfortunate event occurred several years ago along the Mulchatna River, south of the Stony. An Anchorage air taxi operator had dropped a party of three German hunters on a small lake there, then had flown away to leave the party of nonresident hunters on an unguided hunt for caribou, moose, and maybe a stray black bear. Early on the third day, one of the hunters saw movement in the brush along the far shore of the little lake and, having spotted a flash of shiny black, torched off a shot. Hiking swiftly around the lake, he came upon his quarry and proceeded to skin it out.

As the three hunters sat around their campfire later that afternoon enjoying a second cup of boiled bush coffee, a tall American strode into camp. Stu Ramstead, a Registered Alaska Guide who had a headquarters camp in the area, asked how their hunting was coming along. When the successful hunter boasted of the *Schwartzbär* (black bear) he had taken, the skin of which was then draped over the lower limb of a nearby spruce tree, Stu came loose at the seams.

Fleshed clean and spread to dry over the limb was what little remained of Stu's favorite retriever, a black Labrador, for which Stu had paid a sum well into four figures, and upon which he had spent another four to train as a field dog of no small ability. Many of us wonder still at the restraint of Guide Bramstead, widely known to be a man of small patience and large action.

Then there was the young Texan, name of Smith. Smitty was an Alaska resident and, as such, was not required by law to enlist the services of a Registered Guide. Smitty wandered into his tent camp on the shore of Lower Russian Lake late one afternoon, packing a snow-white hide and the horns of what he boasted was clearly a new world-record mountain goat. The record at that time was something just shy of eleven inches in length, and this set of horns was clearly nudging sixteen along the outside curve. Trouble was, they were pale yellow, not the shiny black typical of all mountain goat horns. Smitty, you see, had bonked a Dall ewe sheep, without doubt a hanging offense among some, and certainly a most serious offense under the laws of the state.

I had my own mishap early one evening just outside the town of Dillingham. This fishing village lies at the mouth of the Woods and Nushagak Rivers, where the tides, when low, present an awesome "beach" of gray silt. Almost the texture and fluidity of quicksand, this muddy silt offers nothing short of disaster to anyone walking across it. Unless, that is, the walker is prepared to walk without pause until he has reached higher, drier, and more solid ground.

I had flown with a Swiss husband and wife from Lake Aleknagik to Dillingham for some grub, and circumstances wouldn't allow me to use the airport with my amphibious Cessna 206. I chose to land in the tidewater bay, then taxied up to beach the floats on the gray silt exposed by the receding tide.

I shut everything down, then had my back seat passenger pass me the long rope coiled in the baggage area behind the aft seats. Then I stepped out, tied the line to the left front float davit, and stepped down onto the quick gray silt to carry the line to a fishing boat beached high on the exposed silt beach. Climbing aboard and quickly tying off to make a tight safety line, I told my male passenger to step off the float and, while holding the safety line, walk quickly to the boat. I cautioned him, in no uncertain terms, to keep walking once he had stepped off that float!

He did just fine for about half the fifty-foot distance, then, for some reason, he stopped dead in his tracks—and immediately began sinking!

No amount of encouragement would get him moving, and he was clearly sinking in place. Once he sank below his knees, he would remain there through the next tide, which would surely drown him. If he didn't simply sink right on out of sight where he stood!

I stepped off the boat and backtracked to him, forcing him to bend forward over my lowered shoulder. When he did, I pulled the tops of his hip boots and heaved upward for all I was worth. It worked—barely—and, even though the silt had climbed to the tops of my own boots, I was able to carry him to the boat where he was safe and sound. His wife did much better.

I found out later that he had suffered a bad scare as a lad, when a horse he was riding became mired in the mud and had to be destroyed.

During one moose-hunting season, I supplied a camp at Underhill Lake on the other side of the Alaska Range. I had helped set up camp for two Scandinavian hunters and an outdoor writer, and had just flown in to drop off more grub and to check on the party's well being.

As I lifted off the lake in the Cessna 206 floatplane, I spotted what appeared to be a small tent camp on the north end of the lake. I turned over the camp and spotted two men on the ground waving at me frantically. I throttled back, checked that the flaps were still at 20 degrees, and descended for another landing.

When the aircraft settled down from the step, I turned and taxied back to the two hunters, shutting down the big engine and coasting to the shore near them. It turned out to be a German hunter and his ten-year-old son, and they were in a bit of a fix. Their pilot, from the small town of Kenai, had flown the two of them to Underhill two weeks earlier. His instructions were to leave the father and son alone there to hunt moose and caribou, and to return in seven days to pick them up.

Immediately upon the charter pilot's return to his home base in Kenai, he rolled his airplane into the hangar for an engine change—and promptly forgot all about his charges, left on the other side of the Alaska Range and more than 250 miles out in the bush. I assured the older hunter and his son that I could take them, along with their camp gear and as much of the moose meat as I could haul, back to Anchorage. And I'd do it right that minute!

It didn't take long for the three of us to break their small camp and load the Cessna. Soon we were winging our way past the Stony River and climbing into the west end of Merrill Pass. Both the hunter and his young son were greatly relieved. The boy's father tried very hard to pay me for the trip, but I told him that I had to make that flight anyway, and it didn't cost me one dime more to take them along.

Besides, they had paid their dues. The torment of being utterly alone and not knowing if you'll ever get back home is always payment enough. When a pilot drops his clients off somewhere in the great Alaska wilderness and takes off again to leave them there, an unsettling feeling pervades the camp. Among a group of hunters, this feeling may pass, relatively unnoticed. But if the client happens to be alone, it strikes him immediately. Many questions come unbidden to mind.

Will his pilot make a safe trip back to his base of operations? Will he crash on his way out? Does anyone else in the whole damned world know exactly where I am? Will the pilot forget that he set me down in this lonely spot? Will he crash on his way back in to pick me up?

If the weather turns sour, the client can expect the pilot to be a little late. Maybe even a day or two late. What if the weather is crystal clear and sunny where he is, but the pilot still doesn't return on schedule? Has he crashed? Forgotten me? Often the client doesn't understand how the weather could be nasty where his pilot happens to be, yet sunny and bright at his camp. This happens a lot in Alaska. Each of Alaska's many mountain ranges can hold a weather system on either of its slopes. It may be severe clear at Anchorage, but down to the ground at Aniak, on the other side of the Alaska Range. At other times, it can be sunny and bright in Aniak, but scabby as all get-out over the range in Anchorage. That's true of almost any part of Alaska, and it's hard for the nonresident client to appreciate this.

Most likely, the client arrived in Alaska from some distant point by way of commercial air carrier. The weather seemed clear over the North Pole, right? But flying at 40,000 feet in clear air and with all the sophisticated navigational aids available to the airlines is a world far different from flying around the Alaska bush at 200 feet in rain, snow, fog, or some other meteorological phenomenon that severely limits visibility. And mountain passes, where flying can be somewhat risky to begin with, seem to trap the worst possible weather patterns.

My German clients seemed to be the least understanding of the restrictions weather can place on a bush flight. On several occasions I have loaded some of these impatient clients aboard and started a flight when I absolutely knew we had no chance of making it through the weather to the selected camp area. It was usually not until they lost sight of everything but the back of the spinning propeller that my clients wondered what the hell they were doing up there in the first place. Sometimes they would then dredge up the temerity to scold me for not knowing better than to fly on such a bad day! Imagine that!

In defense of these impatient clients, I would often remind myself that those from Europe and other really distant places had arrived on special excursion flights. If they didn't make the return schedules, they would be obliged to pay a lot of additional money for their return flight tickets. This penalty sometimes amounted to thousands of dollars. Certainly we were obligated to try to maintain those commercial flight schedules for them.

It was almost midnight one mid-September night when the telephone beside our bed started to ring insistently. Sometimes our European clients lost track of the time difference between their homes and ours, and we were liable to get calls at almost any time of the day or night.

This call, however, was from one of my assistant guides. He had taken a party of three for a saltwater fishing trip out into, and beyond, Resurrection Bay. He kept his own boat slipped in Seward, and we had agreed that breaking up a long hunting trip for these clients might be a good idea. They could get hot showers, have a restaurant meal instead of camp chow, and get a little taste of Alaska open-water fishing in the bargain. Alaska, after all, boasts 400-pound barn door halibut and king crabs approaching five feet across. The saltwater fishing is really quite good, if you don't mind the cold and wet of ocean boating.

As it turned out, my assistant had gone a little wild in his pursuit of saltwater fish, having passed Rugged Island and gone right on out into the North Pacific Ocean. Since his outboard cruiser wasn't much of a seagoing vessel by any stretch of the imagination, the clients had been more than a little apprehensive. After a few hours of being tossed around on genuinely rough seas, they had returned late to the pier just a little on the terse side. The clients, my assistant said, insisted on being airlifted back to Anchorage immediately. And they did mean IMMEDIATELY!

Well, *horse* feathers! Seward was sixty-five air miles from Anchorage through the Kenai Mountains. I wasn't about to fly to Seward only to end up taxiing around in the dark at the city docks trying to find these disgruntled folks. I told my assistant I'd drive down in the station wagon to pick them all up. I had been flying all day and wasn't looking forward to a 256-mile drive right then. Sometimes the service industry isn't all it's cracked up to be.

After a two-and-one-half-hour drive to Seward and a one-hour search of the docks for the right boat, I finally located the party. They were all warm, snug, and comfortably sound asleep aboard my assistant's vessel. They were quite surprised to be awakened, since they thought they were to remain aboard until I arrived the following morning, as we had originally scheduled. They admitted that they had been just a little uneasy in the open sea, but told me that it was my assistant, not them, who had so badly wanted to return the same night.

I should have fired that assistant right there on the spot, but I didn't. It would be two more years before I learned, the hard way, that I should have gotten rid of this deadbeat immediately. Besides,

I had paid him even more for the use of his boat than he had asked. I made mistakes with this fellow all along the road. I am sorry to admit that my wife had warned me about him at the outset. He later ended up costing us more than three-quarters of a million dollars.

During the last part of June in 1984, I had contracted to place a three-man party of German visitors at a lake west of Anchorage and behind Mt. Susitna, known locally, and affectionately, as The Sleeping Lady. Herr Schrettl, the spokesman for this group, informed me that they wanted to spend a week or so at the lake, then float the Talachulitna River, a swift-moving stream that flowed from the lake to the Skwentna River, to eventually join the Yentna and the Big Susitna Rivers. I would pick them up at King Bear Lodge downstream along the Yentna and a few miles below Skwentna.

I had explained to Herr Schrettl that he would be camping in bear country—most of Alaska is, after all—and the party would have to be most careful about their cooking, food storage, and general camp cleanliness. We warn all of our clients about bears and Herr Schrettl didn't seem the least bit fazed by it.

Two days later, I received a call from one of the pilots serving the lodge located at Judd Lake. He said that Herr Schrettl had notified him that the bears had drunk all their beer, and would I please provide them with another case or two? Black bears seem especially selective at times, and sure enough, the bruins had found the beer stash. Not only that, but they had meticulously punched each and every one of the full cans, draining them all of their contents. I could only guess at the state of the bears after their little beer bash.

I flew in another two cases of their favorite beverage and arranged to bring one more load of supplies before their upcoming river float trip. I also flew the three of them along the river route to point out one area along the rushing stream where I could safely make a river pickup in the Stationair floatplane, if the need should arise. I wanted to show them two sets of rapids that they would have to negotiate with some care, too. I knew the Metzler rigid inflatable boats would take the water, but the boaters themselves would have to be both cautious and smart while navigating these particular stretches.

My clients insisted that they were not newcomers to this sort of undertaking and had every confidence in not only enjoying the exhilarating trip but of meeting me downstream on schedule as well. With that exchange behind us, I returned the party to Judd Lake and left for Lake Hood.

A few days later, I received an emergency call related to the Schrettl party. It seems that they had met with some minor disaster or another during their trip down the swift stream and had ended up at the Skwentna River with no beer, no equipment, and no clothing other than their skivvies. I can only surmise their embarrassment at having to approach someone, half-naked, and request that I be called to help.

I lit out right away, of course, with fresh clothing and the miscellaneous other items I knew the party would need. Embarrassment aside, I knew that the water in any Alaska river is truly cold, almost never reaching 50 degrees Fahrenheit, and that proper clothing and footgear were the first order of business. I also threw in some more beer, knowing that no German outdoorsman can survive many hours without a healthy ration of that brew.

I met the party at the mouth of the Talachulitna River and told them not to worry about the boats. The boats were a little beat, of course, but I had thought to bring spare oars, so that part of the matter was settled. The group insisted on pursuing their original plan, and I subsequently left them camped again on the sand bar at the mouth of the Tal. They were even then preparing to begin the next leg of their ninety-mile river float trip.

Several days later, I met the group as arranged at King Bear Lodge, where my friend Bear Piekarski had treated the gentlemen to sufficient quantities of beer and an exciting king salmon fishing trip to properly cap their Alaskan adventure. The clients took all the jokes and jibes over their lost clothing very well, but passed up requests that they pose in their skivvies for lodge guest photographers. Can't say that I blame them for that.

Chapter 18

BUSH THIEVERY

*M*y guess is that your image of the Alaska bush pilot is one of an adventurous young man, keen of eye and steady of nerve, big Ray-Ban sunglasses pressed up under the bill of a properly creased ball cap, and presentably crisp in his pressed khaki pilot shirt and slacks, maybe with a nice pair of Clark desert boots or polished jodhpurs to finish the picture. In some cases, I suppose that's true. For the most part, however, it truly isn't!

Your bush pilot will most often be a little older, will not be so clean shaven as you might have wished, and very likely has been too busy during the past few days to have taken many hot showers. Since he does a lot of his own aircraft maintenance, his hands will be a bit oily, and his nails certainly won't be clean. His clothes won't be clean, nor will they be pressed, except by his own body weight as it presses him firmly into his seat up forward and on the left side of his airplane. His Clarks will have long ago given way to the hip boots he is almost always seen wearing (he'll probably go through three pairs each season), and his ball cap, crushed but not clean, will read "John Deere" rather than "NY." And it sure as hell won't read something like "I ♥ NY."

And, while I hate to admit it, there are a lot of bush fliers who are downright thieves! Not the air taxi operators, and not the real bush pilot. Their futures depend upon their good names and reputations. No, it's the everyday Alaska flier who no doubt holds another job and flies only when he can find the time.

His airplane is usually an ill-maintained little ship, sometimes a Super Cub, but more often something with a little less power and performance. And he'll steal anything that's not welded down, growing in place, or actively aflame when he spots it.

When Bob Spelta caught a wingtip in a tall cottonwood tree while leaving a river sand bar, he was killed in the crash. His back seat passenger survived. The little Super Cub with tandem tires was left hanging high above the ground, suspended from the tree limbs. Somehow, the passenger was able to make it safely down to the ground, leaving the unfortunate pilot strapped in the plane.

The Cub was soon spotted high in the cottonwood, and a 10th Air/Sea Rescue team from nearby Elmendorf AFB was able to chopper in a crew to rescue the injured passenger. Since the pilot was no longer living, he was not considered eligible for "rescue," under the strictest definition of the term, and was left for later extraction by a commercial helicopter company.

Bad weather hampered this helicopter extraction, and it was several more days before the commercial flight crew could reach the scene. When they did, they saw that the radio gear and all remaining hunting equipment had been stripped from the hanging plane. Bob's body had been left at the base of the tree for easier access by the helicopter crew. Finally, even the special "tandem gear" wheels had been stolen from the plane. And all this in dreadfully bad weather, less than fifteen flying minutes from downtown Anchorage. I have no doubt that, given a few more days, even the airplane engine would have disappeared.

That very thing happened when an Anchorage pilot encountered minor engine troubles over Chakachamna Lake at the mouth of Merrill Pass. Making a precautionary landing on a convenient sand beach, the pilot was later lifted off by a passing plane. When the owner returned several days later with the needed engine parts, the engine was gone. And a 230-horsepower Continental engine is a heavy load to be manhandling around on a sand bar, not to say that loading it into another plane would have been easy.

More aggravating still, take the pilot who landed along the Yentna River for a little fishing excitement. Fishing downstream, he was soon around a river bend and out of sight of his little Piper Pacer. When he had fished his way back to the plane, he found all the radios missing! Says he never heard a thing.

Bush thievery is a way of life in the far North. The wise pilot tries his very best to avoid having to leave his ship unguarded overnight in the bush, but there are times when he has no choice. I can think of a couple of instances when I found myself in this very predicament.

One sunny fall day, I flew to our lodge at High Lake, deep in the Talkeetna Mountains. I had bent the floats of my Super Cub rather badly, and had called a helicopter to have the Cub air-lifted from the site of the mishap at Madman Lake across Devil Canyon to our lodge property. I planned to pick up the floats, strap them to the floats of the Stationair, and return them to Anchorage for the necessary repairs.

When I arrived in the Stationair, I saw a floatplane tied off at the edge of the lake. This was unusual, since most visitors tied up at the steel and concrete boat dock where davits had been installed for just that purpose. I thought it more than a little odd to find the plane tied so far from the lodge itself.

I coasted to the dock and tied up just as the lodge caretaker, Bob Jones, arrived to meet me. When I asked about the visitors, he told me that he had talked to them, and they told him they had come to pick up the floats. They told the caretaker that I had given the floats to them. The caretaker, of course, had no way to verify their story. Moreover, the two gentlemen were armed. This is not unusual in Alaska. In fact, state law requires that all Alaska pilots carry firearms and other emergency gear in their planes at all times. These two gentlemen, however, seemed to be a little surly at best. He hadn't wanted to provoke an incident, and I didn't blame him for that. Well, *damn* it! I had paid almost $9,000 for those floats, and I sure as *hell* hadn't given them away!

I knew the two thieves were busy taking out a million screws to remove the hardware from the floats themselves. This would take quite a while. As long as they were doing my work for me, I decided to give them a little more time. I strolled up to the lodge with Bob and sat down to a cup of Alaska coffee and a few good chuckles with him and his wife, Pat. When I thought I had given the thieves enough time to remove most of the screws, I set aside the cup and wandered back out of the lodge.

I approached the two unshaven men, gave them my usual "Howdy," and then asked what they were up to. They answered that someone had given them these floats, and they were removing all the smaller parts so that the whole mess could be put inside, or tied outside, their floatplane for the trip out of High Lake.

I told them the story sounded a little lame, since I owned the floats, and suggested that they might be well advised to just scoot on out of there pretty quick. I also suggested that they might want to avoid High Lake in the future, summer or winter, for any reason whatsoever.

The bigger of the two threw his wrench down and put both clenched fists on his hips. Then he told me in no uncertain terms that they wcrc taking the damned floats and there wasn't much I could do about it.

I slipped my Parkerized Ruger .41 Magnum from its shoulder holster and let it hang loose by my side. Then I told them they had two choices. The first was to leave right now, without the floats. The second was to hang around for just a few more seconds and then leave all stuffed down inside the float lockers of my Cessna Stationair. I told them I figured that I'd have to cut them into smaller pieces to get them in there, but I reckoned I could manage that, too. I was pretty sure that we still had a meat saw in the screened meat house somewhere.

I also reminded them that since they were on a bush theft run, I was willing to bet that no one knew exactly where they were. And that I could arrange to move their little plane to some distant lake for them. When they didn't return home, and their plane was finally found, no one would ever know what had happened to them. After all, they were pretty deep in grizzly country. And, by the way, do either of you guys have any kids who might miss their daddy? They decided it wasn't worth the effort, cranked up, and lit out.

Much the same thing happened later to a Metzler rigid inflatable boat that I had cached at High Lake late one summer season. A nosy black bear had found it and chewed twenty-one holes in the thing. I had several boats and decided to just leave that one at High Lake until later in the season when I would fly it out and patch the holes. It would be as good as new. Well, almost as good as new. Certainly good enough for freight hauls. The little devils cost around $2,400 each, and I wasn't going to toss that one away without at least trying to patch it.

When I returned for the boat, however, I learned that thieves had once again intervened. Someone had told the caretaker that I had given the damaged boat away if the recipient would only fly it out and take it off my hands. This time, however, the caretaker had taken the name and address from the thief's driver's license. The man lived in Valdez, Alaska, 115 miles east of Anchorage, tucked deep into a bright little fiord. It was also almost 250 miles from the lodge, but I'd just have to make the trip. Those boats were worth the extra time, but dang it anyhow—that was an additional 250 miles I didn't really need.

I notified the Alaska State Troopers, officially reported the theft, and then advised them that I was going to Valdez to get the boat back. We firmed up a schedule, and the troopers said they would have a man there to meet me when I arrived.

When I did arrive in Valdez, right on schedule, the troopers had done better than that. The trooper was waiting on the dock with my boat. I thanked him, offered to buy his lunch, which he was too busy to eat anyway, and lit out back to Anchorage, the deflated inflatable stored safely in the baggage area. I later patched every one of those twenty-one holes, and the boat served me for several more years.

Chapter 19

LOST FLIERS

*T*here is many an opportunity for a pilot to get lost in the Alaska outback. While it can be said that the flier's "environment" is fixed, since it is always within an air mass, this is only partially true.

You should understand that the pilot's environment includes anything and everything that he can touch or see. And many things, in fact, that he neither can touch nor see: that distant mountain range, for instance, that so influences winds and cloud cover in the pilot's area.

When descending on instruments through the clouds preparatory to a landing, the controller may say something like, "Cleared for the approach. Report the airport in sight."

When the pilot later sees the airport, he may respond, "We have the environment."

When a pilot has made certain that his cockpit is neat, clean, and orderly, he is said to have cleaned up his environment. The pilot's "environment," then, is anything and everything that could possibly have an influence on his flying or his ground operations. Consider the low-time pilot in an environment such as the Midwest, for example. He lights out on his first cross-country solo flight, driving a small two-place Cessna 150. After having preflighted his little craft, and double-checked both the fuel and oil quantities, he is ready to go. But, is he?

It is always a good idea for the pilot to carry a pen and a pad of paper of some sort, perhaps one of those knee-nav pads that straps to the pilot's leg and is always available. And, in spite of the pilot's familiarity with the area surrounding his home field, he should always carry a flight chart of some sort, either a sectional or WAC chart. Unless he's flying in Alaska where the larger scale WAC chart is all that a pilot needs, a sectional chart is the better choice because of its greater detail.

The pilot should also check several other things before taking off. For instance, he should check to make sure that all the lights on the aircraft are working, including all interior and instrument lights. He should also check the ELT battery. No matter how short the planned flight, he should not take off without a working Emergency Locator Transmitter. Not ever.

Even if the pilot plans to leave the ground at eight o'clock in the morning and return no later than two o'clock the same afternoon, he should carry a working flashlight. And he should keep the flashlight and an extra set of batteries within easy reach.

On long flights, the pilot should have close at hand all the current sectional charts that contain the areas over which he can expect to fly. He should fold the charts to show the specific areas over which he will pass. As the pilot flies from one chart to the next, he shouldn't simply throw the last chart over his shoulder, as some pilots do. He may be forced to reverse his course and head for home again. If the weather turns sour, maybe even becomes turbulent and with reduced visibility, he won't be able to loosen his seat belt to reach into the back of the plane to retrieve the charts he has already tossed back there. He might just as well have left them back on the ground or pitched them out the window.

It is wise for the pilot to have drawn a line on the charts that lays out his intended route of flight. For Pete's sake, *don't* draw that line with a red pen or pencil! Yeah, I know, it's quicker to find that red line on the blue or tan or green background—but not in the dark, when the cockpit lighting might be giving off red light. If that's the case, your red line will have disappeared completely. It has now become invisible, and might just as well have been omitted in the first place.

I always thought it was a good idea, too, to jot down the expected time en route between identifiable points along the route. It you expect to cross the railroad twenty-three minutes after passing the last town, and haven't yet crossed it after twenty-eight minutes, something has gone wrong. The winds are higher than forecast—or you are off course by some appreciable measure. Well, you know all that anyway. This isn't a student handbook, and I have no business trying to tell you how to fly.

I have always thought that flying in Alaska was much easier than flying in the continental United States. Alaska pilots always have a mountain range, a pass, a lake, a stream, or a coastline to guide them. On a clear day, it's pretty hard to be flying in a valley and simply wander away from it or to be following a river and then just simply lose it. It's possible, but it's pretty difficult. Maybe what makes following such landmarks easier in Alaska is the fact that we don't usually fly very high. If you're flying in a valley, and staying below the ridges on either side, it really is pretty hard to just wander out of the valley and get lost.

If you spend all your time up there at 2,000 feet—or even higher—

you have impressed upon your subconscious mind a clear picture of what the ground below you is supposed to look like. You are probably used to looking five or ten miles ahead of your airplane. The lakes and rivers stand out clearly for you, and contact flying is pretty easy. But when poor visibility takes you down to 100 feet, where most pilots spend very little time, everything looks a whole lot different.

Let me hasten to say that I'm not encouraging you to plan flights at this skimpy altitude. I am suggesting, however, that being forced down to that altitude is always a possibility. In and of itself, it shouldn't lead you to do something as silly as crashing your airplane. If everything else is still working, all you've lost is a little visibility, right?

Streams that weren't even visible from 2,000 feet suddenly become creeks or rivers flitting past beneath your hurtling little craft. And every puddle, formerly missed completely, now takes on the proportions of a lake that you think you remember having seen from the higher altitudes. This may sound silly, but that's the way it is. If you're not used to seeing these landmarks from only sixty feet up, you may find yourself in hot water if the weather turns scabby on you.

A little bump in the landscape can easily take on the proportions of a genuine hill, or even a mountain. If you're caught down there at 100 feet, a 200-foot hill disappears into the overcast. The landmarks multiply by the hundreds, and each of them seems very familiar to you when you are passing them at 100 miles an hour or more, 100 feet in the air, and can only catch a quick glimpse in passing.

Elsewhere in this book I mentioned flying through a blinding snowstorm at an altitude of ten feet. I had noticed the shadows of three spruce trees blink past the right wingtip. What I didn't mention was that these were the only trees in a ten-mile length of that beach. I certainly knew they were there, having already passed them dozens of times, and I knew what part of the beach they were located along. From 2,000 feet I am not sure that most pilots would even have noticed them. They weren't much of a "landmark" in all that open Alaska country, where the usual low humidity can put visibility out there beyond 200 miles.

A number of years ago, a young pilot started his first solo cross-country flight from Cantwell, located about seventy-five miles north of Talkeetna, along the Alaska Railroad to Palmer and back. The first town he would cross in his flight would be Talkeetna.

His route took him directly along the Alaska Railroad and the Anchorage-Fairbanks Highway for most of the way, if he cared to follow them carefully. Immediately after liftoff, his route took him through a valley only about three miles wide, and with 6,000-foot mountains rising just off either wing, it seemed. It's a beautiful trip, especially in good weather. It can be a little discouraging when the weather turns particularly sour. With no scenery to distract the pilot, the gray environment coupled with the sure knowledge that quite a lot of really hard rock is piled up very high on either side can be a little depressing, even stressful, to many pilots.

At the same time, I was flying one of my float-equipped Cessna Stationairs out of Anchorage. It was raining and spitting snow, and low stratus lay heavy in a broken layer along the hills around Talkeetna. These "hills" quickly become the Talkeetna Mountains, which tower 4,500 feet above the flatland in this area. I was flying at about 3,000 feet.

I had just reported passing Talkeetna when I heard the other pilot on the same frequency. He was calling Talkeetna and asking what his position was. Talkeetna, of course, couldn't help him with that, since it was the pilot's job to know where he was and to report that position to Talkeetna.

I broke in to tell Talkeetna that I would locate the pilot, and then asked the pilot to come up on 123.45, a frequency not assigned to air-to-air communications, but one that is usually not crammed with traffic in Alaska.

When he transmitted on 123.45, the needle of my DF-88 Direction Finder swung to point directly toward his airplane. In order to be sure I had a good fix on him, I engaged him in some conversation, asking first where he was coming from, then where he was going, and finally what features he saw around him.

He told me he was out of Cantwell, was headed for Palmer, and was at that time flying over a river. He thought it was the Big Susitna, but he couldn't see the mountains that he thought should be there.

I realized that he had skirted around the right side of an "island" of land on his way south. The railroad had disappeared to his left as it dodged around that same hill. Having lost the "iron compass," as air mail and barnstormer pilots used to call the railroad, he was a little confused. But the road was still there.

Soon he had come upon a big river, and he decided that this was the Big Susitna. In this area, though, the Big Su is relatively narrow. He described the river he had come upon as quite wide and filled with so many sand and gravel bars that it was difficult to discern the river's main channel.

More than that, the distance between mountains on either side of his plane seemed wider than it should be. Now he wasn't at all sure where he was flying.

By then I had locked onto his transmissions and turned toward his aircraft to follow the DF-88 needle. In only a few more seconds I saw his small plane below me.

I knew he was only minutes from Talkeetna, but it would be possible for him, in the poor visibility we both had, to fly right on past the town and miss it completely. If he did that, he wouldn't see much for almost another hour, at which time he would hit the shore of Cook Inlet and really be in trouble.

I told him to look out under his left wing for my Cessna 206 floatplane. I descended to take up a position off his left side and ahead of his plane, then I told him to follow me. I would take him right down the centerline of the Talkeetna runway, which in fact was only about fifteen nautical miles ahead and 35 degrees left of his present heading. In the poor visibility, he would probably have passed within two miles of the airport without seeing it, or the town, at all. If he had been using his Omni, he would have crossed the TKA VOR about eight minutes after making a small but necessary course change. Unfortunately, his instructor had decided that he would teach radio navigation after the first solo cross-country flight. In this case, just a little too late.

There would be no need for me to land. I flew along the strip at an altitude of about ten feet, from which the lost pilot could easily spot the runway. Unless the situation was really critical, I wouldn't have landed on that gravel runway with my floats anyway. Such a landing was possible, but I risked damaging the float hulls on the heavy Cessna. I circled around to continue my own flight as he touched down at Talkeetna. He transmitted his thanks, and the day began looking a little better for everyone.

In August 1982, I needed another pilot to help me ferry several passengers and their gear from Summit, north of Talkeetna, to my main camp at Kelly Lake, 100 miles east of Talkeetna, a flight of about 175 miles. I had recently met a young commercial and sea-plane rated pilot with his own Cessna 206, just the person I was looking for. I called my new acquaintance and asked if he would be available to help me for a few days, beginning on the following Monday morning. He said he would be glad to help, and we agreed on a charter price.

I hadn't flown with this pilot, but was told that he had plenty of Alaska flying time. When we flew as a flight of two from Lake Hood to Summit, I talked with him on 123.45, getting as much information from his transmissions as possible. I decided that he could carry the freight, which included baggage, gear, and some groceries, while I carried the passengers. That turned out to have been a good idea.

After leaving Summit, we flew south over the Alaska Railroad, hanging a left about five miles below Devil Canyon, just before reaching the Big Su. We were slightly north of the river itself, at that point, flying along the mountain slopes there. We picked up the canyon in another few minutes, flying generally east above the Big Su toward Kelly Lake, about forty-five minutes away.

After passing Fog Lakes and Mount Watana, I noticed that the other pilot had decided he was flying too slow and had pulled ahead. I asked if he was familiar with Clarence Lake, where President Carter had fished for Arctic Grayling with my guide friend Chris Goll. He said no, and I pointed the lake out to him. Of course I didn't care if he knew where the president and his secret service agents had caught a batch of grayling. I did hope the news would clue him in to his present position, because I was pretty sure he really didn't know exactly where he was at that time.

It wasn't long before the other Cessna was only a distant speck in the sky ahead, and I asked the pilot if he was sure he could find Kelly Lake. He was pretty confident about that, but when I later arrived over the lake, his Stationair was nowhere to be seen.

I called the pilot again and found that he was pooping around some miles north and east of us, completely lost now, and getting a little low on fuel. Seems that he hadn't topped the tanks before departure, planning to fuel up at Lake Louise, close to Kelly Lake. Now, however, he was wasting fuel flying around trying to get his bearings in this unfamiliar country. He had spotted Lake Louise, all right, but from there on out the world around him was a complete mystery.

I had already pinpointed his transmissions with the DF-88, and I flew the needle until I saw him circling five or six miles ahead of me. I performed some quick calculations and gave the pilot a new heading, telling him to follow it closely on his gyrocompass. Then I altered my own course to intercept his heading. When we met, I led him directly to Kelly Lake, and we both got on with our business.

After we had stored the gear, put away the supplies, and made sure that our guests were well settled, we flew a few miles south to Lake Louise. We topped off our tanks at Evergreen Lodge, a place owned by Paul Holland—a skilled pilot, an excellent guide, and friend. At least I though we had both topped off our tanks. As it turned out, my chartered pilot had skimped a little on his fuel load again.

I had to make a stop at Black Lake—a body of water almost as green as grass—on the way back to Anchorage. That meant that we would be flying the upper Susitna River in the downstream direction again, west and then south. The other pilot kept asking how much farther to Talkeetna? He finally admitted that he hadn't put on too much fuel at Louise, and thought he might really be better off to add a few gallons at Talkeetna.

I called ahead and arranged for the gas truck to meet us at the long, narrow lake that lies just over a small ridge and directly east of Talkeetna's larger airport. This was not an unusual procedure, and I had often done that myself when in that area. When the other pilot topped off his tanks, I found that he required seventy-five gallons to fill his ninety-gallon tanks. By that time, I was pretty sure that he didn't know how to use his mixture control or his EGT gauge. He very likely wouldn't have made it back to Lake Hood without an unplanned precautionary (or emergency) stop on some deserted lake, begging me to fly fuel back to him. At this point, I probably would simply have left him to the bears. As it was, we returned to Lake Hood as a flight of two, where I simply thanked him for his help, paid him off, and went ahead with my own business. He never flew with me again, of course.

Several weeks later, the co-owner of his airplane tried to leave Lake Hood one evening with one passenger and way too much freight. The overload was obvious from the depth to which his floats sank in the water during the engine warm-up and slow taxi. Several of us watched the heavy plane taxi and then work hard to get up on the step. A few seconds after liftoff, the overloaded floatplane slammed into a two-story apartment building just across the street in Spenard, a suburb of Anchorage. Both occupants died in the crash. The pilot clearly had climbed above ground effect, but I don't know how. I also guessed that he had begun to raise the flaps, much too early—a big error if that guess is correct. Enough said.

Many years ago, another friend of mine flew north along Alaska's west coast with an off-duty airline captain in a Cessna 180. My friend planned to sell some new First Alaska Investment stocks in Nome, Kotzebue, and other far North cities and villages.

They were soon flying in heavy snows, and visibility faded with the daylight. As it grew darker and darker, it was all the two could do to keep the fuzzy coastline just off the right wingtip as they flew northward along the east side of the Bering Sea. The pilot was occasionally flying through fog. Each time the plane broke out in the clear, the two could see the coast off to the right, lighter against the black of the frigid Bering Sea beneath them.

After a particularly long time flying in the white, the little Cessna broke out once again. This time, however, the coastline was off the *left* side of the airplane, exactly where it *shouldn't* have been. Moreover, the compass now showed the aircraft headed north, then west, then south, then east, and once again north as they followed the shoreline around in an irregular circle.

It took several long minutes for the pilot and his passenger to agree that they had drifted some miles offshore and were now flying around an island in the Bering Sea. It must have taken some real intestinal fortitude to leave the comfort of that little dab of dry land and fly again across the cold Bering Sea on a compass heading toward the mainland. With no navigational aids, that was real contact flying. Not the kind of flying one ever wants to take on.

The good news is that the flight ended safely, and my friend went on to sell a considerable number of stock shares. In fact, he sold $10,000 worth to one buyer, left him, and then reconsidered the sale. He returned to talk the buyer into declaring that $10,000 as a 10 percent down payment on $100,000 worth of the stock. That stock would later prove worthless, and my friend is to this day persona non grata in that northern village. He now lives far, far away in southern California.

Sometimes the lost pilot isn't really lost at all. Take the flight I was making one day from Lake Hood to Kelly Lake, which usually takes one hour and ten minutes or so. Just after departure, Anchorage Departure Control advised me that an aircraft had been reported overdue in Glennallen, not far off my route. Would I keep one eye open for the missing aircraft and keep one radio tuned to the guard frequency? I certainly would.

After the guide's wife filed the missing aircraft report, a radio and aircraft search had immediately been set in motion. This was somewhat unusual because as I've mentioned before, such efforts were not normally made at the request of the pilot's wife. But this pilot was a well-known Alaska guide and commercial pilot. Almost everyone in Alaska knew the guides in those days, and this particular fellow was among the big leaguers. He was considered a capable guide, an able outdoorsman, and an experienced bush pilot. It looked as though something truly serious might lie ahead.

Passing behind Sheep Mountain on my way to Kelly Lake, I picked up an ELT on the number two comm radio and immediately turned on the DF-88 Direction Finder linked to that radio. At that point, the signal was coming from dead ahead. I might not have to swing too far off my original course to locate the troubled airplane and its pilot.

The needle led me up the Susitna, then away from it as the river curved east. Soon the river joined my course again, and in only moments the needle swung around to point behind me. I was crossing the little strip at Susitna Lodge, just downstream from the point where Valdez Creek joins the Big Susitna. When I looked down, I could see the guide's Cessna parked and tied down at the lodge strip. It was clear that he had just decided to land there for some reason. I called the lodge on the CB radio and was promptly told that the guide didn't want to be found, and if I notified anyone of my find, he would seek me out one day and blow me away. My Cessna had excellent King radios, and that transmission was coming from less than half a mile away. I knew exactly what that meant.

The guide had his girlfriend aboard and, without his wife's sure and certain knowledge, had decided to spend a few hours, including the previous night, at the lodge. In fact, he had been there a whole day now, seemingly unaware that his ELT had been touched off by his hurried and bumpy landing. Shame on him. He should make smoother landings. I'd let someone else mention the ELT to him. With the many satellites that track these little transmitters from afar, it was bound to attract more attention very shortly.

I had no idea whether or not he was a good shot, but I presumed that, as a guide, he might very well be. I also doubted he would shoot me on sight, but there is always that chance. I promptly forgot that I had found him and went ahead with my own business.

One sunny day on my way to the foot of the Tokositna Glacier, on the southern slopes of Mt. McKinley, I had swung past Chelatna Lake. Crossing the moraine of Kahiltna Glacier, I saw a Super Cub parked on the glacial silt below. The pilot was waving at my passing Cub.

Now, spotting a Super Cub at that remote location would not, in and of itself, cause me to stick my nose into someone else's business. On the other hand, seeing the pilot waving at a passing aircraft told me that he wanted to discuss something with another pilot, however important or unimportant the topic might be. In this case, the little Cub didn't seem to be damaged in any way, so maybe he just wanted to bum a cigarette. Still, it was up to me to find out.

I circled, pulled down full flaps, and set my Cub down near his. After shutting everything down, I climbed out to shake hands with the pilot whom, it turned out, I knew quite well.

He told me that he had run a little low on fuel and had made a precautionary landing at the foot of the glacier, in hopes of flagging down a passing aircraft. Neither of us had containers that would allow me to drain fuel from my own plane's tanks and transfer it into his. I told him I would fly to Talkeetna and hustle back with ten gallons of 80/87 octane for him. His next request revealed his real problem. He asked if I would also—uh, by the way—maybe throw in about four quarts of forty-weight detergent oil, too?

So, that was it! He had sufficient fuel, all right, but had run so low on oil that he had to land at the toe of the Kahiltna Glacier before his engine seized. In the real scheme of things, that location might as well have been on the dark side of the moon. My passing had been sheer, blind luck.

While many of us would chuckle over this for years to come, the situation could have been dramatic indeed. I was happy to be able to help him out, even though I would later be among those who laughed at his predicament. Let me say, though, that we've all done some dumb things in our flying days, and the chiding was all in good fun.

The most famous of all contemporary Alaska pilots, Don Sheldon, once landed near High Lake in either a four-place Aeronca or a Stinson on floats. The lake wasn't quite big enough to allow his uninterrupted departure, and he ran out of water, slamming his aircraft onto the far shore. From that point on the lake was nicknamed "Eight-G Lake" after the forces with which Don and his airplane must have met the far bank.

Running low on fuel is one of the pilot's cardinal sins. Running low on oil may be even worse, since all pilots keep one eye on fuel consumption, but not all of them keep an eye on the oil gauges. They should, of course, but those gauges don't move much over hundreds of routine flying hours. Many pilots become a bit complacent about those gauges.

Instrument flying demands that a proper, and an all-inclusive, scan of the instruments be continuously made. Attitude instruments demand the pilot's utmost attention, with the quality control instruments close behind. Engine instruments are of no less importance, since almost everything related to a flight depends upon the power plant and its condition. I myself include the engine instruments in every fourth scan of the panel. Because I was a smoker, I had installed hard-wired carbon monoxide detectors in the Cessnas. These, too, were a part of the instrument scan, even though I have never seen a positive carbon monoxide indication in all my years of flying. The Cessnas, though, closed up pretty tight. We flew in severely cold weather, and for weeks on end, would fly with full cabin heat. Carbon monoxide under those conditions would have been a most serious intrusion.

While I have never been lost while flying—I can't say the same about driving around in a car—several times I have been in such a pickle that I couldn't get back on schedule. At those times, I was certainly lost, by definition, to others. That is to say, *they* didn't know where I was.

I was supplying a spring hunting camp near Turquoise Lake a number of years ago with one of my helpers, Clay Prince. Clay Prince, a remarkable young man, reminded many of us of the comic strip hero Steve Canyon. Clay had been an excellent student in high school and a very hard worker at Gil's Aircraft, where I first met him. He expressed an interest in working in the bush, and he worked very hard for me, without complaint and always with a most cheerful demeanor.

When Clay asked if I would recommend him for admission to West Point, I didn't hesitate. I contacted Alaska Congressman Don Young and Senator Ted Stevens on Clay's behalf, requesting that they recommend Clay to West Point. I was pleased to learn that Clay was accepted to the prestigious school.

Shortly after that, and before Clay could begin his classes, he was involved in a sky diving accident near Eagle River, Alaska. The accident left him paralyzed from the neck down. It was a tragic accident, but it was not enough to discourage Clay. He struggled against all odds, and the last time I saw him, he was not only up and walking, but promising one day to run as well. There are few like Clay Prince, and I know that, somewhere in Texas where he later moved, others are as proud to know him, as was I. But back to the point.

We had flown around for half an hour or so looking for a suitable landing area, before I finally selected a very small cinder ridge hard beside a tiny, shallow lake that, we later found, produced marvelous lake trout fishing. The lake was much too small for floatplane operations, and my chosen landing site was less than 200 feet long. It was all of 20 feet wide, but dropped off dramatically at one side and at both ends.

We could only make the approach from the west, where the cinder patch dropped almost straight down some fifty feet or so to still another small lake. Landings would always have to be made toward the east, and takeoffs would always have to be made to the west. Period.

It was spring, and I had just had my mechanic replace the Cub's winter skis with big 25x11x4 tundra tires. In order to secure the huge tires to the small hubs, he had inserted a plastic rim. Sharp, fine-threaded one-inch screws usually penetrated the plastic rims and attached directly to the thick beads of the huge, low-pressure tires. The tires, by the way, carried between four and five pounds of pressure. The big tires had inner tubes, with their usual protruding valve stems.

It takes a lot of energy to turn something as large as those tundra tires when they are at rest. Braking with them is proportionally poorer on the same account. As a bush-equipped plane approaches its landing, the big tires are not turning. They are certainly not spinning at the speed that will accommodate the forward speed of the aircraft immediately upon touchdown. The wheels must quickly begin to spin at the rate of the aircraft. Resistance to this rapid change causes the blue smoke to rise from the tires of a landing jet airliner as the wheels make contact with the runway.

In the case of the Cub's big tundra tires, both the outside tires and the inside tubes are still at landing. When the tires themselves hit the ground, they are forced to turn in a hurry, but are reluctant because of their relatively large mass. The valve stems, almost fixed to the turning wheel hub, force the tubes inside to begin moving quickly. Although the tubes have begun to rotate, the tires themselves are slow to respond. As a result, the valve stem will be torn off, and the tube deflates, causing the damned tire to go flat. To prevent this the big outer tire is secured to the rim by the stainless steel screws mentioned above.

But my mechanic had neglected to insert these critical screws. And I was in too much of a hurry to think about checking this very small but infinitely important detail. Small detail indeed! When the Cub touched down for the first time on that little strip beside the lake, the valve stem on the right wheel assembly was instantly torn off. The tire went flat, and the little Cub rolled only about thirty feet before coming to a lurching and lopsided halt. The plane tipped down on the right side, and I was reluctant to look out the window at the big wheel, which I knew had either hit an unseen hole in the cinders or was flat as a pancake.

After we had climbed out and kicked the gravel for a while, Clay and I gathered several large rocks, placing them near the big right wheel. I raised the wheel off the ground by lifting the outboard end of the right wing struts, and Clay placed the rocks beneath the Cub's axle, holding the wheel off the ground.

I removed the wheel and verified that there would be no way that the tube could be repaired. That meant we were grounded, unless we could figure something out. I was thinking of filling the tire with moss and tundra, but there was none to be had.

I decided to pack the tire with my sleeping bag, a custom-made, two-person, down-filled bag made by Holubar of Colorado. The whole thing would have to be inserted, one small section at a time, through the four-inch hole that fit over the small Cub wheel hub. I spent hours and hours at this task, only to end up destroying that expensive sleeping bag and scattering eight or ten pounds of white goose down all over that part of Alaska.

When I didn't return on schedule, Peggy called Dave Klosterman, of Alaska Bush Carrier, asking if he could try to locate the Cub and its occupants. She knew about where we would be, and Dave thought he could pinpoint us without too much trouble. To a busy air taxi operator, this was a hell of a lot of trouble, but Dave took up the task right away.

AUTHOR RESTS AFTER WRESTLING
WITH A FLAT TIRE, MIDWAY BETWEEN
TWIN LAKES AND TELEQUANA LAKE
ON THE WEST SIDE OF MERRILL PASS
AND THE ALASKA RANGE, MANY MILES
FROM ANY MAINTENANCE FACILITY.
THE STRIP WAS A LAVA BED THAT
WAS ONLY 250 FEET LONG.

I had contacted a Japan Airlines Boeing 747 en route from Anchorage to Tokyo on 121.5, the emergency frequency, the moment I heard the big jet flying overhead at probably 40,000 feet. That pilot, in turn, radioed Anchorage, and the whole rescue was set in motion. Having successfully made radio contact with someone, Clay and I were satisfied that we would soon be back in the air. We proceeded to set up the Coleman stove and whip up a little end-of-the-day meal. After that, and after kicking myself a few more times for my all-too-casual foolishness about inspecting my mechanic's work, we settled in for the night. The singing of a nearby family of wolves lulled us to dreamless sleep.

Not long before this incident, Anchorage had opened its first brewery. The beer, named Prinz Bräu, had used Dave Klosterman, along with another good friend of mine, Harry Geron, as photographic models in its initial advertising campaign. One day after our accident, I heard a Cessna 206 somewhere in the area, and I turned on the Cub's radio and made a call on guard. I asked if anyone could hear N1858A.

A voice came back in my ears, saying, "Hey, Mort, how ya doin'?"

When I asked who the other pilot might be, the response came back, "This is the Prince Boy from Prinz Bräu. We'll be there in about six minutes."

Certainly the best news I'd heard in quite some time.

Dave circled us to get a feel for our plight and to look at the nearby puddle of water that was at best a marginal place to land his Stationair. Then he just lined up on it and landed! I didn't think it was big enough for his Cessna, but he certainly knew better than I.

Dave had a mutual friend aboard, Herr Paul Schneider, from Köln (Cologne), Germany. He also carried a new 25x11x4 tire and tube, a few tools, some sandwiches, and a package of cigarettes. All we needed now was a chocolate cake with candles! He had given a lot of thought to what he would bring to our remote location.

When Dave and Paul left, Clay and I began to mount the new wheel. Ten minutes later, we were off and flying, back toward Merrill Pass and home. Just another one of those days . . .

Quite a few of Alaska's fliers get themselves into a bit of trouble by not thinking far enough ahead. The tendency to fly directly from point A to point B, a habit ground instruction fosters, is one of the number one causes of pilot error. Say, for example, a pilot needs to fly to some point on the west coast of Alaska. He calculates the distance, the length of time he expects the flight to take, and the amount of fuel required for the trip, and then he sets a compass heading that will give him the course he needs. In Alaska this course may vary by more than 30 degrees between magnetic and true headings. Then he takes off, headed toward his destination. Let's say his flight to the coast has taken him four hours. He has a five-hour fuel capacity, and that had looked pretty fat at the beginning of this flight.

When he finally reaches the coast, the village he is looking for is not dead ahead of his airplane, where he thought all along that it certainly would be, and he must now decide whether to turn north or south along the coast to finally reach his destination. But, which way is the correct way? Which direction should he turn? He turns north.

If he has made the wrong choice and flies fifteen minutes without coming upon the village, should he turn back? Or, should he proceed northward, as he is now? Remember, it will take him fifteen minutes simply to get back to the point where he first reached the coast. He will then have flown four and one-half hours, be getting pretty low on fuel, and still have no idea where that damned village really is! Since turning back looks pretty grim, he convinces himself that the village could not be far ahead, and he decides to give it just ten more minutes on a northward heading. And so he does.

When he still has not found the village, he has already flown four hours and twenty-five minutes with only five hours fuel aboard. By the time he arrives back to the point where he first hit the beach, he will be down to ten minutes flying time. Will he hit the village within the next ten minutes? After all, it's damned empty and lonely out here where he is right now. Or will he decide, after five more minutes, to make a precautionary landing before he runs completely out of fuel and has to make a risky emergency landing, perhaps along a length of beach that is not as good as the stretch over which he is now flying.

It takes only one flight like this before the pilot learns that long flights into unknown or little known areas should always have as a target some point either to the left or right of the final destination. Consider it a required waypoint, if you will. When the pilot finally arrives at that point along the river, creek, or coastline that he now knows can lie to only one side of that waypoint, he should have no question about the direction in which he must turn. Until the pilot has become intimately familiar with the country below, there is no other way in which to guarantee a safe and timely arrival at the destination.

Several years ago, I had flown commercially to Springfield, Illinois, on a business matter. While there, I visited the local airport, in search of a sectional of that area. I stopped in at a local fixed base operator's facility to see whether or not they sold charts.

It was a Sunday, and the place was quieter than its Alaska counterparts would have been at such a time. In the corner, however, and huddled over a gaggle of sectional charts, was a young lady who was crying her eyes out.

I thought for a moment that she had received bad news about some friend, acquaintance, or relative who had perished in an airplane mishap of some sort. After striking up a conversation with her, and asking if I might be of some assistance, she tearfully told me the story.

She had departed from a city north of Springfield on her first solo cross-country flight, and was supposed to land at another city some twenty-five miles west of her present position. She had not been instructed in even the basics of radio navigation, and was now at a complete loss as to how she should continue her trip. In fact, she considered that she had been lucky as hell to have spotted this airport at Springfield, and was just about to jump on a Greyhound bus for her return trip home.

I asked her to point out the aircraft she had been flying. It turned out to be a fine little Cessna 150. The little dude had a full instrument panel, and should have been more than adequate for navigation. After having asked her a few simple navigation questions, however, I understood that she didn't have the foggiest idea what all those radios did.

I told her that it was quite legal for her to fly while carrying me, a licensed pilot, as her passenger to the city she had originally been looking for. I told her that if she could spare that much time, I would show her how to find that city, how to get back to Springfield, and to ultimately return to her home field. She was still very frightened, but decided that my qualifications, substantiated by the fixed base operator, would get her safely at least to the nearby city and back. So, off we went.

I pointed out to her how she might find the correct VOR frequency on her sectional chart, then had her tune the navigational radio and verify the station identifier. After she had done that, and understood clearly what she was doing up to this point, I had her rotate the knob on the navigational head that would call up the heading indication she needed. I pointed out the "To-From" flag and explained how she could tell whether the station was ahead or behind the plane, and how to center the needle to select the proper course. Then I had her set her gyrocompass to the correct setting, using the liquid-filled compass as the basis for the proper setting.

As soon as she was comfortably settled in on the proper course by carefully flying the Omni indicator needle, I had her turn north by 45 degrees and watch the needle displacement. When it had turned sufficiently off course, I explained how to tell how many degrees off-course she was at that time, and how to properly turn again to pick up the correct course, rolling back on course as the needle centered itself once more.

She successfully navigated the rest of that leg and her return trip to Springfield. When she departed Springfield for her return flight home, she was a confident and capable student pilot. Looking back only an hour or two, she could hardly believe she could have been so upset over something so very simple. Her instructor had never taught her how to use her nav equipment. Now, what sort of instructor would send her off on her first solo cross-country flight, over absolutely flat and featureless country, without a background in at least the very basics of radio navigation? Not a very good one, I can tell you. And I had to wonder what else she would miss before finally getting her private ticket and flying off toward another uncomfortable situation—or even a disaster.

Chapter 20

Maintenance
and Mechanics

I have made it a habit over the years to do as much of my own maintenance work as was permitted by Federal Aviation Regulations. It's not that I think I'm a better maintenance hand than a licensed and experienced Airframe and Powerplant Mechanic. It's because no one else will take as much of an interest in my airplane as I. If I find a mechanic who is willing to spend the time to do what needs to be done, and to do it exactly right, I also find that I usually can't afford to have the work done.

Don't get me wrong—I certainly ask my mechanic to perform all my engine maintenance, whether it is preventive, routine, scheduled, or a last-minute emergency. But I will install all my own safety wire, and I insist on doing the small things that we can all pretty well do for ourselves if we would only bother to take the time. Besides, any time spent on the little maintenance headaches translates into a better understanding of the airplane and its systems. For instance, you should be able to take care of the brakes, miscellaneous hardware and fittings, oil changes, minor wiring, and other non-structural matters. And it's easy enough to change a lamp on your airplane, even one on the wingtip. Changing small but important matters such as the ELT battery, isn't a difficult job, either.

I didn't always do my own minor maintenance work. For a long time I simply trusted my mechanic to do everything. But one too many minor mishaps convinced me that doing what I could when I could was more than worthwhile.

My first airplane was an Aeronca Chief, N9459E, a small 65-hp, two-place, side-by-side that I had purchased with a partner in 1957. The plane cost $1,400, and it was worth every cent, but probably not much more, in those days.

When it came time for the plane's first annual inspection, I delivered it to a mechanic my partner and I had come to trust. He performed the annual quickly and economically. He was already familiar with the little beast, and knew its peculiarities and needs. I trusted that he took care of everything satisfactorily.

Not many hours after that annual—in fact, only *four* hours after the annual—I was flying with Eugene P. "Bud" Graves, a hunting companion and good friend. We had flown up the Yentna River on the first day of moose-hunting season to see what we could find in the way of a small bull for the winter's larder.

In those pre-statehood days, it was perfectly legal to fly until spotting some game, land nearby, and take the game. In those days, Anchorage boasted a permanent population of only around 7,500 souls. When the town's population soared to 260,000, the number of hunters tiptoeing out of town, with varying degrees of stealth and ability, increased dramatically, especially during the fall moose- and caribou-hunting seasons. The state finally came to its senses and stopped this fly-and-shoot practice. It is no longer legal to fly and shoot on the same day, and I agree with that restriction in the interest of good game management.

At any rate, we were flying at about 400 feet AGL when we spotted a moose, wading chest deep in a grassy swamp, eating the soft underwater salads that moose favor above all other meals. He seemed to be just what we were looking for—not too young but no older than four years old. We were about to circle for a landing on a small sand bar along one of the river's backwaters when the engine quit. Dead as a stone and silent as a tomb.

Bud asked what we were going to do. I told him we were going to land, of course, and began to set up for a dead-stick glide to a small sand bar directly ahead of the plane. I told him it might be a good idea for him to tighten his seat belt for the landing.

We were gliding downwind, however, and I quickly figured out that a dead-stick landing wouldn't work. In fact, I could already see that we wouldn't make that sand bar anyway. There were two large spruce trees straight ahead, and I decided to fly between them. I figured the trees would shear off the wings, and the airplane would slow down. Then it dawned on me that flying an airplane without wings would be little better than flying an arrow. I trashed that idea as quickly as it had popped into my head.

I had just room enough to turn 180 degrees to the right and line up into the wind before we were too low to make any other maneuvers. I held the little Chief off with backpressure until we were just about at the tops of the eight-foot willows beneath us. And that's all there was in all directions. With the exception of the two spruce trees I had voted out a moment earlier, willows covered the landscape. There was no open area in which to land the plane.

So we settled into the springy little river bottom willows as softly as a feather. Our forward roll was less than four feet. The gear collapsed on impact, slamming up to lock both doors closed. The Ruger .357 Blackhawk Single Six revolver that I had placed on the baggage compartment lid behind me slid off the shelf with enough force to break through my side window and into the willow swamp. The broken pilot's window and the landing gear—which was not hurt badly at all—were the only damage to the tough little airplane.

With everything shut down, we sat and listened to the sound of dry willow leaves falling on the fabric of the upper wings. At that point in my young life, it was the saddest sound I had ever heard. I remember thinking that this flight was on a Wednesday, and that I was going to make my last payment to the bank for this little ship the following Monday morning. We carried no insurance in those days, and it would have cost more than $2,000 to chopper the airplane out for repair. We would just have to write it off as a loss. My first airplane. Oh, well . . .

I contacted the Civil Aeronautics Administration to request an investigation into why the engine had failed. Turns out that the sediment bowl had completely fallen off the flying airplane. Fuel from the wing tanks traveled through the lines to where the bowl should have been and then went overboard through the bottom of the engine cowling. Without fuel to the cylinders, the engine had simply quit. I had thought of using the primer to force fuel directly into the cylinders, and looking back on it, I wish I had tried that. I don't know why I decided against it. Using the primer probably would have saved the little airplane. The real question, though, was what had caused the sediment bowl to just drop off in the first place?

It is certainly possible that the mechanic hadn't properly secured and safety wired the sediment bowl back in place during the annual inspection. Either way, I was from that day forward vigilant about verifying all maintenance work for myself.

Occasionally, though, I would slip up on this little chore. Take, for example, the time the brakes failed on my Cessna 170A, N5417C. I had discovered a pesky leak in the brake system of that ship, and had taxied the airplane to my mechanic's hangar. He said the work would only take an hour or so and suggested that I just slip across

Fifth Avenue to Peggy's Airport Café for some pie and coffee. Since in those bygone days the café's pies were better than excellent, and the coffee above reproach, that sounded like a good idea to me. My partner, Jack, and I walked over to the café for some refreshments and a little hangar flying.

When we returned a while later, the Cessna was ready. We climbed aboard, started the 165-hp heavy-case Franklin engine and brought up ground control for the clearance to taxi. We were cleared to Runway 24. We would run through the magnetos and carburetor heat checks next to the old Reeve Aleutian Airways hangar, on a concrete runup pad.

At that time, the city dump was located just off the end of the runway, and very close to where we would be running up. That was before the age of landfills, when solid waste simply piled up at the garbage dump. One of the flight hazards at Merrill Field—which was at that time the busiest airport in the United States, surpassing even O'Hare and La Guardia for daily takeoffs and landings—was the incredible number of resident seagulls. In fact, I later hit one of the poor fellows while landing at Merrill in a 250-hp Piper Commanche, N6823P. It scared the wits out of me, too.

As we approached the runup pad with the Cessna, I throttled down and tapped the toe brakes on the big Clevelands. No response. Tapping the pedals had no affect whatsoever. They had come completely loose from the brake cylinder hardware on both sides.

I pulled the mixture control full lean, stabbed the master switch off, switched off both mags, and yelled for Jack to bail out and grab a wing strut before we sailed right off the end of the strip and into the pile of trash just ahead. We both hit the deck running, each grabbing a different wing strut and dragging our feet until the four-place Cessna finally gave up and slowed to a full stop, only eight feet shy of the dump.

A look behind the rudder pedals revealed that our mechanic had failed to install the safety pins that held the clevis heads and actuating rods together behind those pedals. Once that rod-to-clevis connection had fallen loose, probably 2,000 feet behind us, we were without any brakes at all. We had almost lost our precious airplane for lack of two danged safety pins, for cryin' out loud! Ever since that day, I've done my own brake work.

I had flown a newly purchased Cessna 180, N3140C, from Lake Tahoe to Burbank, California, for some minor maintenance work, new radios, a new voltage regulator, and the installation of new 8.50x6 tires and tubes. After landing at Burbank, I taxied up to Pacific Airmotive, right on schedule, and arranged to leave the airplane for the few days it would take the mechanic to complete the work. Usually, the first thing such an outfit will do is remove the battery and stick it on a trickle charger. Beyond being a goodwill gesture, that small service will guarantee a full-hot battery for the customer's later departure. It is a small service, but one that almost all customers appreciate. It's those little things that count, right? But when it came time to leave, one of the mechanics told me that the voltage regulator hadn't really needed to be changed out, and he had saved me some money by simply polishing the points with an emery file. I didn't trust that at all, since I was about to fly this plane through the Canadian wilderness to Alaska and directly out into the bush. But I decided to wait and change the regulator out myself when I got back to Lake Tahoe.

When I had ordered the 8.50x6 tires and tubes, I was told that no one made tires that large for the six-inch Cessna wheels. Since I had been flying those tires for years, I knew better than that. I finally convinced the facility that these larger tires were available, and suggested they call back east to verify it. They did, and were able to order the tires and tubes immediately.

With new tires, new radios, and a few other goodies, I was ready to return to Lake Tahoe and, within the next few days, to fly north through Canada and on to Alaska. I would be departing from the Burbank maintenance facility, headed for Lake Tahoe, just after dark.

Everything was just peachy on takeoff, but by the time I had passed the hills just north of Los Angeles, I was no longer able to transmit a signal. The voltage regulator had stuck on me again, and the battery wasn't getting any electrical charge at all from the generator. By the time I passed Palmdale, Mojave, Edwards AFB, and China Lake, I could no longer receive transmissions on any radio. And, by the time I had reached Lone Pine, I was only running the instrument lights to conserve energy. I was saving the nav lights for my later landing at a controlled airport.

I made a precautionary landing at Lone Pine around nine o'clock in the evening, without using the landing lights, but no one there had a new regulator for me. I had left the engine running, because I was afraid I might have had to prop the damned thing, alone and in the dark, if I had shut it down. I wasn't ready for that just then. Hand propping a 230-hp Cessna 180 isn't an easy job for a lightweight, and at 159 pounds, I fall into that category.

I took off from Lone Pine without lights or radios and climbed up to 12,000 to avoid the mountains I knew I would have to cross farther along this route. There wasn't a whole lot for navaids in that neck of the woods, and Lake Tahoe, which is surrounded by some serious peaks, sits at about 6,500 feet MSL. The lowest pass into Tahoe is above 7,000 feet. With higher peaks and ridges all over the place, I knew that it wouldn't be safe to fly below 12,000 feet.

After a time, the red instrument lights began to dim. I thought that the battery would soon be gone. I squeezed my tired eyes—*and the instrument lights came back up!* When that happened a second time, I finally figured out that my eyes probably weren't getting enough oxygen at that altitude. My smoking didn't help, either. I thought the instrument lights might last for a while longer if I didn't use them too much. For the next two and one-half hours, I flew my route in the high dark, passing Mono Lake on the right and Mt. Whitney on the left, to the south shore of Lake Tahoe, where I landed and bedded the airplane down for the rest of the night.

The following day, I flew to Reno, Nevada, to get a new voltage regulator. When I landed at Reno, though, the left tire blew! A flat of one of the main gear tires on a taildragger can make for a testy bit of ground handling if the pilot isn't on top of the controls. I knew I had made a good landing and couldn't figure out what had caused the brand-new tire to fail. The Cessna 180 has a great rudder, and between that control surface, the power of the 230-hp engine, and the brakes, I was able to control the aircraft without too much difficulty. But, I was now sitting in the middle of Reno's active runway with a dead airplane. The tower was less than thrilled with this, but there wasn't much I could do about that at the moment. Taxiing the crippled craft was out of the question.

The tower sent a tow truck immediately. Once I was clear of the runway, I took a look at the tire to see why it had blown. It wasn't too hard to figure out. When the mechanic had installed the new tires and tubes, he had pinched the big tube of the left main between the tire and the rim. Landing on the hot runway was enough to stretch that pinched tube too far, tearing the tube and causing the flat. It is likely that the decreased air pressure at Lake Tahoe, which caused higher comparative pressure in the tires, had saved my bacon on the landing the previous night. I added a new rule to my little black book: change the tires and tubes myself.

Nine days later, Hollywood film editor Basil C. "Brad" Bradbury, my friend Jay from Lake Tahoe, and I were en route to Alaska from Lake Tahoe when the thermocouple for the CHT (Cylinder Head Temperature gauge) failed. I stopped at Redmond, Oregon, for a replacement, and soon we were off and running once again. Needless to say, the maintenance work at Burbank had left a little to be desired.

I only had two more maintenance incidents with this airplane, the second of which baffles me still. It happened while the same passengers and I were in the Canadian wilderness, climbing south out of Watson Lake en route to Fort St. John, on a return trip from Alaska to Lake Tahoe.

At 9,000 feet on our way to 10,000, the engine suddenly quit. Full dead in an instant. We were heavily loaded and already far from the Alcan Highway, the nearest road. In those few seconds, as I scanned the instrument panel for a clue to the problem, I recall seeing no safe place in which to land. After five or six seconds of almost deafening silence, the engine came to life as smoothly as ever, and it never failed again. Who knows?

The first incident, could have been much more serious. I won't tell you that it wasn't largely my own fault. The Alaska outback presents a wildly disparate collection of places to land your plane. At Chinitna Bay, where I had selected a site for a spring brown bear hunt in 1965, we operated from sand and gravel beaches and bars, grass meadows, mud flats, river bars, and one nearby, and pretty run down, airstrip called Iniskin. An oil exploration outfit had built the strip a number of years before.

N3140C was not equipped with a float kit, which may or may not have helped us out of our little predicament.

We had flown up the narrow valleys created by East and West Glacier Creeks, little rivers that pour swiftly down from the nearby mountains. Our camp itself was on the south slope of Mt. Iliamna, a volcano that steams, rumbles, and shakes the earth twenty-four hours a day. We were really hoping for a break in the weather, since Basil C. "Brad" Bradbury, whose name you will find many times in the *Book of Boone & Crockett Big Game Records*, was field testing a new line of fishing equipment for a prominent sporting goods manufacturer. Our world, though, was still completely frozen. There were virtually no open bodies of water in which to fish.

During the twenty days we had been at Chinitna Bay, the weather had bounced between pretty good and absolutely miserable. On those miserable days, winds and driven snow kept us indoors, worrying about the plane's safety. We had hauled the plane as high as possible on the beach, and then tied as securely as we could to a stand of large Sitka spruce.

I took a short flight south across Chinitna Bay itself one afternoon only to discover two small kayaks pulled up on the rough gravel beach there. Landing on the beach, I shut the Cessna down and stepped out. I was surprised to meet Harold and Bea Watts, two good friends from Seward, Alaska, neither of whom I had seen for many years. By mere coincidence we had all selected the same isolated bay in which to putter around. The two of them were out on their annual kayaking expedition.

Harold was the developer of the .405 Watts cartridge, a heavy rifle caliber well known to most serious hand-loaders, while Bea was the city clerk for Seward, where they had both lived for many years. A marvelous couple—quiet, interesting, and always cheerful—they were investigating the surrounding area and had pitched a small tent on this remote little beach.

That stretch of beach was particularly rough and rocky, and the Cessna always bucked and bounced on takeoffs and landings there. I shared a cup of tea with my old friends before I took off, after telling them that I would drop in from time to time to see if they might want anything from Anchorage.

After takeoff, I climbed northward to cross to our camp on the opposite shore, where the beach consisted of smooth, hard sand and small gravel rather than the rocky beach I had just left. I was thankful for that. I had climbed to only 200 feet, since I would be letting down again in a few minutes. The air was as smooth as silk that morning.

As I reduced the power to about 1,200 rpms for the shallow descent to our own little piece of Chinitna Bay beach, the Cessna began to shudder and rattle so much that I had a hard time reading the instruments. I advanced the throttle again, and everything seemed to smooth out. I looked over the instruments, but saw nothing to indicate that anything was wrong with the power plant. As I reduced power again, the horrible shudder and heavy vibration returned, this time making one hell of a racket. What in the world?!

I had almost reached the north shore, so I just shut down the 230-horsepower mill and pulled full flaps. Seemed I would have to land the shuddering beast to find what the problem really was.

The landing went just fine. I was able to coast to a stop right before our cabin, which was set back only a few yards from the shore and nestled beneath the big spruce trees. At this spot, the beach ended at a twenty-foot-high pile of huge boulders that created a protective pocket during periods of high winds.

I shut down and climbed out to look inside the engine cowling, but I didn't even get that far! Of the myriad small screws that hold the cowling in place, there were only two left. *Only two!* It's a wonder that the cowling hadn't broken free and wrapped itself up in the spinning propeller or folded itself across the windshield.

There was no chance at all that we could find so many screws of the correct length and thread to properly secure the cowling. I had heard that the Cessna 180 didn't fly all that well without its cowling, and I certainly wasn't ready to test fly it in a bush environment more than 180 miles from the nearest maintenance facility. This put me in a bit of a pickle.

I finally decided that the only thing I could do was whittle new screws from splinters of the Sitka spruce that protected our little cabin from the elements. And that is exactly what I did. For the rest of that day, I sat on the beach and whittled, whistling and humming tunelessly as I shaped several handfuls of makeshift cowl screws. Well, I guess calling them screws is a bit of a stretch. They were more like tapered pegs, but they could be screwed in, forming the necessary threads as they went.

I secured the cowling and tied the Cessna down for the night. I had to make another Anchorage run the following morning, at which time I would see whether or not my custom, handmade, wood screws would hold the airplane together for the one-hour-and-thirty-minute flight. If they didn't, I had no idea what I was going to do about that cowling. I could always land on some other lonely beach, but then what?

The truth is that the spruce pegs worked so well I was almost reluctant to spend the money for the expensive, stainless steel screws that the cowling required. After landing and taxiing to the hangar where my maintenance facility was housed, a small crowd gathered to admire what looked for all the world like a porcupine on wheels. I took a good ribbing about that, but what the hell . . . it had worked, hadn't it?

A costly maintenance error was made to my Cessna Stationair amphibian once after I had flown it from Alaska to Florida. In Florida, I had rented a hangar so that the severe Florida sun wouldn't completely destroy the Imron paint or cook the expensive avionics and electronics inside. At about that same time, the plane was due for its annual inspection before it could be re-certified as airworthy. I made an appointment with a nationally known maintenance and repair facility that had a shop adjacent to my hangar.

In Alaska, I was used to paying between $700 and $1,000 for the annual inspection of a Cessna Stationair. This time, the bill came to $5,500, most of which was for work that wasn't at all required. I complained and cried, but had to pay the bill anyway. The facility

This photo was taken while flying over the camp at Chinitna Bay, which is located near the trees behind the Super Cub's left wing strut. This was where I whittled several dozen Sitka spruce "screws" to hold the Cessna 180's engine cowling in place.

bench tested a lot of the plane's electronics and avionics, most of which was brand new equipment. These tests weren't required for another two years, and I thought that I was being taken advantage of. Worse, however, was what the facility did with the engine.

At the time of this inspection, the engine had seen only about 350 hours of flying time since rolling out of the factory. And, remember, this aircraft wore a Teledyne Continental TSIO-530-M, turbocharged 310-horsepower engine. Since the engine was turbocharged, it required special operating considerations. For instance, a pilot should never shut this type of engine off without idling the big power plant for a few minutes to allow things to spool down a little in the turbocharger side of the house.

Even more important was the first flight of any day. The *Pilot's Operating Handbook* clearly states: "On the first flight of the day when the throttle is advanced for takeoff, *manifold pressure will normally exceed 36.5 inches Hg and fuel flows will exceed 31 GPH if the throttle is opened fully.* On any takeoff, the manifold pressure should be monitored and the throttle set to provide 36.5 inches Hg; then, for maximum engine power, the mixture should be adjusted during the initial takeoff roll to 31 GPH fuel flow." This acknowledges that the engine will *normally* over-boost and develop greater power than it should on the first takeoff of the day; and that the pilot is expected to reduce that power to make sure manifold pressures do not exceed 36.5 inches of mercury. An unattended cold engine could be expected to get 38 inches or more, regardless of the ambient temperature.

These big-league mechanics apparently hadn't read, or chose to ignore, this cautionary note about power settings. Without a word to me, they adjusted the turbocharger power controller down to the point that the engine couldn't possibly obtain full power. When I picked up the airplane, the mechanics failed to mention the power controller adjustment, and it certainly didn't appear during engine run-up prior to takeoff. The mechanics didn't note the adjustment on the paperwork nor did they enter details of this work in the engine log.

It was a hot and muggy Florida day when I loaded three passengers, some scuba gear, and photographic equipment into the amphibian for a flight to the Gulf of Mexico. I was putting together a brochure to advertise my flight service to fishermen, scuba divers, and other water-oriented sportsmen and vacationers and wanted to include color photos. We loaded up and taxied out to the run-up area at the west end of Palm Beach International's shorter east-west runway in preparation for an east departure. With this high-performance single engine aircraft, I very seldom used the longer runway unless flying in IFR conditions.

The engine gave a smooth and satisfactory run-up, and I contacted the tower for a takeoff clearance. We were cleared to Runway 9R for the departure. After aligning the aircraft with the runway centerline and setting the gyros, I checked all seat belts and then advised the tower that we were rolling.

By the time I had realized that the engine wasn't going to achieve full power, I was committed to the takeoff. Immediately after liftoff, the tower, seeing that we were in a bit of trouble, asked if we were all right. I replied that we were fine—just a little heavy on this hot day—and struggled for a bit of altitude. I was finally able to settle things down to 30 inches of mercury, 2,600 rpms and 20 GPH on the fuel flow meter to get the 95 knots of airspeed required for the turning climbout. From there on out, things went more smoothly.

When I returned to Palm Beach International, however, I had a little talk with the maintenance folks and demanded that they adjust the controller back to where it had been, should have been, and by George, was going to stay!

That not-so-little maintenance boo-boo could easily have damaged property and cost lives. There are not many open spaces around Palm Beach International for emergency landings, and that heavy aircraft could never have made the turns necessary for a safe landing back on the airport itself.

The same maintenance facility lost my only copy of the Wipline Amphibious Floats operating, parts, and service manual. Said they'd never had the thing. Then how, I asked, had you done the required annual inspection and certification? Those people were a real disappointment, and the entire experience was so discouraging that I moved my aircraft to another field. For a $5,500 annual inspection, the maintenance facility had unwittingly put several of my passengers in real jeopardy.

When I later had an O-ring failure in the right float hydraulic landing gear system, I fixed it myself, putting everything back into factory-new condition. Never had a problem with it again. The O-ring apparently failed because the above-mentioned maintenance facility hadn't greased certain parts of the nose wheel retraction assemblies. They didn't seem even to understand how the danged system worked! I found that incredible, and more than a little disappointing.

In my many years as a pilot, I have encountered good mechanics and not-so-good mechanics. One lesson I've learned is to never take good maintenance for granted. I had always enjoyed excellent maintenance work at a particular Merrill Field facility. This shop had maintained my 1978 Cessna Stationair and my 1984 turbocharged Stationair. I was always particular about routine oil changes. I consistently changed oil at the twenty-five-hour mark, regardless of the aircraft, and in spite of some advice to the contrary.

Once I had loaded nearly 1,000 pounds of groceries into the turbo-206 for a trip to Painter Creek Lodge. I was about to leave Merrill for the ride through Lake Clark Pass toward Iliamna, King

Salmon, and Painter Creek, a trip of slightly longer than three hours and thirty minutes.

Upon my arrival at Merrill the day before, I had requested an oil change on the plane. This was a rather involved procedure, requiring the removal and replacement of some of the turbocharger and waste gate elements. Before I departed, I checked the oil, as is always my habit. The new oil must have been super-clean, because I couldn't see any of it on the dipstick. I tried it again. Still I could see no oil on the stick.

Climbing down from the big amphibious floats, I walked into the hangar and found my mechanic. I asked whether or not he had made the oil change, and he replied that he had. I asked whether he *personally* had performed the change. He told me that he had drained the old oil and had then asked another mechanic on his crew to add the new oil and replace the filter. At that point, I invited him out to check the oil level for me, since the sun must have been in my eyes, and I couldn't find any evidence of oil on the dipstick with my failing vision, which he knew wasn't failing at all.

When my mechanic removed the dipstick and looked at it, he knew right away that the oil reservoir was completely dry. He turned white as a sheet, and it was easy to understand why. If I had taken off with no oil in that big engine, I would have made it about as far as the airport limits before the engine would have seized up, dumping the heavily loaded amphibian into the creek off the end of Merrill's Runway 33.

Maintenance. Do as much of your own as you are able. And when you aren't able to do the work yourself, at least pay close attention to the work and its quality. After all, people do make mistakes, don't they?

During a round-trip flight to the Bahama Islands, I found I had to pump the gear down upon arrival in the islands, once again after departure, and finally once more when I arrived back in Florida.

The pump on that Cessna installation is directly behind the left side of the pilot's big control wheel. To operate it, the pilot must pump it at least fifty times with his left thumb. This is very difficult to do in flight, and there is little room behind the control wheel for doing so. Cessna could have found a much better place to install that hydraulic pump.

The ashtray in that model is in an awful place, too. It's located immediately adjacent to the fuel control valve at floor level. Jeez . . . it seems to me that this is a definite fire hazard. And, if you fly instruments, you know that bending over in that direction and then straightening up quickly will induce vertigo and spatial disorientation almost every time. Didn't anyone ever tell Cessna that? Well, I did, by telephone. They promised to move the ashtray on the subsequent models. I don't know whether they ever did or not. One would think sparks from a cigarette and fumes from a leaky fuel selector valve wouldn't be a good mix.

A pilot never knows what sort of spare part he might need in the bush. I learned early on to always carry spare instrument and nav light lamps along with me, either taped to the fuselage behind the headliner or in the glove box, if there is one. And I never fly without spare fuses, of course. I even began carrying spare micro-switches in the Stationair.

I once flew from Lake Hood through Merrill Pass to a small puddle south of Two Lakes where I set up a temporary hunting camp. Occasionally, I would have to make a trip to resupply that camp, and it was during one of these resupply flights that I had flap trouble in the Stationair.

After making a water landing, I raised the flap control lever, but the indicator needle didn't move. I looked out the window, and sure enough, the flaps were still at 20 degrees, the recommended maximum for floatplane landing operations. Full flaps—40 degrees of those barn door flaps—would guarantee flipping the plane when the nose-low attitude dipped the float noses into the water.

I moved the selector lever into the full up then the full down positions. The flaps responded to the last directive, and they came down to 40 degrees. But nothing I could do would raise them again. Well, I certainly couldn't operate the Stationair on floats with those huge flaps locked in the full down position!

I was now stuck on a lake more than 100 miles from the nearest city, and on the wrong side of Merrill Pass. What to do now, I wondered? After unloading and tying the Cessna down on a log ramp I had made for it, I pondered the situation for a time.

The flap system on the Cessna Stationair is electric rather than manual, as they are in the Cessna 180 and 185 models. I knew that the flap circuit had a problem, and that no other system in the plane had been affected. That very likely translated into a problem with one of the seven micro-switches in the flap circuit.

I finally located the switch that appeared to operate the flaps, but it was located in a place I couldn't reach. I found that I could raise and lower the flaps by operating a micro-switch in the right wing, outboard from the floats, with a long screwdriver. In the end, I simply raised the flaps, since I knew the airplane would both take off and land without them, then flew the aircraft back to Lake Hood for a change of switches.

Once there, however, I discovered that the faulty switch really was one of those located directly behind the pedestal on which the flap control lever is mounted. It was easy to change out and adjust, and I did that myself without further problems. It had been a pain in the neck, though, and certainly could have been much worse. Ever after, I have carried the spare switches. They are quite small, weigh next to nothing, and are worth their weight in gold in an emergency.

There are a few other items that a pilot should never be without. One of these is stainless steel wire—the kind used in safety wiring certain elements on the airplane. Duct tape is another, and I always carried a roll in the back of my Cubs. In the absence of duct tape, newspaper is an excellent patching material for a fabric-covered plane. Just wet the paper and spread it flat over the ripped fabric. Allow it to dry completely, and then just fly away. It does work, though using newspaper almost got me in hot water once. I had left my Chief at Merrill Field one evening with such a patch on a torn elevator. When I arrived at the plane the next morning to make permanent repairs, the Civil Aeronautics Administration had already placed a red tag on the pilot's window noting that such newspaper repairs were not considered airworthy. No kidding? Well, I didn't think it was airworthy either, but there had not been a repair facility nearby when the river bar willows had punched their way through the fabric.

I've known some pilots who've built complete vertical stabilizers by cutting up five-gallon avgas cans and duct taping the flattened pieces in place. It looks terrible, but it will get you back home in a pinch. Out in the bush, your best friends will always be your ELT and your radios. It is my heartfelt recommendation that you keep both in tiptop shape. In spite of all, try to keep an eye on your own maintenance needs and those who perform that maintenance for you.

There may come a time when you are far from a facility or a mechanic and badly in need of some type of maintenance. It happens every day in Alaska, and it may happen to you one of these days, regardless of where you choose to fly.

Take the cold and windy day in 1982 when I flew to Shadow Lake where I had a grizzly-hunting cabin high in the Talkeetnas. Shadow is a small lake, by most standards, even though it was plenty big enough for the Stationair's use. Full-load departures were out of the question, but half-loads were comfortable, and bigger loads could be split and transferred, half at a time, to nearby Stephan Lake. On this occasion, I was carrying only one passenger and a small amount of freight. Departures from Shadow were made either to the north or the south, depending upon the winds. Takeoffs toward the south allowed sufficient room for a comfortable idle turn at the north end to align the plane for the takeoff run. To takeoff to the north, however, pilots had to taxi southward into a narrow, doglegged shallow that was only fifteen or twenty yards across. A turn for the north takeoff run at the south end, depending upon wind velocity and direction, meant that the pilot would have to go to full idle, sometimes reducing the power to one magneto, or even completely shutting down the engine to allow the wind to turn the plane.

Shadow Lake is located at almost the very top of a mountain, so there is not water flow through the lake, and all the underwater rocks are quite rough and sharp. I had taxied into the south cove for the turn required for a north departure. The wind wasn't cooperating at all, and even on one mag, the plane was pushed up onto some shallow rocks. For all practical purposes, the plane was barely moving when we hit the rocks, but I could feel the bump on impact. I knew I had better have a look. I taxied back to the cabin and tied down the Cessna.

I ran my hand along the float bottom and found a dimple in the right float. I removed the float compartment cover and discovered a hole about as large as the end of my thumb. At least it was a puncture and not a gash. Even so, water was flowing freely through the hole and into that compartment. The float wouldn't take on enough water to sink, but the added weight would be a problem. I would have to fix the danged thing. But, with what, I wondered?

I hunted around the cabin for a time and finally decided to make use of a few items I was transporting. I cut the heavy handles from two aluminum cooking pans and removed two bolts from one of the GI surplus steel bed frames. Then I used the leather punch blade of a Swiss army knife to drill two matching holes in the handles. From the pair of old hip boots that had been hanging in the cabin, I cut a patch with a sharp hunting knife. I folded the boot piece over to make a double thickness patch about two inches wide and four inches long. Then I cut a second patch to match the first. I wasn't going to like the next step very much!

Armed with the Swiss army knife, I stood hip deep in the frigid water, which was probably less than 40 degrees, and drilled two holes through the hull, deep under water, matching the holes in the two pot handles. That done, I proceeded to cut matching holes in each of the double patches. Now I was ready to bolt the whole mess together.

I put one patch on the inside and one on the outside of the float to cover the hole. Next, I placed one panhandle inside and one outside, and bolted them in place over the makeshift patches. Since the screws themselves had slotted heads, much like stove bolts, I could tighten them using the screwdriver blade of a big Swiss Army pocketknife. As the folded rubber patches were compressed, they would provide enough resistance so that I shouldn't need a wrench to hold the nuts in place and prevent them from turning.

I thought for sure I was about to freeze to death. I was shivering like a wolverine passing porcupine quills. I had no feeling in my fingers, but I could tell that the resistance on my knife-blade screwdriver was increasing with every turn. I finally pumped the float compartment dry and went inside for some hot coffee.

An hour later, the feeling had returned to my hands. I walked out to have a look at the repairs. Sure enough, the float compartment was still dry. The patch would hold until my mechanic could install a proper and permanent riveted patch in an hour or so. Just another day in the bush.

There have been times when I've done extensive work on my airplanes. Immediately after the fiasco at Drift River, a series of boo-boos admitted earlier in this book, I stripped the fabric from my Super Cub, N1858A, and tore the entire plane down to its bare fuselage tubing. Everything came out or came off. There was nothing left but the fuselage perched forlornly on its landing gear and the oversized 25x11x4 tundra tires. The plywood floor panels came out, the wings and tail feathers came off, the seats came out, the panel came out—until the remains represented the very first phase of its original manufacture.

After brushing the tubing and checking all the welds, I added structural elements to strengthen the landing gear and tail areas, and added another structural steel tube diagonally above the baggage area and immediately behind the skylight. I also had a smoked brown skylight installed. I found the green skylights of those more contemporary Super Cubs truly depressing during bad weather flights. I poured boiled linseed oil throughout all the tubing to prevent future rust and corrosion. I designed a brand new panel, one that would accommodate full IFR capability, including glide slope and marker beacon features. I also added a remote indicating compass and an artificial horizon and gyroscopic compass. A full and sophisticated radio switching system was designed, and a complete radio stack, including ADF, DME, and transponder units, was constructed for a rack installation to be installed later below the instrument panel, ahead of the stick, and between the pilot's lower legs. I ordered a new, larger engine and a new and longer propeller designed to forty-two-pitch—a float, or takeoff, prop, as they are

279

AFTER THE BLIZZARD AT DRIFT
RIVER, I STRIPPED THE BIGFOOT
SUPER CUB DOWN TO ITS BARE BONES
AND COMPLETELY REBUILT IT, INSTALL-
ING A FULL INSTRUMENT PANEL, A
LARGER ENGINE, AND SEVERAL
ADDITIONAL BUSH MODIFICATIONS.
MY MECHANIC'S SON GOT A KICK
OUT OF FLYING THE CUB SKELETON.

termed. To be accurate, a *Borer* prop, I think designed by Alaskan Roger Borer. In short, the new airplane would only vaguely represent Piper's original.

I had a full-width piano hinge installed on the metal panel above the baggage area. The hinged top, with quick-release fasteners, would enable me to load freight and baggage with ease.

I abandoned the wing-mounted landing lights and designed a system that allowed a high-intensity "driving light" to be installed at the center of the landing gear. Many told me that this light would break during the first landing but, since it was mounted directly behind the propeller, I thought it had all the protection it needed. After all, the prop would have to go first, wouldn't it? That light turned out to have been a very practical element, serving me exceptionally well for a long time. I was surprised that Piper hadn't thought of it years before. Besides, the new light didn't reflect off the back of the prop during nighttime or IFR operations.

During final assembly of all these bits and pieces, I kept a close eye on things. After having listened to hours of hangar flying tales over the years, one of the things that was high on my priority list was the trim system installation and rigging of the wings. I'm glad that it was.

During the installation of the flap cables, I discovered that one cable had been wrapped around the outside, rather than the inside, of a cable keeper adjacent to one of the pulleys. The flaps would still work, but the cable wouldn't be running inside the pulley trace and would soon be worn through. I corrected that error immediately.

After the trim and flap cables had been installed and safety wired, I checked the elevator and elevator trim operation. I discovered that the trim had been rigged backwards, and that when the trim control was moved to the nose-up position, the trim itself had traveled upward rather than downward. This forced the elevators into a downward position, creating a tendency for the nose to drop. Clearly, this rigging was backwards and would have exacerbated any nose-down condition. Or any nose-up condition, for that matter.

Let's say the Cub was heavily loaded and, during takeoff, I needed to trim the nose down a bit. When I rolled in the necessary trim, the nose would have gone even higher. Now I would have rolled in all the nose-down trim I could manage, and the nose would have been forced as high as it would go. I'm not sure that stick pressure could have overcome this climbing tendency before the airplane had stalled and spun in under full takeoff power. I do know that such strain would test the elevator strength.

It was theoretically possible for an empty airplane to be forced over onto its back during a climbout by trying to increase nose-down trim, only to actually be feeding in nose-up trim. It had been known to happen, in fact, right on the runway at Anchorage International Airport.

I was having a terrible time convincing the mechanic that he had rigged the trim backwards. After an hour of haggling, he finally saw the light. I re-rigged the trim cable myself, but I still have sober moments recalling that argument over something so very basic. Other pilots had paid a very high price indeed for this backward rigging.

The complete rebuilding included all new fuel lines, too. I didn't want anything "old" to remain on that Super Cub. It would cost $20,000 for the rebuild, and I wanted a "new" airplane when it had been completed. And I had one, I can assure you.

When the new fuel lines were being installed, each joint was treated with Fuel Lube, a non-fuel-soluble lubricant with the consistency of water pump grease. If avgas would dissolve it, there was no point in using it, was there?

What I didn't observe, I suppose because I was looking elsewhere, was that the mechanic had dipped a connection directly into the can of Fuel Lube in order to coat the threads. He didn't notice that he had picked up a glob of the stuff that had completely sealed the pipe, blocking it off to the point that fuel couldn't flow through it. And still the rebuilding continued . . .

The morning of my flight test, I preflighted the craft and started the engine. Static run-up had already been completed, and the prescribed number of ground hours had also been reached. The new little Super Cub, bright yellow with red trim—horrid colors maybe, but easy to see in the all-covering snows of Alaska's winter months—was now ready for the flight test. No passengers.

Because I wanted a departure that would take me over uninhabited land, rather than over a busy part of the city, I requested, and received, clearance for a Runway 15 departure from Merrill Field. I taxied to the run-up area and went through the magnetos, carburetor heat, and full power checks, then requested the takeoff clearance. I got that clearance right away.

I notified the tower that this was a test flight, something they already knew, and taxied into position, holding long enough to set the new gyro compass to the runway heading. I slowly advanced the throttle to add power and took the Cub off smoothly, without flaps.

Almost as soon as the Cub had lifted off, the tower reported black smoke coming from the exhaust stacks. I immediately requested a precautionary landing on Runway 24. The request was instantly approved, and I turned onto the downwind leg for that runway.

I landed without a problem and taxied back to the hangar to check things out. All seemed in order, so I went through the pre-takeoff business again. Everything still seemed all right, and I departed south and east to get away from the city for a couple hours of concentrated systems and aircraft flight controls testing.

I found the rigging itself was out by some appreciable amount, and I wanted a hands-off trim condition for cruise configuration. We would have to check the rigging.

All instruments seemed to operate with their ranges, and the radio installation was perfect. I had installed a helicopter cyclic grip on the top of the Cub's control stick. I had personally installed wiring inside the control stick, connecting it to the radio transmitter button on top of the cyclic grip, one of the reasons I had installed that grip in the first place. This also proved to be a good idea. All wiring, except a very short run of cord from the big David Clark headset to the wing root panel on the left side, had been carefully concealed and cable tied. The interior was smooth and free of any loose wiring. Suddenly, the engine quit . . .

I was flying at 6,000 feet and over the east coast of the Kenai Peninsula, slightly east of the mountains that ran like a spine down the peninsula's full length and beyond. The east side, the very steep sea side of these mountains, had no beaches for safe landings. Instead, the mountains and glaciers dropped directly into the seas. I hoped I wouldn't soon have to put down somewhere in the water along the mountains, and I began to review the possible reasons for the engine failure only an hour or so into its maiden flight.

I had recently switched from the left wing tank to the right wing tank. One of the first things for me to do now was to change tanks again, and I immediately switched back to the left tank. The engine started right away. When I switched back to the right tank, the engine ran for a few minutes and again stopped. When I switched again to the left tank, the engine started and once more ran smoothly. I decided that there was some obstruction in the fuel line leading from the right tank, and I would have to return to Merrill Field and have it checked out. I reversed my course and returned to Merrill without any further problems.

An investigation of the fuel system revealed the plugged fitting in the right wing tank feed line. After the fitting had been removed, cleaned and reinstalled, that problem was forever cleared up.

The rigging was a different matter, and one that I decided only I could correct to my own satisfaction. It has always been my habit to purchase both the parts and the service manuals for any aircraft that I own. That was true, too, for this Super Cub, first manufactured in 1952 as an agricultural model designed for crop dusting. Within the service manual for the Cub resides a complete set of instructions for the rigging of the aircraft. This deals with wing dihedral as well as with other matters having strictly to do with the rigging.

With Peggy helping me, since I didn't want to trust anyone else with this fine-tuning chore, we leveled the aircraft and went through the complex procedure of jury strut rigging and adjustment. When we were finished, after almost a full day of measuring and adjustment of the threaded rods at the jury strut connections where they join the fuselage low on the cabin, I flew the Cub again. Once more we had to fine-tune the little plane, and this time it was absolutely perfect. It was rigged so closely that I would later discover I could initiate shallow turns by leaning one way or another in the cabin, and climb or descend by leaning back or forward in the seat. I realize that all aircraft exhibit this same response, but not to the extent that the little Cub responded.

New foam seats had been designed and constructed, by the way, and flight in the Cub would forever after be much more comfortable than before. I'll still admit, however, that a ten-hour day in the front office of a little Piper Super Cub is a grueling, thankless, and painful experience. The widest part of a Super Cub is only twenty-four inches, and that is right at the front of the pilot's seat. Not much stretching room for a tired, stiff, and bored pilot at the end of a long day in the saddle.

I had also installed full aerobatic seat and shoulder harnesses in both the pilot and the passenger seats. Completely redesigned electrical systems, along with breaker and switch panels, had been in-stalled at each wing root. All breakers and switches had been marked by attached plates, white lettering on black plastic, for easy reading under any lighting conditions. All in all, it was a premier Super Cub, though admittedly a little on the heavy side. But, I only weigh 159 pounds, wringing wet, so the added weight didn't really cut perfor-mance by all that much. My Cub would take off with ample fuel in ninety feet. Some Cubs, of course, could make it in only forty-two! I didn't think a distance of sixteen long paces would make that much difference in the bush, though I admit the better performance could be fascinating. No matter, since I knew I could fly out of any place that I could safely fly into. I didn't know any pilots that could safely and consistently land in forty-two feet. Unhappily, I would later bend the hell out of that little Cub, but it would be once more repaired to a like-new condition. With a lot of help, that is . . .

Chapter 21

Troublesome Loads

There have been times, I am sure, when each of us has flown loads that were in some way troublesome. Whether internal or external, and whether heavy or light, there are just some loads that present problems for the pilot. Advertising banners, often called banner tows, are certainly troublesome loads. Routinely, they are quite manageable, but if something goes south for a banner-tow pilot, the situation can become much more ominous. If a pilot towing a banner has to make an emergency landing, the pilot's first instinct is to get rid of all that laundry tagging along behind the plane. But where to dump it without endangering someone on the ground? The long metal post located at the very front end of the banner is not only heavy, it makes a pretty good spear in a free fall. If there is any time at all for the maneuver, the pilot will most assuredly try to avoid dumping a banner in a school yard, a shopping center parking lot or on any traveled street.

During the summer of 1959, while serving my architectural apprenticeship with Robert E. Hanson, AIA, of Fort Lauderdale,

Florida, I received a telephone call from a young lady in Daytona Beach asking if I could pick her up and fly her to and from Fort Lauderdale. She needed to make the trip on the following Saturday morning, and my schedule had a big hole in it, so I told her I would be happy to help. We arranged a time for our meeting in Daytona.

When I arrived in Daytona Beach the following Saturday, I saw that she had with her a miniature poodle, which had been dyed a god-awful shade of pink. He, or she, or it—whatever the little beast might have been—was generally the opposite of any idea I ever had in regards to the appearance of four-legged creatures, of whatever size or shape. I'm sure I would have felt the same way if her pet had been a pig, a horse, or a moose. It just appeared unseemly to me somehow.

At any rate, we stored her suitcases in the baggage area of N4249F, the Cessna 172 that I had rented earlier that morning from Sunny South Aircraft at the old Broward County Airport in Fort Lauderdale, and placed her little pink friend in the back seat. The dog was traveling without a cage or carrier of any sort, but the weather was good and the air quite smooth. I was confident that we could make the two-hour-and-fifteen-minute flight without pitching the little devil out somewhere along the route.

The young lady, Ms. Tanya Graef, was one of those gorgeous Florida gals who reminded me of the much-touted California Girl— blond, deeply suntanned, and athletic. Her grandfather wrote law textbooks. She was sort of a beach bum with money, I suppose. At any rate, we enjoyed the bright and sunny flight.

As we neared West Palm Beach, she turned to look at her disfigured little pet, only to utter a quiet exclamation. When I looked back to see what the problem was, I saw that the little critter was getting sick all over the back of the plane. On the seats, on the carpeted floor, on the seat rails, on the upholstered side panels . . .

I've had an aversion toward most canine passengers ever since.

My trepidation over carrying the little buggers has been borne out several times since that first doggy flight. I've carried wet dogs, sick dogs, injured dogs, dogs that have been shot, and dogs caught up in the lure and fascination of animal husbandry. This latter experience occurred when an Iditarod dog musher asked if he could winter at our lodge on High Lake. That area enjoys deep snows rather early in the season, and he thought it would be a good area in which to top off his team's training program.

The musher agreed to pay all flight expenses to transport him, his team, and their support materials. And, he agreed to act as caretaker for our lodge property until February, when the Iditarod 1,000-mile dash from Anchorage to Nome would begin. Since I knew the aircraft loads would be pretty heavy, I agreed to meet him, his handler, and all his gear at Big Lake, fifty road miles, but only a fifteen-minute flight, north and slightly west of Anchorage.

It was way down in the fall—October 22, 1978, to be exact—when I met Dick Petersen, the musher, and Bob Jones, his handler, at Big Lake for the transfer. Dick had twenty-five dogs, one sled, two steel kennels, several bundles of dried salmon, and two heavy tarpaulins to transport to High Lake.

In the first load, I flew fifteen of the dogs, the two steel cages, a couple of green tarps, the sled—which was tied outside the airplane to the right float struts—two bundles of dried salmon, and Dick and Bob, who had to handle the dogs while in flight. It's not nice to strap live dogs to the floor during flight, you see. It's not acceptable to cram them down into the float lockers either. To accommodate this load, I had removed all the seats except my own.

Several of the sled dogs were males, and two of these were a little larger than the breed's standard forty-five pounds. We loaded the larger males toward the front and right behind the musher, Dick, who was seated on the floor where the co-pilot's seat usually stands.

The load was particularly heavy, but the air was crystal clear and the temperature was hovering around two-dogs cold, so I knew the engine would perform at full capability. Besides, Big Lake was about eight miles long with relatively flat land all around it.

With everyone and everything in place, I started the big engine and let it warm up with the float heels on the beach. I waited until the oil temperature needle had moved well above the peg before I added enough power to slip free of the beach, drop the water rudders, and coast out into the lake. We would depart from Big Lake Lodge, situated on the lake's east shore, toward the west. The highest piece of ground of any significance between Big Lake and Russia was Beluga Mountain, and that hump, standing at about 3,700 feet MSL, was more than thirty miles away. The huge Alaska Range was in that direction, too, but it was scores of miles away. All we had to do was to clear the thirty-foot spruce trees at the lake's west end, eight miles ahead.

I added power, raised the water rudders, and leaned to the correct fuel flow. I was using 10 degrees of flaps to help get the load up on the step. I horsed and rocked and horsed and rocked with the control yoke, but I could not get that load up over the hump and onto the step. On and on the heavy Cessna plowed, throwing heavy water every which way, bellowing like a bull alligator.

I always adjusted the throttle to 1,000 rpms at the beginning of any float taxi so I could look back from my window to see where the water line was in relation to the deck at the float heels. As long as the entire top surface was above water, the plane, of almost whatever type, would usually rise to the step and fly away. On many occasions, I had lifted loads when the heels were awash, so I knew this was possible. In today's case, the heels were definitely awash, but I kept thinking of that long, uninterrupted eight-mile waterway ahead of me. I was *convinced* that this load would fly.

As we passed by the first cove to our north, and then several of the smaller islands near the middle of the lake, I began to wonder whether or not I could ever coax the plane up. I hoped that burning a small amount of fuel would help. Mathematically speaking, I was sure it would work, but math is an exact science, and my shifting load was not.

Dick and Bob were both busy trying to keep the fluid gaggle of animals pressed as far forward as possible. This was a little like trying to stack marbles, though, and they were only partially successful. The center of gravity was changing from moment to moment, a happenstance that didn't help me in the least.

We had been throwing heavy water for more than six miles, almost twelve full minutes, before I could see the spray begin to move aft along the floats. When that begins to happen, the airplane is about to roll over onto the step, and from there on out the takeoff is virtually assured. That rollover occurs at just about 40 miles per hour. When the overloaded Cessna finally came up and settled over on the step, I raised the flaps to reduce drag and gain enough the speed for the wings to lift the plane off the water.

It was just at this moment that the biggest male realized there was a bitch in heat all the way back at the rear of the cabin. And he had every intention of romancing that sweet thing, if he could only get to her.

When the large dog got away, both handlers grabbed for him, shifting the load aft just enough to tip the aircraft back off the step. This takeoff was becoming a cross between a Chinese fire drill and a Lebanese goat rope. I was not at all sure of the ultimate outcome. But I did know that the spruce trees on the shore ahead were looming larger than ever and that we were rapidly running out of wiggle room. It boggled my mind that an eight-mile takeoff run might not be quite enough for a Cessna Stationair.

Suddenly the plane felt appropriately slick on the water, and I lowered the flaps to 20 degrees for the takeoff. The heavy plane sluggishly left the water, but I wasn't going to allow it to climb above six feet or so until I had built up some additional airspeed. We were married to ground effect, and I wasn't looking for an early annulment.

The Keystone Cops comedy of errors continued behind me, and the heavy Cessna teetered on the sharp edge of a stall even as the trees grew bigger and blacker in the windshield. At the last possible moment, I eased in a little backpressure, and the floats cleared the treetops by no more than two feet. When I was five or six feet above them, I leveled the plane out and we flew at that altitude for the next one and one-half miles. I was afraid to roll the wings far enough out of level flight to begin the shallow right turn that would put us on the course northward toward High Lake. We continued to travel on the ragged edge of the oscillating stall for about two more miles before I felt the airplane settle reluctantly into something only vaguely akin to stable flight.

It was several more miles before our airspeed built to the point that I could comfortably close the cowl flaps against the cooling of the frigid outside air. The engine had been overworked, and I wanted to be as kind to it as I could be.

When we arrived at High Lake, the sun was already beginning to throw long shadows across the water. Where the sun shone, the water was clear, cold, and calm. Where the water lay black and still in shadow, the lake was already covered with a thin sheet of new ice. This sheet moved with the shadow line, and we could actually watch the lake freeze.

I landed and we unloaded as quickly as we could. If the lake froze completely across, it would still be no problem for the Cessna and its floats, but we had one more trip yet to make. I would have to break the thin ice on the next landing, and once again during the last takeoff of the day—which would actually be at night.

The last flight in, with a much lighter load, went without a hitch, though I had to break through the new ice on both the landing and the takeoff. Before long I had left the freezing lake for Lake Hood. Since Lake Hood sits at only about 120 feet MSL, it wouldn't freeze for some weeks yet. As I flew the return trip, I could see smooth, hard ice covering the float decks, sides, and fittings. I could see the water rudders, too, and sure enough, they were frozen in the up position. I wouldn't be able to steer the big airplane on the water once it came down off the step after landing at Hood. The biggest problem, though, would be that ice on the float decks.

When Approach Control gave me to Lake Hood Tower, I explained that the water rudders had frozen on takeoff and that I would have to shut down in the middle of the lake and walk the floats to kick the rudders down before I could taxi in to tie down. When they approved the shutdown, I reminded them that all the airplane lights would go off at that time and I would be a sitting duck in the middle of a dark body of water. Please, I reminded them, don't let anybody run over me, okay?

The float decks were covered with about a half-inch of very smooth, and very slippery, wet ice. The trip aft to kick the water rudders loose was the most dangerous part of the day. There are no handles along the painted metal fuselage of a Cessna 206, and the exterior is particularly smooth. I fully expected to slip off and was already planning my cold, wet swim to shore. I certainly couldn't climb back aboard the icy floats. In the end, the exercise went reasonably well. Although it took several frustrating attempts to kick the ice from the water rudders, my worry had largely been for nothing.

* * *

A number of years ago, I made a resupply flight to Ted and Mary Gerken's Iliaska Lodge on the north shore of Lake Iliamna. Rather than mess around with the state strip, where the FAA had its Flight

Service Station, or the smaller and much closer village strip at the small enclosed lagoon there, I decided to land on the gravel driveway at the lodge. It was plenty big enough for the Super Cub, and I had made arrangements with Ted well in advance. The landing went well, and I loaded up a few supplies for a camp I was running in the Stony River country.

After the obligatory coffee, cookies, and bush chatter, I prepared to depart. The load was packed in, and I placed my big, red Kelty expedition backpack atop the rest of the stuff, lashing it all to the seat. I strapped in under the big aerobatic harnesses and torched the little engine off.

After warm-up, I taxied from Ted's hangar-cum-workshop to the end of the driveway and then turned back to face the three-story lodge building dead ahead of the Cub. The lake was about 100 feet beyond the lodge. I pulled down two notches of flaps and advanced the throttle. For some reason, the engine would only give me about 2,000 rpms, and I thought the throttle might be stuck. I pressed it forward harder, but nothing happened. By that time I was already committed to the takeoff.

Outbuildings, including Ted's tall hangar on the right, bordered both sides of the driveway. To the left was a small hill. The driveway wasn't very long, of course, but I hadn't thought that I'd need much takeoff room in the high-performance little Super Cub. The load certainly wasn't a heavy one, but it looked as if I had been wrong.

With the three-story building towering smack dab in front of the spinner, and no time to abort the takeoff, I glanced back to discover that the throttle control along the window ledge in the back seat area was stuck under one of the shoulder straps of the big Kelty backpack. The pack was strapped down, and there was no way to take up the slack at the moment. It looked as though I was about to become a new weather vane for the lodge.

I pulled down full flaps and yanked the Cub into the air, barely popping up over the lodge roof, and immediately dumped the stick forward again. The little plane and I just seemed to bounce over the lodge and dive toward the huge lake beyond. It felt exactly like riding a basketball. I wondered how much of a splash we would make in its 2,000-square-mile surface.

With the nose lowered, I rode the Cub downward for as long as it took to pick up just a bit more airspeed. When I leveled out again, I must have had no more than two or three feet between the big tundra tires and the surface of the huge lake. And then we were off and running again, climbing to turn on course as though nothing untoward had happened at all.

Ted had watched all this and later determined that the maneuver hadn't really been an attempt to buzz the lodge, but one that circumstances, whatever those might have been, had required. Ted flies the bush, too, every day of every summer, and he knows what it is to find himself pinched somewhere between a rock and a very hard spot. And, like the rest of us, he has bent one or two along the way.

I remember trying very hard to fly to Seward from Anchorage one cold winter day. I was driving a little two-place, 90-horsepower Aeronca Champion on skis through the mountains that divide the Kenai Peninsula from north to south. It was a particularly windy day, and Seward normally closed its airfield at 16 knots anyway. The winds were certainly higher than that, and Seward was going to be impossible even if I did ride it out that far. I finally gave it up near Kenai Lake and turned to return home.

I was glad to leave the mountains over Turnagain Arm and turn west over the little village of Hope. When the wind is out of the east as it was that day, that trip can be especially bumpy—the mountains act as a natural wind chute between the Gulf of Alaska and

Turnagain Arm. In only a few more minutes I would radio Anchorage and begin planning the penetration and approach to Merrill Field.

Although the Champ had no ashtray, I was nonetheless smoking away, now and then flicking the ashes out into the slipstream that cascaded bumpily along outside my left window. A lot of us did this, and we had always escaped the obvious.

The only thing inside the airplane other than me that day was a one-quart can of oil. I had earlier pitched the can all too casually into the baggage area, and now it was becoming a real problem. The turbulence had grown severe, and the oil can had become virtually ballistic, slamming the floor on its way down, and smacking the headliner on its way back up. I was afraid it was going to bonk me on the head bone at any moment. And the Champ was now bouncing so hard that I was afraid to try tossing the very short cigarette butt out the window—and my seat belt had begun to lose its grip.

That was in the days before the metal-to-metal seat belt was required in light aircraft and manufacturers were still installing those old friction jobbies. This one wasn't holding at all. Each time the airplane dropped, I would be slammed upward against the belt's limit. Each time the plane was tossed upward, the belt loosened just a wee bit more. It was now so loose that I had to duck my head each time I was thrown upward to keep from slamming into the overhead with enough force to knock me senseless. My casual planning with the oil can and cigarette had now placed me between a rock and a boulder.

I finally said to hell with the finger-burning cigarette butt and tossed it out the open window with my violently thrashing left hand—a risky maneuver that worked. Then I let go of the stick so that I could tighten the failing seat belt—a maneuver that didn't work! I slammed into the headliner several times, then began worrying about coming completely out from under the belt and getting tossed overboard! Man, what next?

Just past Campbell Point, the air settled down long enough for me to secure the aging seat belt again, and the rest of the flight was almost academic. I vowed never again to travel with loose baggage, though. And, I would never again fly without a proper seat belt, either. I decided right then and there that aerobatic harnesses were the ticket. And they are.

I've talked a little bit about a few of those Alaska modifications that make flying the bush much easier. There is a wealth of such modifications—longer, flatter props, for instance, big Scott tail wheels with heavier springs, beefed up landing gears, and structurally improved aft fuselage assemblies—and each one unquestionably improves flight safety. To the serious outback Alaska flier, such modifications are mandatory. All are legal, though many require special FAA certification and a new Weight and Balance sheet. All of them make good sense, whether or not you fly the bush.

I had long ago removed the rear control stick from my Super Cub, N1858A, but hadn't yet gotten around to buying and installing the modification that placed a fiberglass housing over the protruding stick stub at the rear seat. That little stub wasn't really in the way, but it definitely should be covered if I were to haul freight safely.

I was a day late and a dollar short with that modification when I loaded a moose aboard the Cub late one fall afternoon. I was at the foot of Tokositna Glacier, loading in a light rain. I would fly the moose meat from the silt and gravel bar, where the small hunting camp had been set up, to nearby Talkeetna. Someone would meet me there, load the meat onto a pickup truck, and drive the meat to Anchorage where the hunter's family could pick it up. All the required Transporter Report forms were in order, and everything was now a go.

The strip was too short for almost anything but a Super Cub (there are a few notable exceptions, including the Tern, a two-place plane built in Anchorage), but it was even suitable for a loaded Cub. Heck, almost anything larger than a postage stamp is suitable for a loaded Cub!

I strapped in and warmed up the engine. I pulled down half flaps—this Cub had one extra notch on its flap settings—and then powered the Cub around to align with the little strip. When I advanced the throttle control to full power, the Cub responded immediately, and I was on my way.

Within seconds, I was off the ground and climbing to 200 feet for the twelve-minute flight over flat country to Talkeetna. It was just after dark, though not quite as black as it would soon become. Only about two minutes into the flight, I hit a surprising bump of turbulence, probably caused by a stray blast of cool air scooting down the glacier behind me. Whatever had caused it, I felt the heavily loaded little plane lurch only once before the nose was suddenly pushed violently toward the ground.

At 200 feet, I didn't have a whole lot of altitude to spare, and didn't want to give up one foot of what I did have. I came back a little on the stick—*but it didn't want to move!* A fresh moose ham weighing probably 140 pounds had slipped forward off the pile of butchered and bagged meat behind the seat to jam itself down over the protruding stub left behind after I had removed the rear control stick. I reached behind me, but there is no way a man of my size and weight can lift that much dead weight backward and upward with only one hand. I might be in some real trouble here. . . .

Even using both hands, I could just barely apply sufficient backpressure on the stick to keep the nose up and the aircraft in level flight. But, would the strain I was placing on the stick be too much for its thin-walled material? What if it suddenly bent? Or even broke off completely?

The answer to that question was really easy: I would plant the loaded Cub nose-first into the nearest piece of real estate. It would only be a matter of seconds. Let's see now—200 feet at maybe 800 feet per minute equals—WHAT??? *Why, that's only 'bout fifteen seconds!* Of course, maybe the angle of incidence could be held below 15 degrees, in which case I ought to be able to walk away from it. Unless the meat behind me decided to shift forward and smash me flat. Aw, Jeez, this just wasn't my day. . . . Why hadn't I just found the time to install that little thirty-five-dollar fiberglass housing, anyway?

The stick was made of sturdier stuff than I had imagined, and I was able to coax the loaded plane into Talkeetna. The landing was a bit of a tightrope walk because, if I reduced the power by much, the nose tended to drop like a stone, and I wouldn't be able to hold backpressure against it. I had already rolled in as much elevator trim as I could manage, and that helped a little, but it was still a tough landing. I applied power to keep the nose up on touchdown, and the big tundra tires accepted the landing with style, grace, and a remarkable amount of forgiveness. I flew the empty Cub back to Anchorage that same night. And I installed the new stick housing before noon the very next day. It hadn't been very smart of me to hoard the thirty-five dollars when that stick cover modification was such a potential lifesaver. And I could always have found the spare time to make the half-hour installation.

* * *

It was late in the year when I found myself flying back from the Ugashik Lakes area of the Alaska Peninsula. Upper and Lower Ugashik Lakes lie between King Salmon and Port Heiden, tucked to the east against the mountains. The narrows that connect these two lakes, a stretch of clear, cold water less than a quarter of a mile long, are home to some world-class Arctic Grayling fishing. In fact, the world record grayling came from this short stretch of water.

I had flown down to pick up two of my assistant guides who had accompanied a client, one of the National Rifle Association's directors and a handgun hunter, on his caribou hunt. The hunter had taken a fine caribou with his scoped .44 Magnum Dan Wesson revolver with a seven-inch barrel, a new weapon on the market at that time. At the end of the trip, I would still have to clean out the camp and return my crew to Anchorage.

We had loaded the meat, horns, and equipment aboard N756VR, the float-equipped and normally aspirated Cessna 206 Stationair, and the four of us had piled aboard. My two assistants would split the caribou meat for their winter larders.

We pilots always seem to have enough room in a crowded airplane because we try very hard not to pile freight on or around our own seats. It's a matter of self-preservation, you see. For this trip, I had also left the front passenger seat vacant for the client's use. My assistant guides, though, were going to be a bit cramped. For the three-and-one-half-hour flight, they would have to make themselves as comfortable as possible while stretched atop the meat and camp gear. During the flight, the two of them would drink an entire bottle of Scotch whiskey that I had brought for them. They had worked extremely hard and had certainly earned the season end's little tot. Well, not so little, maybe. But I knew that my guides, Dan Boga and Al Mollo, could handle it in stride. These guys could call up moose and track fish under water. They were good at what they did, including the frequent and sizeable ingestion of burning liquids.

We stopped at King Salmon for some fuel, and then lit out for Lake Clark Pass and Big Lake, north of Anchorage. When finally we reached Big Lake, the eight-mile-long stretch of water sparkled under sunny skies at its west end, but it was fogged in clear down to the surface at the east end, where Big Lake Lodge was located. It was

After a successful handgun caribou hunt, a group of us loaded the Cessna 206 floatplane at Lower Ugashik Lake for the return trip to Anchorage's Lake Hood. From left to right are assistant guide Fred Cook, a former Mississippi policeman who is deaf as a post; client and NRA Director Phil Johnson, who was field-testing a new handgun for a big-name firearms manufacturer; assistant guide Al Mollo, reputed to have the ability to call bull moose and to track even small fish; and Dan Boga, who can carry a 200-pound pack from sunup to sundown, even though he wears a Tenz pain-blocking unit for spinal injuries.

there that my two assistants would climb stiffly down to meet their families. Well, no problem. We landed in the open area on the west end of the lake and taxied toward the fog. As I passed one of the small islands in the middle of the lake, I set up a compass course I knew by heart, throttled down to absolute idle, and poked the Cessna into the gray, wet darkness.

The instrument taxi, for that's what it was, would last for about two miles at probably 10 miles per hour. That meant about twelve minutes in the white, with each second of that depending upon my holding a compass heading with absolute accuracy. The heavy Cessna, though, was as stable as a rock, there was no wind to worry about, and I had every confidence in the results. If I missed, of course, I could well slam into the boat dock and the avgas pumps that were located just to the right of the lodge itself.

Out of nowhere the lodge appeared, just to the right of the airplane's nose. We were headed on a course that would split the boat-launching ramp, a gravel drive that had been our final destination from more than three hours out.

The lodge had a series of windows on the water side, half of them looking out from the restaurant and the other half from the bar. On this foggy autumn day, every single one of the bar stools was occupied. I could see the patrons' faces as we lumbered out of the dense fog, as if I were looking at a tree full of owls. I don't think I'd ever seen such a collection of wide eyes and open mouths before in my life.

I pulled the mixture control out to starve the big engine into silence, and we coasted to a stop against the shallow bottom. I climbed out and turned the aircraft around to place the float heels on the beach while we unloaded.

I climbed back up onto the left float deck, opened the pilot's door, and slid my seat forward so that my baggage area passengers could crawl out. When I did that, the empty whiskey bottle slipped from the top of the freight pile, bounced out the pilot's door, and hit the float deck with one loud bang before bouncing in a high, end-over-end arc to splash into the lake. No doubt everyone in the lodge bar could see that bottle. To those in the bar, the whole world was blanketed in a very dense fog. As far as they were concerned, I had landed in zero-zero visibility, a miracle in itself, while stone, blind drunk. When I walked slowly into the lodge bar, I slurred my speech as I asked, "Whash th' name a this dang place, ennaway?"

For a moment there, you could have heard a pin drop. I couldn't have paid a single one of those folks to ride with me until they realized that we were only spoofin' 'em. Fortunately the bartender and lodge owner knew me well and knew that I had never mixed alcohol with flying. Everyone had a good laugh over that. I guess there are loads and then there are loads . . .

Chapter 22

THE TANK COMMANDER

*H*is name was Günter Schmidt, he was as big as a house, and he had been a tank commander for the Third Reich during World War II. And, through an unusual set of circumstances, he had also become my client.

His often-stated claim to fame was his skillful marksmanship, acquired while he was busy shooting at Russian soldiers during that long-ago conflict. Like many who had sadly grown beyond adolescence, youthful optimism, and infectious wishful thinking—but not yet into realism and forgiveness—Herr Schmidt still harbored genuine anger at anything Russian. When primed with sufficient Schnapps, he would gather several of his hunting companions into his strong arms and sing into the night every single verse of the "Horst Wessel Song." In short, Herr Schmidt was a real piece of work. And scary as hell, when armed with his very heavy rifle and loaded with his fair share of Schnapps.

Günter had contracted with another of Alaska's Registered Guides for a trophy moose hunt. I had a hole in my schedule. At the other guide's request, I set aside a week during which I could drag the huge hunter around in Game Management Unit 19 on the far side of the Alaska Range.

I had expected to hunt from the other guide's permanent camp, a cabin on a small lake. But I learned after arriving in the bush that I was to drag Herr Schmidt out in the wilds somewhere and plunk him down inside the two-man mountain tent that we were to share for the duration of the hunting trip. Living in such a confined area during Alaska's fall rainy season was going to be rather punishing to Herr Schmidt, not to mention myself. I reckoned that it wasn't going to improve his outlook any. Since he spoke no English and I spoke almost no German, this didn't promise to be much of a whiz-bang vacation for either of us.

I loaded Herr Schmidt and our gear into my Super Cub, equipped with tundra tires, and we lit out from the guide's small tundra strip to find a suitable gravel bar for our campsite. I chose a bar along the Swift River, where we landed and proceeded to set up housekeeping. It doesn't take long for a guide to shake out a two-man tent camp, and we soon had everything in ship shape. It was a good thing, for we were going to live here for quite some time.

We climbed aboard the Cub again to have a look around the surrounding country. We could expect to find both moose and caribou within five miles of the camp. While that would be a long, hard pack with up to 150 pounds of moose or caribou meat on my back each packing trip, it was still well within the range of typical Alaska hunting safaris. Usually, however, the guide hires meat packers for the dirty work so that he can share other activities with his clients.

We took off and climbed northward to scout along the southern slopes of the Neacola Mountains. Both big moose and caribou bulls would still be up in this higher country, trying to escape the black flies and other winged insects of summer. The weather had recently cooled a bit, and we could see "termination dust," the first snows of winter, sneaking down the ridges and slopes toward the tundra below. The snow would drive big bulls down ahead of it.

We saw several large caribou bulls that afternoon, and two rather impressive bull moose. One of them was in a location that made it very hard to accurately judge his size from the air, but if what I could see of him proved true, he was a tremendous bull! Quick glimpses of his huge horns led me to think they were greater in spread than six feet. That would be large indeed. He was still quite high in the small, tight little bowl of a valley that eventually led downward toward Caribou Mountain, a lower foothill below him. But he was feeding steadily downhill, so I fully expected him to work his way into accessible hunting country within only a day or two. It was encouraging, too, to think he might be the last bull down from the higher elevations, since that might also mean he was the biggest, a definite loner until he began looking for the cows. In the meantime, we would keep looking and, occasionally, fishing for our dinners.

The next two days were cool and relatively clear, although I expected snow any evening. I wasn't worried about a sharp freeze, since I had tundra tires on the Cub and we had a world of sand and gravel bars from which to work. Without floats, freezing wouldn't be a problem.

On the third morning, Günter and I found the huge bull down at the mouth of his little valley, moving downhill with every stride. This time we got a good look at him. Another look led me to believe that his horns might be as wide as eighty inches, and that's an awesome set of horns.

I began to search the ridges of Caribou Mountain for a place to land the Cub and set up a spike camp. By that time, same-day flying and shooting was against the law in Alaska, so a second camp would be necessary. I didn't want to wait another five or six days for the moose to work his way to the bottom of the hills. For one thing, there was nothing to keep the magnificent bull from heading directly south, or even southwest and miss our Drift River camp altogether.

Although we could have directed him from the air, that is clearly against Alaska's "Fair Chase" game regulations. Moreover, if a guide can't outsmart a big game animal, then he doesn't deserve to be a Registered Guide.

Alaska, by the way, is most serious about its game management laws. If you are convicted of such a crime, the state can and will seize every single piece of equipment that was used in the crime. For example, if you drove your own car to the airport, the car can be seized. Certainly your airplane and firearms will go. Poaching game, snagging salmon, wanton waste of game animals or game parts, and fly-and-shoot hunting, all carry stiff penalties. Even those guides and hunters who don't philosophically subscribe to the tenets of fair chase know the risk is not worth the potential losses. The laws are clear, and justice is both swift and sure in the far North.

We had circled Caribou Mountain several times, but the only place I could find that might accommodate the Bigfoot Cub was the steep ridge on the north side, running north to south and close up against the mountains at the north end. I decided I could handle that, even though it did look a little bit iffy. There was a low overcast at the time, and it was spitting snow when I decided to shoot the landing and select a campsite. I circled the mountain one more time, finding nothing better than the steeply sloping ridge I had already selected. I told Herr Schmidt, as best I could, since he understood very little English, to tighten his seat belt for the landing.

The approach itself had to be a little screwy. I had to fly directly north toward the mountains, take a steep turn against their southern slopes, and, at the last possible moment, pull down full flaps only about twenty feet away from the face of the mountain itself. From there, I could descend quite steeply without power and add full power again almost immediately to land uphill along the spine that lead to the top of the ridge where it flattened out slightly. Getting back out would mean taking off downhill and directly toward the mountain, but the slope was steep enough that a short takeoff was pretty much guaranteed. I was quite sure I would have enough airspeed to turn away from the mountain itself with plenty of time to avoid smacking into its face.

I don't think my passenger enjoyed being carried directly toward the face of solid rock, but he said nothing. I guess he had already heard of these crazy Alaska bush pilots. When I was only a few feet from the mountain itself, I rolled into a steep left turn, pulled the throttle to idle, and lifted the flap handle to lower full flaps and drop the nose. It was a busy moment, but not that unusual a maneuver, really. I monitored the turn by looking upward at the slope through the smoked plastic skylight of the valiant Cub. It was one of those maneuvers that make Cub pilots glad that there is a skylight overhead, because that's what we all are looking through on such a tight turn. And, although I was descending rapidly, I was still looking up at the landing area.

I followed the toe of the mountain at an altitude of about three or four feet, and then added power as the Cub began its climb along the spine on which I would land. Everything was going smoothly, and I was looking hard for bumps, hummocks, and holes that I could not see from above in the flat lighting of the overcast day.

I touched down and was already coming on with the power as we started uphill toward the top. It was clear that we could easily coast to a stop before reaching the top of the ridge, but that would leave me with an extremely short takeoff run. I allowed the Cub to roll out at the top to give me the next few feet. That was a mistake!

AFTER THE LANDING MISHAP WITH THE
GERMAN TANK COMMANDER DURING
THE HUNT FOR A LARGE BULL MOOSE,
TWO MECHANICS REMOVED THE WING
TO ALLOW THE RESCUE HELICOPTER TO
HOVER AS THE LIFTING CABLE WAS
ATTACHED TO THE SUPER CUB. THE
ACCIDENT OCCURRED ON CARIBOU
MOUNTAIN, NEAR STONY RIVER.

The top of the ridge didn't just level out, as I had thought, but dropped eight or ten feet into a hole two hundred feet in diameter. Rocks the size of small cabins, overgrown with moss, tundra, and lichen, filled the bottom of the hole. A few small willows had sprouted sometime over the past million years, too. I hadn't been able to see the depression in the flat lighting, and now I was in deep doo-doo.

The Cub rolled over the edge and down to the first big rock, where it pitched to a halt. We were sitting there with the Cub's yellow tail in the air, its nose and prop against the rock, and the right wing bent upward about 20 degrees at the outboard end of the right aileron. In short, the plane was a mess. It certainly wouldn't fly itself out of this one!

We climbed out, and Herr Schmidt wondered nervously, What the hell are we going to do now? Well, Günter, we're going to get your big moose, what else? We might be here for a while, and we're certainly going to need something to eat, right? Günter was shooting the biggest hand cannon I had seen among German hunters. Oh, I had seen the .450 African, the .460 Weatherby, and a few of the English elephant guns. But Herr Schmidt's *nuen-komma-etwas-oder-andere* was one big smoke pole. At more than nine millimeters, it was certainly capable of smoking the big bull moose.

Günter had told us all many times that he might very well be the best shot in all of West Germany. He didn't recognize East Germany at all, of course. He repeated his claim to unchallenged marksmanship skills, then asked if I would now please just turn around to face the moose and stand very still for a moment. The huge animal, maybe 1,600 pounds on the hoof, was more than 300 yards away, and while his chest was more than three feet square, that was still quite a distance for an offhand shot.

Instead of using his usual hunting stick, Günter laid the huge rifle across my left shoulder, aimed for only a moment, then torched off the loudest explosion I had heard in a long, long time. I lost sight

A HELICOPTER LIFTED THE BROKEN
BIGFOOT SUPER CUB FROM THE
MOUNTAIN RIDGE TO A NEARBY GRAVEL
BAR FOR BUSH REPAIRS.

of the moose at the loud report. Even after my senses had returned, I could not see the huge animal. I asked Günter where it had gone.

"*Tot,*" he replied. "Dead. I shot him, isn't it so?"

Oh, yeah, sure. Where did you hit him.

In the neck, naturally.

It seemed that it was incumbent upon a German hunter of quality and gentility to dispatch such a grand animal with skill and humanity. The neck shot would kill the moose instantly, quite humanely, he pointed out. Yeah, yeah . . .

Sure enough. When I walked to where I had last seen the moose, he was flat on the ground. Well, not quite flat. He was upside down with all four feet in the air. The huge bullet had knocked him off his feet, and his massive horns were jammed into the soft earth, holding him in place in a perfectly inverted position. He had indeed died instantly, and Herr Schmidt had indeed hit the monster in the neck, breaking his spine. It was the most incredible shot I have ever seen! Well, *Weidmannsheil,* Herr Schmidt! Good hunting indeed!

I assisted patiently while Herr Schmidt went through the ritual of cutting and placing the successful *Duetsches Jäeger*'s (German hunter's) three twigs. The first, placed in the animal's mouth, represents the moose's last meal. The second, placed atop the carcass, represents a good and legal kill—in this case an emergency taking for our own food supply. The third, placed in the successful hunter's hat band, was the congratulations, the *Weidmannsheil*, to which the hunter must be accorded. When all was in order, I cut open the critter and cleaned him out for future use.

And then the fun began in earnest. We were far from our little tent camp and even farther from the guide's main camp. And my little Cub needed attention as quickly as possible. As soon as the word leaked out, the site would become a prime target for numerous Alaska vultures—those flying thieves of the outback who strip anything of value from every aircraft mishap they can reach.

After leading Günter back to our Swift River campsite, which was several thousand feet below us and six or eight miles away, I was able to contact a helicopter. He was returning from some contract work he had undertaken at Aniak, downstream along the Stony River from the Cub's location. He carried me to Sparrevohn, a few miles south, where I was able to contact my mechanic and arrange for him to fly over in his custom Cessna 170B to make the necessary repairs. Then I arranged for the helicopter to sling the Cub down the few miles to the gravel bar where our tent camp was located. I had left the tent for the mechanics' use. The helicopter pilot stood by and helped me prepare and sling the Cub for its dangling ride to the campsite gravel bar where the mechanics would make the necessary repairs.

The two mechanics arrived on schedule, and we got to work on the Cub. The severely bent right wing was first on the agenda. The mechanics removed the wing and laid it upside down on the gravel bar. I stepped carefully atop the lower surface, now facing the sky, and jumped up and down until I had taken out enough of the bend in the spar to render it flyable again, in my judgment. I don't believe this is a universally recognized maintenance technique, but it does work in a pinch. The mechanics mounted the wing onto the fuselage, replaced the gear and the prop, and cleaned out the air intake, which was stuffed with tundra, moss, and small willow leaves. Before long, the Cub was ready for the journey back through Merrill Pass and home to Merrill Field. I would eventually have to replace the right wing, of course. When the time came, I was able to find one of the newer models, featuring fifteen ribs instead of the original thirteen. The entire bush repair operation had taken only three days, including the time spent flying bits, pieces, and parts back and forth through Merrill Pass.

The mechanics did a marvelous job, despite sleep deprivation. In the flurry of activity initiated by their arrival, I had neglected to tell them about the pack of wolves traveling in the area. All night long these huge canines would prowl the gravel bar, woofing, snarling, growling, snuffling, and generally scaring the hell out of the two mechanics. Neither was eaten by the wolves, in spite of some of their serious concerns about that.

This story wouldn't be complete without mentioning the size of the trophy horns—seventy-six inches! They were so very impressive that the other guide stole them. It would be two years before the Alaska Department of Tourism intervened, retrieving and shipping them to their rightful owner, Herr Günter Schmidt, Bundes Republic Deutchland, Tank Commander (Retired).

Chapter 23

ALL IN ONE FLIGHT

*I*t is said that everyone has to learn *sometime*. And the pilot always hopes to be alone, not carrying a passenger, when lesson time comes! In spite of this, I went ahead with one flight very early in my flying career that I should have never attempted. Oh, I learned a lot during that long flight—actually a whole series of flights—but it was a dreadful mistake on my part to have taken the job in the first place. Especially since I had a passenger aboard almost the entire time.

By the time this trip was finished, I was so absolutely embarrassed that I actually forgot to apologize to the client. Looking back on it, I suppose he had enjoyed himself. It is doubtful that he understood just how many times I actually stuck his neck out during the whole episode. If I knew where he was today, I would apologize to him, for sure!

I first met Charlie Hubbard in April 1957. Charlie was an architect who had come to Alaska to work with E. B. Crittenden, FAIA,

Fellow in the American Institute of Architects. At the time I was working for Crittenden as an architect's apprentice.

Now as I recall, Charlie had been born in Northern Rhodesia. His mother had been Vice Consulate and Financial Advisor to the Union of South Africa. Charlie told exciting tales of growing up in darkest Africa, with lions marauding through his bedroom at night and elephants grunting in the high grass nearby. His provocative tales included polar bear–hunting trips by helicopter out of Norway—an activity that turned me off even in those long ago days—and other such exotic outdoor activities.

Despite all that Charlie had seen and done, his lifelong dream was to take one of Alaska's mighty brown bears. The earth's largest living carnivore, the brown bear had held sway over Charlie's imagination since early childhood, he claimed, and now that he was finally within petting distance, so to speak, he certainly wanted one of those big bears. I sort of put my nose in the air and told him that just about anyone could get one of those dern things if he really wanted one. Why, heck, I could lead him right to a brown bear, if he was that determined to find one of the big scallywags.

Now, keep in mind that I had yet to even see a brown bear up close. In fact, I don't recall whether or not I had seen one at all, from either near or far. Having already put my foot in my own mouth with this casual "anybody-can-do-it" comment, I didn't recognize that the time had come for me to back off a little. But, when Charlie offered to pay for the airplane rental, it was close to impossible to back down. Besides, I really *did* believe that it shouldn't be all that hard to find a brown bear. Why, hell! To hear the old-timers tell it, the bruins pretty much grew on trees in the Alaska outback.

I told Charlie that the best place for bears was probably way down on the Alaska Peninsula—around Port Heiden, maybe—but heck, Charlie, you don't want to go that far. Do you? He certainly did! It seemed that no distance was too great to discourage Charlie. Well, in for a penny, in for a pound . . .

At the time, I had amassed the grand total of seventy-six hours and twenty-five minutes of flying time. That averages somewhere around two and one-half flying hours *per month* since having earned my private pilot certificate. I had agreed to fly to a place nearly 600 miles from my home field, through mountains I had never before laid eyes on, to chase bears I knew absolutely nothing about, in an area so devoid of civilization that we wouldn't see people for days on end. And, at this point in my flying career, I had yet to venture more than 200 miles from home. I must have been out of my tree to agree to this sort of foolishness.

With Charlie's money in hand, though, I boldly went to Barton Aviation at Merrill Field, the flight school where I had staggered my way through the minimum requirements to earn my private pilot certificate. With only the ability to safely stall, spin, take off, and land, I rented a Cessna 140 for the trip. I told Bill Barton that we were going to "visit" in King Salmon for a couple days, and we'd be right back. Now, that's pretty casual, but this was Alaska and it was a pretty casual place, especially in those days. Bill may have guessed what we were up to, but I doubt it. He surely wouldn't have let something like a Cessna 140 go flying off into the bush. With six-inch tires? I doubt it! Besides, it was a side-by-side two-place, cruised at 120-mph or better, and had a pretty high stalling speed. It just wasn't the thing for flying the outback, even if it did only burn about four and one-half gallons per hour.

I spent almost the entire night before our planned departure going over sectional charts covering our route of flight. I was afraid of missing the opening into Lake Clark Pass, skeptical of finding Pilot Point or even Port Heiden, and had never even been to Iliamna—Alaska's largest lake and the halfway point in our flight south toward the Aleutian chain, birthplace of the world's worst weather.

While poring over the flight charts, I had consumed more than my fair share of black Alaska coffee. By the time I met Charlie at Merrill Field, I had probably consumed several gallons of the strong stuff and had slept only a few nightmare-ridden hours. This whole thing was a mistake, but I had talked my way into it up to the tops of my hip boots and could find no face-saving manner in which to back out at this late date. It never dawned on me to just take my lumps like a man and back out of the deal.

Early on the morning of May 7, 1957—it was a mild and bright Tuesday morning—Charlie and I lifted off Merrill Field in the little green-and-orange Cessna 140, N81098, and crossed Knik Arm to Point McKenzie, turning southwest to fly down the west shoreline of Cook Inlet. About twenty minutes out, I found the little village of Tyonek and considered making a rest stop. Why did I drink all that coffee, anyway?

I thought a first leg of only twenty minutes might not seem like much of a start to Charlie and decided I could just hold on and grit my teeth until we found Iliamna at the southern end of Lake Clark Pass. But that wouldn't be for another two hours! We were too far south along the beach for me to turn back, so on we went.

Not five minutes later, I knew my kidneys would never hold out until Iliamna. I began to look for a likely spot along the beach to serve as my first landing place. I had never before landed on a beach, and the idea of that first landing didn't cheer me up much. Besides, this stretch of beach was covered with thousands of rocks, some of them the size of a modest Alaska duplex, and I couldn't have found a place to land anyway. Even the seagulls were passing up this stretch of beach. Oh me, oh my. I would never make it to Iliamna without a pee break— something had to give here.

I trimmed the little Cessna into something approximating a very gentle climb, then pointed out the airspeed indicator to Charlie.

"Charlie," I said, "See this little gauge right here?"

Charlie nodded, so I said, "If this needle starts to come down, push just a little on this wheel, okay?"

Charlie nodded that he understood.

"And if the needle starts to go up, just pull back a wee little bit on the wheel. Can you do that?" Another nod.

With that, I loosened my seat belt, opened the fly of my Levis, cracked open the driver's door and leaned toward it. It was at this moment that I learned the first of many lessons on this trip: Peeing into the slipstream of a swiftly moving aircraft isn't a good idea. The pee blew right back into the cramped interior of the little airplane. And, of course, once you get the darned thing turned on, you can't just turn it off.

With that embarrassing moment behind me, I resumed control of the airplane. Charlie looked at me and asked, "Is it always like that?"

"Oh, pretty much," I replied with a false dignity that I'm sure Charlie could see right through. But Charlie was such a gentleman. He didn't utter another syllable for about an hour.

It turned out that I had a knack for contact flying, and we found the mouth of Lake Clark Pass without any problem whatsoever. I would later learn through the years that lots of pilots never develop that skill.

Charlie and I moseyed our way through Lake Clark Pass, finally reaching long, clear Lake Clark itself. We passed the lakeside village of Kijik, which lies about midway down the west side of the lake, and then flew past the strip at Port Allsworth (Tanalian Point), a fine gravel strip that in those days was about 2,900 feet long and situated along the east shore. It wasn't long before we also passed the village of Nondalton, right at the south end of Lake Clark, and about thirteen miles farther along we flew past the big airport at Iliamna itself. I turned left slightly to take up a compass heading of just a pinch shy of 160 degrees magnetic, and settled back down for the eighty-five-mile flight that would take us into King Salmon. It was here that we could grab a quick lunch, put on some more fuel, check the weather forecast ahead, and file our flight plan for Port Heiden and the bear-hunting grounds.

My kidneys had settled down and decided to take whatever abuse I was willing to give them. By the time we landed at King Salmon, we had been in the air for exactly four hours and had not seen one living thing. I had sort of expected to see brown bears scurrying around down there like a bunch of cockroaches caught in night-time kitchen lights. Well, we weren't going to hunt here anyway, were we?

After a slow lunch, a lot of talk, and a check of the weather, I went to file a VFR flight plan. I learned that we would be leaving the Domestic Air Identification Zone and crossing into a Coastal Air Identification Zone. That required the filing of a DVFR flight plan, which in turn meant that we would have to indicate our route of flight, all our intended points of landing, and our ETA (Estimated Time of Arrival) back in King Salmon. *And all within five miles or five minutes!* If we missed either of those estimates, we could expect the United States Air Force to scramble two F-89D Scorpion fighters then deployed at King Salmon to intercept and identify us. At which time, of course, we would be found in violation of our flight plan and dealt with accordingly. After all, we were still in the hot times of the Cold War.

Filing such a plan, of course, would be impossible for us. We didn't even know how many *days* we would be gone, much less how many hours and minutes. I told the Flight Service Specialist that we would simply give it up and return to Anchorage. *Without* a flight plan! That was legal enough.

We took off and headed north for about twenty miles, then descended to 200 feet, turned 180 degrees to take up a southerly heading again, and proceeded south past King Salmon toward Port Heiden once more. For the remainder of this trip, we would almost never fly above twenty or thirty feet AGL. That would be plenty anyway, I figured.

I knew I could find Pilot Point seventy-five or eighty miles south of King Salmon, where we could pick up on some grub and some canned avgas. We would fly direct to Pilot Point, crossing Bristol Bay to the west coast of the Alaska Peninsula anyway.

The first edition of the Alaska Airport Directory, no longer in print, showed Pilot Point to have its own little gravel airstrip, measuring 1,000 feet long, 75 feet wide. The following was noted in the remarks column: *"Airfield on ridge with low saddle in middle. East end somewhat washboardy."* One thousand feet sounded long enough, and if there was gravel standing on the runway surface, it would surely support an airplane. I'd just have to have a look at the "low saddle in middle." Alaskans have a knack for understatement.

When we found Pilot Point's little airstrip, set back a short distance from the beach and village, I flew around it several times to check on that low saddle. Clouds had moved in, providing us with flat lighting and no shadows. For the life of me, I couldn't see that low saddle. I decided it had either been exaggerated or someone had been filled it in since the directory was last published.

The strip was lined up roughly east and west—discounting its 20-degree east variation, that is. I decided to land toward the west and set up for the left traffic pattern like a good boy.

The Cessna 140 is a pretty hot little airplane, everything considered, and our approach speed was around eighty or so. I came in low over the scrub willows with all the flaps I could get, which wasn't very much in that little tin airplane. My approach had been low to begin with, and my descent was pretty shallow as a result. I had no room for a steeper, low-airspeed approach and short-field landing, really. That was a mistake, no question about it.

As soon as I had crossed the last of the little willows, I was over the strip. It began heading downhill for the low saddle at about the same rate I was descending for the landing. By the time I hit the strip I was already midway along its length, with a skinny 500 feet in which to finish the landing. The Cessna's wheels bounced against the uphill side of the low saddle, and my brakes didn't work well unless the wheels were firmly in contact with the earth.

When I had lost enough airspeed to finally become anchored to the runway, I stood on the brakes and poured power across the little tail to keep the Cessna from pitching right on over onto its fragile little back. When I had finally brought the little rocket to a stop, we were only four feet from the willows at the far end of the strip.

I sat there for a moment, pretending to cool the 90-horsepower engine, then lit a cigarette. Charlie asked if he might have one too, although I knew he didn't as a rule touch the things. As soon as we stepped out and stretched our cramped legs, a young Aleut lad came running out of the willows holding a camera. Well, well, well.

"Hi there, young fella! Don't get many airplanes around here, huh?' I asked.

"Naw, ain't that. My dad didn't think you'd make it. He thought you were too low and too hot, he said," the boy responded with a huge smile.

We followed the boy downhill to the village, located right on the beach. The lad's father owned the local store, and we picked up on some grub and a few nonessentials, as well as some canned avgas. When it came time for us to depart, I knew the little Cessna wouldn't make it off the strip with the load I had placed aboard. I would have to land on the beach near the village and put Charlie aboard there. Besides, this would be my first beach landing, and I didn't want to put Charlie through the unknown, so I had him walk back down from the strip to the beach to wait for me there.

The takeoff and the beach landing went much better than I had expected. I found the beach to be relatively cool, without the pesky thermals that always rise from hard-surfaced runways, and even some gravel runways. The sand was also a bit softer and more elastic, making for a smoother landing.

We spent a little too much time at the beach, and before I knew it, the tide was coming in. With no beach experience, I hadn't thought about the tides. Holy Moly! I would later learn that all outback pilots carry tide tables when flying near the coasts. By the time we were ready to blast off, the beach was too narrow to taxi downwind for an upwind takeoff. So I'd be taking off downwind in a really poor-performance, overloaded aircraft. I was learning a lot on this trip, but I was sticking my passenger's neck out at every turn in the road.

The engine was plenty warm so, after we had both belted in securely, I advanced the throttle and started the takeoff roll. The salty Bristol Bay was just off the left wheel, and a sand cliff was no more than about eight or ten feet off the right wingtip. The takeoff looked more than a little questionable.

It seemed that every fourth wave was a little larger than the preceding three. Each time this fourth wave came ashore it rolled up high enough that the left tire squirted through the water, spraying water up into the prop blast, which in turn threw it all over the windshield. The waves also pulled strongly at the left wheel, trying their best to drag us into the surf. With the tail already in the air and the left wheel periodically dashing through the surf, I didn't know if I could get the plane off the ground.

Suddenly, the little Cessna just flew off and away we went. The downwind takeoff and the squirrelly downdraft coming over the thirty-foot cliff just off the right wingtip made the whole operation questionable. All's well that ends well, I suppose.

We were soon turning to our southern heading again and looking for Port Heiden, fifty-two miles farther along the Bristol Bay beach. Heiden had been an Army Air Corps B-29 base during World War II, and the runways there are both long and hard. Made of crushed volcanic rock, they may be among the best runways in the world.

The only real concern at Heiden were perpetual winds that swept across the flat country that surrounded the village. It was normal to encounter 30- or 35-knot winds. When landing at Heiden, pilots had to be aware of offshore winds that might blow them off the beach and into the cold waters of Bristol Bay.

We had each seen our first brown bear—a relatively large sow with one cub—on the flight between Pilot Point and Port Heiden. We flew close overhead to have a better look. The big sow couldn't see the plane—bears have notoriously poor eyesight—but the old gal's hearing was nothing less than superb. She followed our sound inbound, and when we passed her, she was chasing us and jumping for all she was worth. For a fleeting second I wondered what would happen if the engine failed, and I had to drop the plane within easy reach of the irritated bear. Not a pleasant thought at all.

Charlie and I stayed in the hangar at Heiden, sleeping on the concrete floor and taking our meals, tourist fashion, with Paul, the Reeve Aleutian Airways station agent, and his wife. Pretty easy living for two bush hunters, really.

On our second day there, one of Alaska's honest-to-God hunting guides came in with his client and a small brown bear hide. The bear squared only about six feet, too small for a nonresident client to take, but the guide didn't care much. He got paid, and the client didn't know the difference, it seemed. A good bear would approach nine feet or so, and a really big bear would square ten feet or better.

That same day, Charlie and I flew across to Strogonoff Point, a long sand spit that protrudes into Meshik Bay near the village of Port Heiden. Between Heiden and Strogonoff lies a sand island, frequently crawling with hair seals waiting for salmon runs that will pour into the bay. We could see hundreds of these mammals as we flew past the island to Point Strogonoff.

We followed the beach southward from the point, and within minutes we saw a grand, silver-tipped brown bear wandering north. We circled him once and decided to take a closer look. I landed straight ahead on the beach, putting the little Cessna down relatively close to the water in order to land in wetter, harder sand. Like the majority of beach landings, this one was smooth and easy. The beach was steep enough that I touched down one wheel at a time. I turned the Cessna, and we taxied north along the beach to within about a quarter-mile of the bear, which was still working slowly northward, now more or less away from us.

This stretch of the country was nothing but sand, providing no cover for our stalk. As we got closer to the bear, I realized that he was bigger than I first thought and began to look around for something to climb, just in case. But there wasn't any such thing for miles. In those days, I didn't realize that a brown bear could have knocked down any tree I could have climbed anyway.

When we were within about 100 of the bear, he stopped his wandering and simply lay down in the sand. He scooped out a hollow in the sand, folded his paws before him, laid his head on his crossed paws, and promptly went to sleep! His silver-tipped hairs gave the bear the appearance of sleeping in a halo. He was gorgeous! In all my years since, I have never seen a more beautiful animal. We snuck up to within about fifty yards of the bear, Charlie's rifle seeming to shrink by the second. Goodness but that bear looked big!

I had seen no rubbed spots on the hide and decided this was as good a bear as we were likely to stumble upon. I told Charlie that I would whistle sharply to get the bear to stand up. Pretty much like the groundhogs from my early hunting days as a farm kid back in Ohio. When the bear stood upright, Charlie was to shoot him in the shoulders. It had to be a shoulder shot in order to break down the big bones in front and anchor the bear. I didn't want to contemplate a wounded bear on that flat sand patch—they're pretty speedy on only three legs!

Well, I whistled, all right. And the bear continued to snooze. I whistled some more and finally reduced myself to shouting and singing. Still nothing. That was pretty embarrassing. The bear didn't seem to be affected one way or the other by all this commotion. Though not the best of choices, it looked as though Charlie was going to have to take the bear as it lay asleep on the sand.

The bear was quartering rather toward us, and I asked if Charlie could shoot slightly over the bear's head and into the shoulder hump beyond that. Sure, he replied, and settled in for the shot.

I locked my 7x35 Bausch & Lomb binoculars on the bear and waited for the report from Charlie's Winchester 30-06. It wasn't long in coming. I blinked at the sound and couldn't find the bear when I finally turned the glasses back on the spot where he had been. When I found him, I thought Charlie had killed the bear in one shot. That turned out not to be so.

The big bear lifted his rear end up in the air, and then his front legs bolted upright—and the bear was away in a flash. Although I was sure I had seen the impact knock dust off his gorgeous coat, the bear didn't seem at all troubled.

A bear, much like an African lion, can reach almost full speed in his second jump. That speed is greater than the speed of a quarter horse, and a bear can run a horse to the ground in one-quarter mile or less. They can probably run 35 miles per hour at a full tilt. This one was going at least that fast and, fortunately, had started out simply following his nose. That took him on a quartering course away from us at about a 45-degree angle.

I told Charlie to cap him again, and he did. To make a long story short, Charlie had shot the bear through the heart with the first bullet, but the bear just didn't know he was already dead. He had run full-tilt for about 300 yards before he collapsed. Bears are very tenacious of life, I've found. The bear, by the way, squared slightly more than eight feet. Not a really large specimen, but a truly beautiful one.

When it came time to depart Port Heiden, we flew direct from Heiden to King Salmon, a flight of one hour and thirty minutes. We topped the tanks, had a quick lunch, checked the weather ahead, filed our VFR flight plan, and departed northward, toward Lake Iliamna.

By the time we had passed Big Mountain, near the southern shore of the huge, crystal-clear lake, we were into some pretty bad weather. It had begun to spit snow mixed with rain, and rime ice was starting to build on the airframe. More than that, the Cessna's little 90-hp Continental engine sported a tapered shaft. The shaft seal was leaking oil, as these tapered shafts were wont to do, and the oil was now mixing with the rain and snow that pelted our windshield, seriously reducing forward visibility.

Lake Clark Pass was closed in snow, and we elected to ditch our original flight plan and fly east along the 100-mile length of Iliamna Lake toward the mountains at the east end of the lake. There were several passes through these mountains, and I was sure we could sneak through at least one of them.

The weather, though, continued to get worse, and ceilings had now forced us down to only 100 or 200 feet above the water. Visibility was now down to less than one mile, and even at that, we couldn't see anything but water and a dim shoreline just under our right wing.

Both the oil temperature and oil pressure gauges were still well up in the green, so the small oil loss at the worn prop shaft seal wasn't worrying me yet. But the forward visibility was almost worthless, and we were coming up on a small section of the Alaska Range with slopes obscured in the low cloud deck.

This was my first flight into this part of Alaska, and I really didn't have a very good grasp of the terrain. Following our route on the Kodiak sectional was easy enough. The village of Kakhonak was hard to miss, with its 1,900-foot airstrip and the big lagoon behind it. Of course, from this low altitude, the bay looked more like another ocean to us. We couldn't see the end of it at all.

A few minutes later, I knew we were passing a 3,400-foot peak just off our right wingtip. We had been following the lake's south shoreline, and when we ran out of lake and the shoreline began to turn northward, I knew we were finally near the tiny village of Pile Bay. I also knew, from the Kodiak Sectional Chart, that there was a small dirt road leading from the lake up to a small saddle where a small airstrip was located. The very short road appeared to continue past the airstrip, through the narrow pass itself, and then down to the sea on the Pacific side to the tiny fishing village of Williamsport. If we could make it that far, I knew we could skirt north along the shoreline for the next couple of hours to Anchorage.

Even before we had reached the small airstrip at the saddle, and with almost no forward visibility, I could tell the low mountains ahead and off each wingtip were solidly socked in. At the strip, clouds hung down nearly to the ground. I was sure I could see a little daylight, though, just beyond the strip and between the two mountain slopes on either side of the airplane. There was not enough room to turn the swift little aircraft in that narrow space near the strip, but there *was* enough room, I thought, to shoot through the narrow gap between the two slopes. We were again flying at about forty feet, and it looked as if we would be forced just a few feet lower as we scooted through the tiny slot.

Only four or five seconds later, the ground fell sharply away to Williamsport and the waters of narrow Iliamna Bay. From there, we made an immediate 90-degree turn to the left and headed north, skirting past the west slopes of Sugarloaf Mountain. We turned sharply east to fly down Iniskin Bay, took another sharp left to cross the small oil exploration strip set well back into a little valley at Iniskin, and flew directly over Chinitna Bay. From there on out, it would be an easy flight along the flat shoreline flight to home.

After we passed through the tiny saddle at Williamsport, the east side of the Aleutian Range was washed in bright sunshine. There wasn't a cloud in the sky.

All the tense flying had left me a bit tense. I leaned back, put my right foot against the pedestal between Charlie's rudder pedals and mine, and pushed forward to stretch that leg. The airplane took a sudden and dramatic nosedive, scaring the wits out of me. I hadn't realized that the two control yokes were joined behind the instrument panel and from there traveled down behind that pedestal. When my foot was jammed forward on it, the control yokes were thrust forward also, placing the speeding little craft into an immediate dive. Whooooosh! Woke me right up and I recovered from the dive.

Well, Charlie got his brown bear, I hadn't done away with him on my first bush flight, and I had learned a lot during the trip. I had logged sixteen hours and forty-five minutes of flight time, about 22 percent of my total flying hours up to that point.

The entire mess, though, reinforced something I had already known: *Don't begin a vast project with a half-vast idea of what you're doing!* And if I just couldn't get along in the future without doing something really dumb, I always tried as best I could to avoid putting a passenger in harm's way.

Epilogue

*S*everal years ago, Peggy and I decided to take a vacation, something we had never done. Why should we? Living in Alaska is pretty much a vacation anyway, if you can acclimate to the long summer days, long winter nights, and the bouts of dreadful weather.

That year, the last days of April saw three feet of snow remaining in our front yard, so we decided to take the turbocharged Cessna 206 on a short jaunt to Florida to visit some of my family.

When we reached Cincinnati, we discovered green fields, open water, trees in leaf, and cows grazing contentedly on the hillsides. By the time we reached West Palm Beach in Florida, we had pretty well decided to semi-retire to this much warmer clime. I rented a hanger and rolled the Cessna inside, out of the bright sunlight. We found a place we thought we'd like at the Palm Beach Polo Club and put a down payment on it. Then we returned to Alaska to close up things and sell our home there.

FROM WHERE I SIT, THE VIEW OF
VOLCANIC MT. ILIAMNA CAN'T BE BEAT.

Big mistake! Florida is too hot, too flat, and much too humid for me. There's not a rainbow trout to be had here, and I've yet to see a good moose or a grizzly bear. I don't expect to see any Dall rams, either, what with the highest piece of ground around here only fifty-five feet above sea level. And that a landfill!

I miss the cold, clear nights of the far North. Those that come with the cracking of frozen spruce trees and the howl of a wolf family up there on the ridge. When I drive past a swamp, I still expect to see a moose knee-deep in the water. But I don't.

I've too much Arctic blood in my veins now. I've recently designed a series of geodesic domes to replace the old plywood cabins high in the Talkeetna Mountains and at High Lake, and I now look forward to my early return to the Alaska bush. Oh, it will take another year or two, I suppose. But I'll make it. Soon. You can bet your best snowshoes on that!